BIRDWATCHING
IN
GWENT

produced by

Al Venables
Andrew Baker, Dave Brassey, John Coleman
Chris Field, Verity Picken, Steph Tyler

for

Gwent Ornithological Society

Published in 2013 by:
The Gwent Ornithological Society
www.gwentbirds.org.uk
email: secretary@gwentbirds.org.uk

© Gwent Ornithological Society 2013

ISBN: 978-0-9505760-1-5

Editor: W. Alfred Venables
Design and maps: John Coleman, Christopher Field and Verity Picken

Front cover: Whinchat and Red Grouse on the slopes of the Sugar Loaf, by
John Gale
Back cover: Reed Bunting and Bearded Tits at Newport Wetlands Reserve, by
John Gale

Gwent Ornithological Society is a registered charity; No. 1088830

Printed and bound in Great Britain by:
Healeys Print Group
The Sterling Complex
Farthing Road
Ipswich IP1 5AP

Maps reproduced by permission
of Ordnance Survey on behalf
of HMSO. All rights reserved.
© Crown copyright 2013
Ordnance Survey 100047517.

Contents

Walks featured

Contents

List of line drawings and artists

Introduction

THIS BOOK has been produced as part of our celebration of the 50th Anniversary of the founding, in 1963, of the Gwent Ornithological Society (GOS). Its origins, however, go back to the completion of *The Birds of Gwent* in 2008. In that book we had compiled a short chapter on the best bird sites in the county and, in doing so, had realised that there was scope for the future production of a stand-alone book on the same topic. A further three years were to pass before the impending GOS anniversary provided the necessary stimulus to turn this idea into a reality.

The potential for such a book derives from Gwent's superb bird habitats, which are unusually diverse for a county of rather modest size (see separate chapter on habitats). This diversity is reflected in the wide range of breeding birds the county supports: a total of 122 species was proved to have bred during the most recent Gwent breeding atlas (1998-2003) and a further ten probably bred. In addition, passage migrants plus wintering wildfowl and waders, are attracted by the adjacent Severn Estuary and numerous inland water bodies, which include the Newport Wetlands Reserve. In consequence, annual totals of species recorded in the county are consistently just short of 200, while the all-time species list is 301.

A small subcommittee was set up to produce the book and early in our discussions it became apparent that we all greatly admired the *Best Birdwatching Sites* books, produced in recent years by Buckingham Press. We were therefore very pleased when David Cromack gave us his blessing to use much of the style and format pioneered by that series. In our book, however, we wished to make greatest use of the scope for walking provided by Gwent's beautiful and varied countryside, so our emphasis here is on walks that offer the best birdwatching, rather than sites. We hope that this approach will encourage use of the book, not only by birdwatchers, but also by walkers who have perhaps only a passing interest in birds.

Walks were selected by putting out a call to GOS members for accounts of their favourite bird walks/sites, together with birding tips applicable to each particular location. As well as ensuring that all our walks were described by those who knew them well, this approach enabled us to achieve a high degree of membership involvement – a philosophy that has always been a hallmark of GOS projects. All routes were 'road-tested' by members who had no previous experience of the walk in question and, in some difficult cases, were tested again by one or more different people. As a result of this process we have confidence that by use of the route descriptions and the maps, it should be possible to complete all walks without significant problems.

The walks are distributed widely across the county among fifty-five distinct locations; some locations offer two or more alternative routes making a grand total of over sixty-five. Collectively they embrace many habitats, are suited to a wide range of abilities, and provide such choices as: Newport Wetlands Reserve for breeding Avocets and Bearded Tits, plus a great variety of passage waders; Graig Goch Woods for Wood Warblers, Pied Flycatchers and Tree Pipits; Highmeadow Woods for Hawfinches; The Blorenge for Red Grouse and Wheatears; Gobion for breeding Goosanders and Common Sandpipers; or Beacon Hill for Nightjars and Woodcocks. Reference to the Birding Year table will help you decide where to visit at any particular season.

The choice is yours. Enjoy your visit.

The Severn Estuary from Black Rock   *Al Venables*

Acknowledgements

THIS BOOK has been a joint effort and we are extremely grateful to all who have contributed.

Our thanks go first to those who wrote accounts of their local patch or favourite walks – some were so enthusiastic that they submitted several (the number is given in brackets in the list below). The authors were:

Andrew Baker (3), John Bennett, Nicholas Beswick (6), Ruth Brown, Steve Butler, John Coleman (2), Richard Dowle, Chris Hatch (2), Keith Jones (3), Jerry Lewis (2), Luke Phillips (2), Verity Picken, Roger Price, Keith Roylance (2), Darryl Spittle (3), Ed Stevens, Mark Stevens, Lee Taswell, Colin Titcombe (2), Keith Trott, Steph Tyler (7), Al Venables (4), Ian Walker, Lyndon Waters, Alan Williams and Steve Williams (4).

Road testing the walks and checking the maps proved to be vitally important as, on a few occasions, this flagged up routes which needed amendment if our readers were not to get lost. Those who helped were:

Mick Bailey, Andrew Baker, Dave Brassey, Matt Broome, Ruth Brown, Steve Carter, Allan Clarke, John Coleman, Frank Cook, Andrew Cormack, John Davies, Steve Davies, Richard Dowle, Carl Downing, Chris Field, Jeff Hall, Ceri Jones, Keith Jones, John Marsh, Catherine Mendez, Rob Parsons, Jo Penning, Verity Picken, Arthur Pitcher, Keith Roylance, Trevor Russell, Darryl Spittle, Lee Taswell, Keith Trott, Steph Tyler, Al Venables, Lyndon Waters and Lesley Watson.

Chris Jones, our County Recorder, kindly wrote *The birding year in Gwent*. The *Habitats* chapter was written by Andrew Baker, John Coleman, Darryl Spittle, Steph Tyler and Al Venables, and the *Other wildlife of note* section was contributed by Chris Hatch.

We are greatly indebted to John Gale for providing us with such eye-catching covers, to Steve Roberts for the delightful line drawings and to Chris Hodgson and Dave Brassey for the smaller vignettes.

The landscape photographs show just a little of Gwent's beautiful countryside and varied habitats – these were taken by Jonathan Baker, Dave Brassey (the majority), Verity Picken, Keith Roylance and Al Venables.

Proofreaders, whose work was much appreciated, included, in addition to all the authors:
Dave Brassey, Arthur Pitcher, Trevor Russell, and Lesley Watson.

We are grateful to David Cromack of Buckingham Press for allowing us to follow the design and style of the *Best Birdwatching Sites* series.

The subcommittee for the book comprised:
Andrew Baker, Dave Brassey, John Coleman, Chris Field, Verity Picken, Steph Tyler and Al Venables. Al edited and harmonised the text, John produced the maps working closely with Al and Verity, Chris did the page-setting and Verity coordinated the project. Andrew chaired the group and dealt with outside contacts, Dave took charge of photographs and Steph provided invaluable expertise where habitats were concerned.

G WENT IS a fairly small and essentially rural county of about 137,000ha. Despite its modest size it has a good range of bird habitats including moorland, lowland heath and bog, broad-leaved and coniferous woodlands, farmland, sizeable rivers, numerous open water bodies, coastal levels reclaimed from the sea in historic times, estuarine coast and one very small, but ornithologically significant, island.

The major habitats of Gwent together with some of the characteristic birds they support are outlined briefly below.

Moorland and Lowland Heath

G WENT'S MAIN areas of moorland are found in the northwest of the county, on a series of parallel ridges running in a north/south direction. Whilst a proportion of this habitat is in reasonable condition, some areas of Coity Mountain and Mynydd Maen have been degraded by illegal use of trail bikes and four-wheel-drive vehicles.

The more florally diverse areas, containing plants such as bilberry, heather, cowberry, cross-leaved heath, and gorse, support the widest range

The Blorenge. This typical Gwent moorland supports a range of upland species including Red Grouse, Whinchat, Wheatear and Cuckoo. See Walk 6.   *Dave Brassey*

The lowland heath at Beacon Hill is home to typical heathland birds such as Nightjar, Woodcock and Stonechat. Yellowhammer is still reliably found here. See Walk 3.

Dave Brassey

of birds. The best examples of this moorland of high conservation value include The Blorenge, Coity Mountain, the Black Mountain ridges alongside the Honddu Valley and the north side of the Sugar Loaf. As well as containing an abundance of Skylarks and Meadow Pipits, these mountains hold good densities of Red Grouse, Stonechats, Whinchats and Wheatears. Bryn Arw has a dense growth of about 4ha of gorse and is a good place to observe breeding Stonechats.

Another species present in good numbers is the Cuckoo, which in this habitat lays its eggs mainly in the nests of the very common Meadow Pipit. The small trees that are found on the Sugar Loaf and Skirrid Fawr are amongst the best places to observe Yellowhammer, whilst Ring Ouzels can be observed on passage at a few sites, with Trefil quarry probably the most reliable.

Many birds of prey use moorland to forage, particularly the Coity Mountain plateau, which has Merlin, Hobby, Peregrine, Sparrowhawk and Long-eared Owl in the summer with Hen Harrier and Short-eared Owl present during the winter.

Lowland heathland and bog are extremely rare in the county, much of

9

these habitats having been ploughed and/or drained for agriculture, or planted up with conifers. Small remnants remain along forest tracks and in pockets in conifer or mixed woodland in Wentwood, and also in the Trellech area. Here Cleddon Bog survives, the largest of three remaining bogs in the east of the county; hummocks of purple moor grass and wet acid-loving species such as bog asphodel grow here and Snipe occur in the winter.

In recent years the Forestry Commission (now Natural Resources Wales) has cleared conifers from two areas near Trellech; one, Broad Meend, lies adjacent to Cleddon Bog and the other is a short distance away on Beacon

Hill above Trellech. These areas are now once again covered with bilberry, heather and bell heather, with cross-leaved heath in damper spots. Some Scots pine trees were left in groups on the restored heath. Bracken, gorse and silver birch threaten to convert the heath to woodland again but these plants are regularly cleared back or confined to particular areas to allow a mosaic of open heathland with some trees and patches of gorse to thrive. Ponies graze both sites but make little impact on the young birches, bracken and gorse. Nightjar, Tree Pipit and Whitethroat abound on the heaths and bog, whilst Stonechat, Linnet and Yellowhammer favour the gorse and scrub.

Woodlands

GWENT HAS about 19,000ha of woodland, covering just under 14% of the land area. Half of this woodland is broad-leaved, 29% coniferous and 15% mixed, with the remaining 6% consisting of coppice, clear-fell and open ground within woods. Within the broad-leaved total, about 2,250ha are ancient semi-natural woodlands.

In the east, the internationally important Wye Valley woods extend almost continuously for 30km along the Wales/England border, on both the Gwent and Gloucestershire sides of the River Wye and northeast from Monmouth into Herefordshire. There has been some planting of conifers but most of this woodland is protected

by a Special Area of Conservation (SAC) designation and three nationally important types are present: yew-dominated woods with ash and whitebeam on limestone; lime and maple on rich base soils; and beech on neutral/rich soils. These woods are species-rich, commonly containing (as well as the species already mentioned) oak, birch, gean, rowan, wych elm, sweet chestnut and holly, with occasional pockets of hornbeam and with alder in damper areas along the watercourses.

Common woodland birds abound and all three of our resident woodpeckers are present, though the Lesser Spotted may prove elusive. Among the finches, Hawfinch is widespread though easily

Wentwood from Gray Hill. The mix of coniferous and broad-leaved trees supports a good range of woodland birds including Goshawk, Willow Tit, and Crossbill. Firecrest occurs in some years. See Walk 51.

Dave Brassey

overlooked but Chaffinch and Goldfinch are abundant and a further five species should not prove difficult to find. Raptors are relatively common in these woods. Buzzard is ubiquitous, with Goshawk and Sparrowhawk widely distributed and Kestrel and Peregrine not infrequently seen. Tawny Owls are more easily heard than seen, but occur in all Wye Valley woodlands. Springtime makes roding Woodcock easy to spot, though they may be flushed from the woodland floor while walking at any time of year. Cuckoos are much less common in this habitat than a decade ago. In summer, Hobbies hunt in the valley though they are thinly distributed. Other summer visitors include Spotted and Pied Flycatchers, Tree Pipit and a variety of warblers, with up to eight species possible in a day in the field, as well as all three common hirundines, while Swifts hunt insects over the tree canopy. Winter brings good numbers of Fieldfare and Redwing with occasional large flocks of Brambling in the woods and flocks of Siskin and Lesser Redpoll in riverside alders.

The Woodland Trust's plans to improve the woodlands in Wentwood, northeast of Newport, involve the large-scale replanting of broad-leaved species

11

and better woodland management – this bodes well for the future. Elsewhere in Gwent there are two more SAC-designated woods, both in the north near Abergavenny. On the southern slopes of the Sugar Loaf, the Abergavenny Woodlands SAC has excellent tracts of sessile oak on acidic soils with significant beech woodland on neutral/rich soils overlying limestone. Similar beech woodland is found a little to the west at Cwm Clydach SAC, where there is also a rare beech with holly understorey component. Birds in these habitats are similar to those found in the Wye Valley, though finches are perhaps less common, while flycatchers and Wood Warbler are more easily found and Ravens are almost always within hearing distance. Both Whinchat and Stonechat may be found along woodland fringes and one would be unlucky not to see and hear Cuckoos, though they tend to prefer more open areas with breeding Meadow Pipits.

Conifer plantations on richer soils in the Wye Valley and Wentwood consist mainly of larches and Douglas fir, with Norway spruce where the soil is wetter. There are also some areas of larch and Douglas fir in the western valleys though, due to the poorer soils and higher altitudes, the most extensive plantations are of Norway and Sitka spruce. Apart from these species, a wide variety of other conifers occur in smaller pockets.

Elsewhere, Gwent has a further 17 woodlands designated as Sites of Special Scientific Interest (SSSIs). These represent a variety of woodland types, mainly in the north and east – there are only two woodland SSSIs (Silent Valley and Plas Machen) in the western valleys, where historic industrial activities, more recent overgrazing and planting of large areas of conifers have had a significant impact on the original sessile oak woodland of those valleys. The relative abundance of conifers has encouraged breeding Siskin and Crossbill to nest with some regularity, though never in large numbers. While open areas attract Cuckoo and Nightjar in summer, these conifer plantations are generally less productive of birds than broad-leaved woodlands.

The broad Usk Valley and the open, rolling countryside of central and northeastern Gwent are less well-wooded, although there are still many small broad-leaved woods, especially where larger estates exist. The historic absence of large estates in a broad swathe northwest from Raglan is perhaps the reason for the relative paucity of woods in that area, but in spite of that it is fair to say that there are no significant areas of Gwent without some form of woodland. Most of the commoner woodland bird species already mentioned occur in these scattered fragments and parklands, though for the most part at a lower density.

Farmland

FARMLAND IN Gwent now offers rather little for birds. As in the rest of England and Wales, the land is mostly intensively farmed, receiving large doses of artificial fertilisers and pesticides. Whilst Gwent is still largely a pastoral county, old permanent pastures have largely been replaced by rye-grass and white clover leys. Early cutting of the grass for silage for cattle feed has been the death knell for ground-nesting birds such as Curlew, their chicks killed by the machines. Elsewhere sheep are now the favoured stock and on improved pastures

Typical farmland in the Usk Valley. Stock Dove, Barn Owl, Whitethroat and Linnet are widespread. Little Owl has declined in recent years. *Verity Picken*

create a short sward of little value for wildlife. There has been a corresponding decline in numbers of dairy and beef cattle. More exotic animals including red deer, llamas, alpacas and goats have appeared on the scene, albeit in small numbers.

Arable crops are largely confined to the Usk, Trothy and Monnow valleys where maize, other cereals (wheat, barley and some oats) and oilseed rape are dominant. Potatoes and other crops such as flax are sparingly grown. Most cereal crops are planted in the autumn, leaving no stubble and no arable weeds for seed-eating birds over the winter months. Skylarks still hang on in small

13

numbers in arable fields and on leys, whilst a few pairs of Yellow Wagtail breed in cereals and other crops. Lapwing and Curlew have all but gone; Yellowhammer has suffered a massive decline too, now being scarce or absent in many areas, but Linnets are still reasonably common and some Reed Buntings use arable crops, especially in the lower Monnow valley.

Small pockets of land have escaped agricultural improvement, especially on the Trellech Plateau between Monmouth and Chepstow across to Shirenewton and to Wentwood. There, flower-rich meadows and pastures, a haven for insects, are scattered through the landscape. Hirundines hunt over these grasslands and Goldfinches love the knapweed fruiting heads in the late summer. Some rough grassland also persists on slopes below the hills in the west and northwest, and this ffridd habitat, often with much bracken and scattered small hawthorns and rowans, is prime habitat for breeding Whinchat, Willow Warbler, Tree Pipit and Redstart. Elsewhere in the northwest, old open-cast mining sites have been grassed over, creating higher altitude rye-grass pasture where sheep grazing is the predominant land use.

Farmyards are now rather sterile places compared with 50 years ago. They have little spilt grain for seed-eating birds and the use of rodenticides to control rats and mice has an adverse effect on owls and kites. Farm buildings still provide nest sites for Swallow, Stock Dove and Barn Owl, but numerous barns have been converted to human dwellings with the loss of former inhabitants.

Rivers and Open Waters

GWENT HAS an abundance of rivers, lakes and reservoirs. The main river is the River Usk, running down through the centre of the county from the Brecon border northwest of Abergavenny, through the town of Usk and on to Caerleon and Newport, finally reaching its confluence with the Severn at Uskmouth. This river boasts cliff banks, shoals and old oxbow lakes, as well as reedbeds along the estuarine section. It is joined by the Grwyne Fawr in the north, the Afon Llwyd at Cwmbran and the Olway Brook near Usk.

On the east side of the county is another major river, the Wye, which enters Gwent near Monmouth and forms the national boundary with England, running south to join the Severn near Chepstow. The upper section is well wooded and further down are old weirs, sand banks and islands, followed by an estuarine section south of Bigsweir. The Wye has a number of important tributaries, notably, in the Black Mountains, the Afon Honddu, which joins the River Monnow at Pandy; the Monnow then meanders along the northeast county boundary with Herefordshire. Smaller

The fast-flowing Sirhowy River near Graig Goch Woods is home to Dipper, Grey Wagtail and Kingfisher. See Walk 20.   *Dave Brassey*

tributaries near Monmouth include the Mally Brook, River Trothy and several short steep tributaries – White Brook, Black Brook and the Angidy River, all south of Monmouth. In the west the 'Valleys' rivers of the Sirhowy, Ebbw and Rhymney flow down to join the Severn Estuary just west of Newport. These rivers are mainly tree-lined and much cleaner than formerly. The Monmouthshire & Brecon Canal runs through the county between Abergavenny and Newport, and from there northwest to Crosskeys.

The major water body is Llandegfedd Reservoir near Pontypool, but a series of smaller reservoirs and man-made lakes are scattered around the county from Garnlydan and Carno Reservoirs, Bryn Bach Lake near Tredegar, Garn Lakes and Dunlop Semtex Pond in the northwest, Wentwood Reservoir and St Pierre Lake in the southeast, The Warrage near Raglan, Ynysyfro, Pant-yr-eos and Ponthir Reservoirs north of Newport and a host of smaller lakes and ponds. There is also the important Newport Wetlands Reserve to the southeast of Newport.

Waterbirds are well represented in Gwent. The Dipper and Grey Wagtail populations are high especially in the north and west; Goosander and Mandarin Duck breed on wooded upper reaches, Common Sandpiper and Little

15

Llandegfedd Reservoir is Gwent's largest inland water. Great Northern Diver and the rarer grebes favour this site on their occasional appearances. Large winter gull flocks sometimes contain the odd rarity such as Iceland or Sabine's Gull. See Walk 24.

Dave Brassey

Ringed Plover on shoals, Sand Martin and Kingfisher in the riverbanks and in some walls, whilst Great Crested and Little Grebes, Mute Swan, Tufted Duck, Coot and Moorhen nest along slower-moving sections of rivers and the canal, and also at open water bodies. The Canada Goose breeding population has exploded and they are now found on most waters. Non-breeding waterbirds commonly include Teal, Pochard, Wigeon, Goldeneye and Green Sandpiper and, less commonly, Bewick's Swan, while divers, Common Scoter and other rarities regularly turn up at various waters.

16

The Gwent Levels

THE GWENT Levels comprise an extensive low lying area of farmland alongside the Severn Estuary and are divided into the Wentlooge Level to the west of the River Usk and the Caldicot Level to the east. In combination, the Levels constitute one of the largest surviving areas of ancient grazing marshes and drainage ditch systems in the UK. The landscape is entirely hand-crafted, the product of a series of episodes of land reclamation ongoing since at least the Roman period. Despite industrial, commercial and residential 'development' in recent times, the landscape remains largely characterized by flat grassland divided into small- to medium-sized fields by a system of ditches and larger drainage channels known as reens.

The Gwent Levels are of national significance for their wildlife and, as a result, much of the area is designated under a series of adjoining Sites of Special Scientific Interest. The proximity of the internationally important Severn Estuary, with its extensive areas of intertidal mudflats and saltmarsh, and

Typical Levels pastureland near Peterstone. Reed Warbler and Reed Bunting nest along the reed-lined ditches and Lesser Whitethroat in the tall hawthorns. *Al Venables*

17

Uskmouth reedbeds – the only site for breeding Bearded Tit. Aquatic Warbler occurs on passage in some years. Water Rail and Cetti's Warbler are common. See Walk 36.

Dave Brassey

the Rivers Usk and Wye result in a series of interconnected and complex wetland systems.

Prior to drainage, much of the landscape would have been fenland, the only significant remnant of which is now found at the Gwent Wildlife Trust's Magor Marsh Reserve (probably the best spot for Kingfisher in the area). However, even in its present condition, the Gwent Levels are home to a wide range of wetland and farmland birds and, in combination with the adjacent estuary, are the location of many of the most productive birding sites within the county.

The farmland within the area holds small breeding populations of species scarce elsewhere in the county including Lapwing, Barn Owl, and Tree Sparrow. It is also, increasingly, the best area in the county to see Little Owl. The fields are criss-crossed by a system of ditches that host nationally important invertebrate and plant communities and these also provide a network of habitat for Cetti's, Sedge and Reed Warblers, and Reed Bunting.

Various wetland habitats have been created in recent years by the Countryside Council for Wales (now Natural Resources Wales) at the Newport

Wetlands Reserve, which now boasts extensive areas of lagoons, wet grassland and reedbeds. The saline lagoons at the eastern end of the reserve play host to six species of breeding wader (including Avocet) in the spring and summer, and provide a high tide roost for migrating and wintering waders at other times of the year. Much of the central section of the reserve is made up of wet grasslands that support large flocks of wintering wildfowl, particularly Wigeon. The reedbeds make up the western third of the reserve and provide a good opportunity to see Bearded Tit and Water Rail along with Cetti's Warblers in the surrounding scrub and well-vegetated ditches. Outside the breeding season they often host huge roosting flocks of Starlings, which often attract a number of birds of prey.

The Severn Estuary

THE SEVERN Estuary forms Gwent's southern border. It is subject to one of the highest tidal ranges in the world and, at low tide, the exposed area of intertidal mud can reach a total area of 20,300ha.

In winter, the estuary supports up to 80,000 wildfowl and waders, most

The intertidal mudflats of the Severn Estuary at Peterstone Pill are at their best in winter when the thousands of feeding waders may include Dunlin, Knot, Grey Plover and Redshank. See Walk 38.

Dave Brassey

19

of which are dependent on the inter-tidal mud for feeding. The value of the Severn to birds is recognised by its statutory designation as both a Special Protection Area (SPA) and Ramsar site on the basis of internationally important wintering concentrations of Bewick's Swan, European White-fronted Goose, Shelduck, Dunlin and Redshank. Winter numbers of Pintail and Shoveler are also of international importance, as too are numbers of Ringed Plover on passage in both spring and autumn. The first two species listed are of little relevance to Gwent, as they winter high up the estuary at Slimbridge. Others, however, are present in good numbers locally: in recent years Gwent's Shovelers have represented over 60% of the entire Severn population and Redshanks over 40%. Gwent's Shelduck population often peaks at over 1000 birds during winter and the appearance of flotillas of ducklings on the estuary in June and July is evidence of local breeding. Nationally important numbers of wintering Wigeon, Teal, Lapwing and Curlew are also found on the Severn and are well represented on the Gwent coast.

Availability of rocky substrates along the Gwent coast is rather limited so Turnstones are usually few in number. Beaches with a high sand content are also scarce; the only one of significance is near the West Usk Lighthouse so, not surprisingly, this is the most likely place to find Sanderling, but only on passage – Gwent has no wintering population.

Along much of the Gwent coast the estuary is bordered by saltmarshes, often with grazing cattle and a few horses. The saltmarshes hold a few pairs of breeding Oystercatcher, Lapwing and Redshank but numbers of the latter two species have declined greatly in recent decades. During high-tide periods the saltmarshes provide safe roosting areas for thousands of waders that use the estuary. The recent opening of long stretches of the seawall to form the Wales Coast Path is a matter of some concern, as increased recreational use of the seawall has the potential to cause significant disturbance to wader roosts, particularly when people bring dogs. Only time will tell.

Denny Island, a small outpost of Gwent in mid-estuary, has breeding Great Black-backed Gulls (the most marine of our local gull species) and a thriving colony of Cormorants, but true seabirds, which spend most of their life on the open sea, are not normally found in the estuary. During southwesterly gales, however, a variety of seabird species, including Fulmar, Kittiwake and Gannet, may be blown into the estuary. A full list of species, and tips on how to see them, are the subject of the Goldcliff Point walk in this book. Occasionally, considerable numbers of Manx Shearwaters have been observed flying up the estuary in mid-summer as far as the Severn Bridge, usually into an easterly breeze, but this is unusual. It has been speculated that these are exploratory flights by immature birds.

Whatever the time of year, there will be something to interest the birder on the Severn Estuary.

The birding year in Gwent

The walks through the seasons

THE TABLE below gives you a broad indication of the major birding interest on our walks during three different periods of the year – winter, spring/early summer and late summer/autumn. At any particular season, similar habitats will generally experience the same ornithological events, so we have grouped walks into a series of habitat types shown in the left hand column of the table. The right hand column briefly summarises the main bird interest on those walks at that time of year. Thus, in the upper section of the table (winter) the first row shows you the sort of birds (and sometimes behaviours) you would be likely to encounter on our coastal walks at that season.

Winter: November – February

Walk groupings	Species of interest
Coastal walks	Wildfowl & wader numbers peak during Nov–Jan.
Black Rock Collister Pill NWR Goldcliff Lagoons NWR Uskmouth Reedbeds Peterstone Pill/Gout Sluice Farm Saltmarsh St Brides Coast	Large numbers of Teal, Wigeon & Shoveler at NWR sites & Peterstone Pill. Up to 1,000 Shelduck off St Brides & Goldcliff; up to 1,500 Lapwing, 250 Black-tailed Godwit plus Spotted Redshank & Greenshank regular at NWR Goldcliff Lagoons. Large high-tide wader roosts at Collister Pill & St Brides. Water Pipits regular along Peterstone Great Wharf (W of Peterstone Pill). Merlin, Short-eared Owl & Cetti's Warbler regular at most sites. Bittern, Hen & Marsh Harriers, Barn & Little Owls, Bearded Tit & a huge Starling roost at NWR sites. Large numbers of Redwings & Fieldfares feeding in hedgerows on the Levels during Nov–Dec. Winter gales can bring the occasional seabird (Gannet, Leach's Petrel, Fulmar & skuas) into the estuary.

The birding year in Gwent

Winter: November – February

Walk groupings	Species of interest
Inland waters walks Afon Lwyd Brynmawr Ponds Bulmore Lakes Cwmtillery Lakes Garn Lakes Garnlydan Reservoir Llandegfedd Reservoir Nedern Brook St James Forestry The Warrage Wentwood Reservoir Ynysyfro Reservoirs	Wintering wildfowl numbers peak during Nov–Jan. Wigeon, Teal, Goldeneye & Goosander at Llandegfedd Resr. Good numbers of Pochard & Tufted Duck at Wentwood & Ynysyfro Resrs. Goosander at Bulmore Lakes, Garn Lakes, Garnlydan Resr & St James Forestry. Large Wigeon flocks at The Warrage. Large evening gull roost at Llandegfedd Resr occasionally includes Mediterranean & Iceland Gull. Black-throated & Great Northern Divers, and Slavonian, Black-necked & Red-necked Grebes are scarce visitors at Llandegfedd Resr. The Nedern Brook Wetlands (if flooded) may have a good selection of wintering wildfowl that can include Bewick's Swan. Small groups of Little Egret are regular.
River walks Bargoed Woodland Park Bulmore Lakes Castle Meadows Gobion Llanwenarth Lower Monnow Valley River Usk & Olway Brook The Moorings Two Rivers Meadow	Green & Common Sandpipers at various locations, but probably most regular at Gobion, Llanwenarth & The Moorings. Goosanders frequent along the whole length of the Usk valley; also Lower Monnow Valley, Two Rivers Meadow & River Rhymney at Bargoed Woodland Park. Bewick's Swan & Goldeneye at River Usk & Olway Brook. Mandarin regular on Lower Monnow. Kingfisher at Gobion, Llanwenarth & Castle Meadows. Curlew (Feb onwards) at sites in the Usk Valley.

The birding year in Gwent

Winter: November – February

Walk groupings	Species of interest
Woodland walks Highmeadow Woods King's Wood Lasgarn Wood Minnetts Wood Wentwood Wye Valley sites	Marsh & Willow Tits in Wentwood, with Crossbill regularly noted. Great Grey Shrike in the clear-fell areas in some years. Wintering finch flocks of Chaffinch & Brambling, and of Siskin & Lesser Redpoll at Wentwood, Wye Valley woods, Silent Valley & other sites. Hawfinch in Wye Valley sites, Minnetts Wood & Highmeadow Woods.
Upland walks The Blorenge Garnlydan Reservoir St David's Vale Trefil Quarry Waun Afon Bog	Hen Harrier possible at Trefil Quarry & Garnlydan Resr. Red Grouse at all sites listed. Red Kite at sites in the north & west of the county. Short-eared Owl, Hen Harrier & Merlin frequent at Waun Afon Bog.
Lowland heath & bog walk Beacon Hill/Broad Meend	Good chance of Woodcock & Crossbill.

The birding year in Gwent

Spring/early summer: March – June

Walk groupings	Species of interest
Coastal walks Black Rock Collister Pill Goldcliff Point NWR Goldcliff Lagoons NWR Uskmouth Reedbeds Peterstone Pill & Gout Sluice Farm Saltmarsh St Brides Coast	Seabirds – strong southwesterly winds can bring a number of seabirds species (Manx Shearwater, Storm Petrel, Fulmar, Gannet & auks) into the estuary. Best location to view is Goldcliff Point. NWR Uskmouth – Marsh Harrier frequent; resident Bearded Tit & Cetti's Warbler prominent. NWR Goldcliff Lagoons – Avocet & Little Ringed Plover arrive from mid-Mar; Garganey frequent during Apr–May; Tufted Duck breed. Passage waders likely at all sites: Whimbrel mid-Apr–May; Knot & Bar-tailed Godwit late Apr–early May. Spoonbill almost annual at Goldcliff Lagoons in May. Sanderling probable at St Brides during Apr–May. Wood & Curlew Sandpipers plus Little Stint possible at Goldcliff Lagoons in May. Golden Plover, Ruff, Greenshank & Spotted Redshank can turn up any site; rarer waders including Black-winged Stilt & Temminck's Stint most likely at Goldcliff Lagoons. Mediterranean & Little Gulls not infrequent at most sites. Occasional Skua and tern passage through estuary in the right conditions (NE wind). Passerine migrants move through and local breeders arrive widely on coast: Mid-Mar – Wheatear, Sand Martin, White Wagtail, Swallow, Blackcap, Chiffchaff & Willow Warbler. Mid-Apr – Cuckoo, House Martin, Yellow Wagtail, Grasshopper, Reed & Sedge Warblers, Whitethroat & Lesser Whitethroat. Water Pipits (many in breeding plumage) regular at Sluice Farm until early Apr. Oystercatcher & Redshank breed at NWR & other sites.

The birding year in Gwent

Spring/early summer: March – June

Walk groupings	Species of interest
Inland waters walks Bulmore Lakes Garnlydan Reservoir Llandegfedd Reservoir Nedern Brook Wetlands Tredegar Park The Warrage Wentwood Reservoir Ynysyfro Reservoirs	Llandegfedd Resr – Osprey occasionally on passage. Sedge & Reed Warblers arrive at north end. Breeding birds include Coot & Great Crested Grebe. Terns, including Black Tern, are occasionally noted. Tufted Ducks breed at Brynmawr Ponds and other waters. Nedern Brook Wetlands, if flooded, occasionally holds Garganey & Shoveler. Breeding birds can include Coot, Little Grebe, Lapwing & Redshank. Mute Swan, Coot & Reed Warbler breed at Tredegar Park.
River walks Bargoed Woodland Park Bulmore Lakes Castle Meadows Gobion Llanwenarth Lower Monnow Valley The Moorings River Usk & Olway Brook	Osprey occasional on spring passage. Common Sandpipers frequent on passage along all rivers, and breeding on R. Usk. Sand Martin colonies found wherever suitable habitat exists. Lesser Spotted Woodpecker likely at Gobion. Dippers on R. Monnow, R. Rhymney at Bargoed Park, R. Sirhowy at Graig Goch and much of R. Usk above Usk town. Kingfishers & Grey Wagtails frequent at many locations. Look out for Hobby at most sites; Yellow Wagtail & Little Ringed Plover at several Usk Valley sites. Reed Warblers breed at The Moorings.

The birding year in Gwent

Spring/early summer: March – June

Walk groupings	Species of interest
Woodland walks Clytha Hill (mostly farmland) Goetre House Wood Graig Goch Woods Highmeadow Woods King's Wood Lasgarn Wood Llanthony Woods & Valley St David's Vale St James Forestry Wentwood Wye Valley sites Ysgyryd Fach	Displaying Goshawks over many woodland sites during Mar–Apr. Summer visitors arrive mainly from early Apr– early May, including Cuckoo, Wood Warbler, Redstart, Pied Flycatcher & Tree Pipit. Crossbill possible in all woods with conifer content. Wentwood: Firecrest possible; late evening visits for Woodcock & Nightjar in clear-fell areas. Clytha Hill – good range of woodland & farmland breeding birds. Goetre House Wood – Spotted & Pied Flycatchers, Marsh Tit. Hawfinch in Highmeadow Woods, King's Wood, Minnetts Wood & Wye Valley sites.
Upland walks The Blorenge The British Coity Mountain Garn Lakes (upland section) Mynydd Garnclochdy Mynydd Llangatwg Mynydd Maen St David's Vale Trefil Quarry Waun Afon Bog	Generally on most of these walks: Cuckoo, Meadow & Tree Pipit, Stonechat, Whinchat, Wheatear, Redstart, Wood Warbler, Pied Flycatcher & Yellowhammer. Red Grouse on The British, Coity Mountain, Garn Lakes, St David's Vale & Trefil Quarry. Wheatear & Ring Ouzel at Trefil Quarry. Red Kite widespread at sites in north & west of the county. Waun Afon Bog excellent for Grasshopper Warbler.

26

The birding year in Gwent

Spring/early summer: March – June

Lowland heath & bog walk	Stonechat, Tree Pipit, Yellowhammer.
Beacon Hill/Broad Meend	Evening visits in June for Woodcock & Nightjar.

Late summer/autumn: July – October

Walk groupings	Species of interest
Coastal walks Black Rock Collister Pill Newport Wetlands Reserve Peterstone Pill & Gout Sluice Farm St Brides	Seabirds – southwesterly gales can bring seabirds including skuas & terns into the estuary. Goldcliff Point the best location to view. Wildfowl – Teal appear from mid-Jul, Wigeon, Pintail & Shoveler during Aug–Sep. Garganey occasional on return passage. A few Brent Geese anywhere along the estuary from late Sep. Marsh & Hen Harrier, Osprey, Hobby & Merlin appear. Return wader passage from late June with Common Sandpipers leading the way. Other regular waders include Little Ringed Plover, Ruff, Curlew Sandpiper, Little Stint, Green & Wood Sandpipers, Greenshank & Spotted Redshank. Pectoral Sandpiper almost annual in recent years. Rarer waders have included: White-rumped, Baird's & Buff-breasted Sandpipers & Temminck's Stint. Large evening roost of hirundines at Uskmouth reedbeds. Yellow Wagtail numbers increase on the Levels sites. Roosting Starling numbers build up during Oct at NWR Uskmouth. Visible passage of Woodpigeon & many passerine species from mid - late Oct.

The birding year in Gwent

Late summer/autumn: July – October

Walk groupings	Species of interest
Inland waters walks Bulmore Lakes Garnlydan Reservoir Llandegfedd Reservoir The Warrage Wentwood Reservoir Ynysyfro Reservoirs	Wildfowl numbers (Tufted Duck, Pochard & Coot) start to build up, particularly at Ynysyfro Resr, from late July. Look out for Osprey & terns (Common, Arctic & Black) at Llandegfedd Resr; Common Scoter (July/Aug) and Wigeon & Teal from Oct. Passage waders at Llandegfedd, Ynysyfro & Garnlydan Resrs if water levels are low.
River walks Bulmore Lakes Castle Meadows Gobion Llanwenarth River Usk & Olway Brook The Moorings	Passage waders (Greenshank, Green & Common Sandpipers) along the Usk Valley. Hobby frequent. Passage Osprey not unusual.
Upland walks The Blorenge Coity Mountain Garn Lakes (upland section) Mynydd Garnclochdy St David's Vale Trefil Quarry Waun Afon Bog	Returning Hen Harrier & Short-eared Owl from Sep onward at The Blorenge, Garnlydan Resr, Mynydd Garnclochdy & Waun Afon Bog. Passage Ring Ouzels occasional during Oct at any upland location. Red Grouse on The Blorenge & several other sites

Other wildlife of note

G WENT CONTAINS a very wide range of habitats, making it a rich and varied county for wildlife. In this section we highlight some of the more notable examples.

Gwent is home to a number of mammals, among which Red, Roe, Fallow and Muntjac Deer have all recently expanded in both numbers and in range, and Wild Boar are present in the east of the county, particularly in the vicinity of the River Wye. Atlantic Grey Seals are occasionally seen at the coast and in recent years have been increasingly recorded in the tidal reaches of the Rivers Wye and Usk. As in many other parts of the country, Otters are now present in every river system and in all large bodies of water in the county. Introduced American Mink, which had become a problem in recent decades, are now subject of to an extermination programme along the River Monnow and on the Levels. This is allowing the re-introduction of Water Vole to some of its former haunts, and is probably the reason for some apparent recovery of breeding Moorhens on the Levels. The county is also a stronghold for Lesser Horseshoe Bats, whilst Dormice are widespread and not uncommon, especially in central and eastern areas.

The county contains four of the UK's native species of reptiles: Common Lizard, Slow Worm, Grass Snake and Adder, with moorland and lowland heaths being particularly important for the latter species. In terms of amphibians, apart from the common and widespread species, Great Crested Newt can still be found, particularly in lowland areas.

A wide variety of fish is present. Twaite Shad migrate up the Rivers Usk and Wye, although numbers of these, together with those of European Eels, have declined in recent years. Also, Lampreys – the Sea, River and Brook species – all occur.

Amongst the invertebrates, the Silurian Moth and Wood White butterfly are particularly significant, whilst the Hornet Robber-fly is still numerous in the right habitat. Among the dragonflies the Brown Hawker is present near Ebbw Vale, the Club-tailed Dragonfly along the River Wye and the Hairy Dragonfly on the Gwent Levels, while the Ruddy Darter occurs in the south of the county. The Levels themselves are particularly important for their ditch fauna. One unusual arachnid, the Shingle Spider, may be encountered on shingle banks in the River Usk.

Special plants, among Gwent's wide and varied flora, include a number of Whitebeam species and associated hybrids, as well as the Tintern Spurge, Spreading Bellflower and Bulbous Foxtail grass.

Fungi abound: a variety of waxcaps are present in particularly good numbers on limestone grassland on The Blorenge near Blaenavon, whilst the Oak Polypore can be found at a site in Wentwood.

How to use this guide

HERE IS a typical description of a walk with pointers to the several sections and a key to the symbols used in the title bar.

Key points: more information on distance (miles and km), terrain, best season, precautions to take, available facilities, wheelchair access and other useful tips. See following pages for further explanation.

The Title bar gives the following information for each walk:
number and title (walks are listed alphabetically)
appropriate season to visit

Target birds: this lists the species for which the walk is most noted and which might influence your decision to try the walk. The percentage figure (as in Dipper 60%) has been selected by the author of the walk to indicate the rough chance of your seeing the species during a visit of reasonable duration in the appropriate season; it is based on his/her personal experience of the site. The chance of seeing a particular species may also be affected by your own personal expertise and experience in bird identification.

Other likely species: this lists the commoner species you are likely to see in addition to the 'target species', and is organised seasonally. See following pages for definitions of bird groups used.

Recommended route and birding tips: this section guides you through the walk and generally tells you which birds to look out for on particular sections, and the best tactics to employ when looking for them. It may also give you further background information on the site and more detailed information on the terrain. Distances generally in metres (m).

14	**Cwmtillery Lakes**	All year

Key points
- 2.7 miles (4.3km)
- A shorter route provides views of both lakes
- Moderately strenuous
- Stout footwear/wellingtons required
- Telescope recommended
- Toilets by car park
- Free parking at site
- Wheelchair accessible beside lower lake

IN A remarkable feat of engineering, a pipeline delivers water from high in the Black Mountains to the upper Cwmtillery Lake, a reservoir that feeds the domestic supply of the South Wales valleys. Whilst this lake is private, the smaller lower lake is the centrepiece of a popular public park. The walk encompassing both lakes and the valley above them will take a minimum of two hours but a much shorter route will provide views of the lakes and area between them. Habitat is very varied, comprising lakes, woodland, stream, scrub, fields and uplands.

Target birds
All year: Little Grebe 90%, Tufted Duck 90%, Dipper 60%
Autumn/winter: Goldeneye 30%, Pochard 80%, Goosander 50%, Kingfisher 30%

Other likely species

All year		
Canada Goose	Grey Wagtail	Chats
Greylag Goose	Pied Wagtail	Summer warblers
Gadwall	Common woodland birds	Garden Warbler
Teal	Siskin	Whitethroat
Common waterfowl	Linnet	Redstart
Grey Heron	Bullfinch	Tree Pipit
Cormorant	Yellowhammer	*Winter*
Common raptors	Reed Bunting	Snipe
Red Kite	*Spring/summer*	Water Rail
Goshawk	Hobby	Winter thrushes
Regular gulls	Common Sandpiper	Brambling
Barn Owl	Cuckoo	*Passage*
Green Woodpecker	Hirundines	Osprey
Skylark		Curlew

Recommended route and birding tips
From the car park follow the path round the west side of the lower lake, looking in particular for Little Grebes, which breed here, with Kingfisher and Water Rail possible in winter. Continue north on the path alongside the stream that flows between the lakes, where Dipper and Grey Wagtail are possible. The scrubby plantations hold Bullfinches and, in summer, several species of warbler. Cross the footbridge over the stream and re-join the road, then head up the valley to the water treatment plant and the northern lake, which is private but viewable from the path. Cormorant and Grey Heron are regular whilst a passing Osprey is a tantalising possibility in autumn.

80

How to use this guide

Title bar continued:

Appropriate recent Ordnance Survey Explorer or Outdoor Leisure (OL) map number

grid reference and nearest post code for the recommended car park or parking space. Note that in some more rural areas the post code (and therefore your sat nav) may not take you to the exact parking place – follow the written directions if this is the case

total length in miles

Symbols:

degree of difficulty (easy, moderate or strenuous)

availability of public transport

wheelchair access

Title bar symbols used::

 Public transport

𝕏/E   Easy walk

𝕏/M   Moderate walk

𝕏/S   Strenuous walk

   Wheelchair access

OS map OL13 SO217061 (NP13 2LU) 2.7 miles 𝕏/M 🦽   **14**

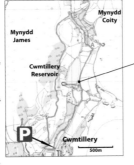

Scan the upper slopes of the valley for passing raptors and Ravens. Chats may be present on the moorland slopes.

If short of time, return at this point along the road to the car park. Otherwise, continue on the public footpath above the east side of the lake to the woods, following the power line across the middle of the meadow. Once in the woods, follow the footpath, turning sharp left at the obvious sign (point A) (beyond here the track is for private access only). The woods may hold Tree Pipit and Redstart in summer, with Brambling in winter. At point B, ford a minor stream and then cross the Tyleri, following the path round the boggy bowl. A public bridleway leads all the way back to the start of the walk over grassy slopes – the landscaped remnants of mining spoil tips. For the very adventurous, another bridleway heads on to the moor at the head of the valley with the possibility of associated upland birds.

Large map: this shows in detail the route you will walk, together with landmarks mentioned in the text. If parking symbols are numbered, these relate to the alternative parking places mentioned in the directions.

Small map: shows location of site within Gwent.

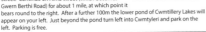

How to get there
Immediately N of Cwmtillery

Leave the A467 in Abertillery at the traffic lights (signposted Town Centre/Cwmtillery), bear right onto Castle Street then, almost immediately, left onto Alma Street (signposted Town Centre/Cwmtillery); after 200m join Gladstone Street before almost immediately bearing left back onto Alma Street at the junction with Foundry Bridge. Continue on Alma Street for another 200m at which point bear left to stay on Alma Street. Continue on Alma Street (which becomes Gwern Berthi Road) for about 1 mile, at which point it bears round to the right. After a further 100m the lower pond of Cwmtillery Lakes will appear on your left. Just beyond the pond turn left into Cwmtyleri and park on the left. Parking is free.

How to get there: this gives detailed instructions on how to get to the parking area(s) by car and (when available) public transport. Numbers of bus services are generally not given as they are subject to change. Directions are usually from only one starting point. Sometimes we have detailed the most straightforward route for those who are unfamiliar with the area, rather than the shortest. Miles are used here, as this is the unit on UK road signs and distance recorders of most cars.

81

31

How to use this guide

Key points – additional explanation

The following terms and expressions are used in Key points and require additional explanation.

Mountain precautions: on mountain walks, mist can descend unexpectedly so take all sensible precautions – warm clothes, food and drink, map, compass or GPS, mobile phone etc. Do not stray from track as there can be deep holes.

Telescope advice: if it is not mentioned, we think it is probably a waste of energy to carry one. Otherwise we have used three advice categories:

Telescope useful – a telescope will not improve your general experience, but might be useful occasionally to identify distant birds such as gulls in a far-off field or a bird of prey perched in a tree.

Telescope recommended – a telescope is likely to improve your general experience significantly, perhaps in enabling identification of species on the far bank of a reservoir or large pool or tracking raptors over an extensive marsh or moorland.

Telescope essential – not having a telescope is likely to be a source of frustration in that you may find it impossible to identify many of the birds you see with certainty, or even to see some of them at all! This is often the case on the coast, particularly if you are looking for birds on the sea or at the waterline when the tide is low.

Wheelchair access: if not mentioned, it does not exist to the best of our knowledge.

Facilities: toilet, café etc. These are not mentioned unless they are on or very close to the site/walk

Definitions of bird groups used in this guide

In the *Other likely species* section of each walk we have often saved space by the use of group names for birds. The list below details which species are included in each group. In some of the walks, certain species may be named individually in the list even though they are included under a group heading also in the list.

Common corvids

Jay, Magpie, Jackdaw, Rook, Carrion Crow (Raven always mentioned individually despite its increasing abundance).

Common farmland birds

Pheasant, Woodpigeon, Collared Dove, common corvids (except Jay), Blue Tit, Great Tit, Long-tailed Tit, Wren, Dunnock, Starling, Blackbird, Mistle Thrush, Robin, Pied Wagtail, Chaffinch, Greenfinch, Goldfinch, Linnet.

How to use this guide

Common finches

Chaffinch, Greenfinch, Goldfinch, Linnet, Bullfinch.

Common garden birds

Collared Dove, Magpie, Jackdaw, tits, Wren, Dunnock, Starling, thrushes, Robin, common finches (except Linnet).

Common passerines

A mixture of common species, typically including Goldcrest, tits, warblers, Nuthatch, Treecreeper, Wren, Dunnock, thrushes, Robin, Pied Wagtail, common finches and others.

Common raptors

Sparrowhawk, Buzzard, Kestrel.

Common waterfowl

Mallard, Moorhen, Coot.

Common woodland birds

Woodpigeon, Goldcrest, Blue Tit, Great Tit, Coal Tit, Long-tailed Tit, Nuthatch, Treecreeper, Wren, Dunnock, Blackbird, Song Thrush, Robin, Chaffinch.

Hirundines

Sand Martin, Swallow, House Martin + Swift (not a hirundine but convenient to include here).

Regular gulls

Black-headed Gull, Common Gull (winter only), Lesser Black-backed Gull, Herring Gull.

Summer warblers

Chiffchaff, Willow Warbler, Blackcap (other species usually mentioned separately).

Thrushes

Blackbird, Song Thrush, Mistle Thrush.

Tits

Blue Tit, Great Tit, Coal Tit, Long-tailed Tit (other species mentioned separately).

Winter thrushes

Blackbird, Fieldfare, Song Thrush, Redwing, Mistle Thrush

The birdwatchers' code

Around three million adults go birdwatching every year in the UK. Following *The Birdwatchers' Code* is good practice, common sense and will help everybody to enjoy seeing birds.

1. Welfare of birds must come first
Whether your particular interest is photography, ringing, sound recording, scientific study or just birdwatching, remember that the welfare of birds must always come first.

2. Habitat protection
A bird's habitat is vital to its survival and therefore we must ensure that our activities do not cause damage.

3. Keep disturbance to a minimum
Birds' tolerance of disturbance varies between species and seasons. Therefore, it is safer to keep all disturbance to a minimum. No birds should be disturbed from the nest in case the opportunities for predators to take eggs or young are increased.

In very cold weather, disturbance to birds may cause them to use vital energy at a time when food is difficult to find. Wildfowlers impose bans during cold weather; birdwatchers should exercise similar discretion.

4. Rare breeding birds
If you discover a rare breeding bird and feel that protection is necessary, inform the appropriate RSPB Regional Officer, or the Species Protection Department at the RSPB, The Lodge, Sandy, Beds SG19 2DL. Otherwise, it is best in almost all circumstances to keep the record strictly secret to avoid disturbance by other birdwatchers and attacks by egg-collectors.

Never visit known sites of rare breeding birds unless they are adequately protected. Even your presence may give away the site to others and cause so many other visitors that the birds may fail to breed successfully.

Disturbance at or near the nest of species listed on the First Schedule of the Wildlife and Countryside Act 1981 is a criminal offence.

5. Rare migrants
Rare migrants or vagrants must not be harassed. If you discover one, consider the circumstances carefully before telling anyone. Will an Influx of birdwatchers disturb the bird or others in the area? Will the habitat be damaged? Will problems be caused with the landowner?

6. The law
The bird protection laws, as now embodied m the Wildlife and Countryside Act 1981, are the result of hard campaigning by previous generations of birdwatchers. As birdwatchers, we must abide by them at all times and not allow them to fall into disrepute.

7. Respect the rights of landowners
The wishes of landowners and occupiers of land must be respected. Do not enter land without permission. Comply with permit schemes.

If you are leading a group, do give advance notice of the visit, even if a formal permit scheme is not m operation. Always obey the Country Code.

8. Keeping records
Much of today's knowledge about birds is the result of meticulous record keeping by our predecessors. Make sure you help to add to tomorrow's knowledge by sending records to your county bird recorder.

9. Birdwatching abroad
Behave abroad as you would at home. This code should be firmly adhered to when abroad (whatever the local laws). Well behaved birdwatchers can be important ambassadors for bird protection.

(Reprinted with the permission of RSPB)

Birdwatching Walks
in
Gwent

Key points

- A linear walk of up to 3 miles (4.8km)
- Easy walk
- Mostly on hard-surfaced paths
- Interesting river birds all year
- Wheelchair access on surfaced paths
- Telescope useful
- Café and toilet facilities spring – autumn
- Frequent bus service

THIS IS a short walk that follows the Afon Lwyd upstream from the Cwmbran Boating Lake as far as the Cwmbran railway station. Although the river and lake are the main features of interest, the area also includes playing fields and parkland.

The walk has birding interest at any time of year but, as it is popular with dog walkers, it is best done at first light before other walkers arrive. There is a hard-surfaced footpath for most of its length but it is often necessary to leave the footpath to view certain sections of the river. These sections can be muddy and slippery underfoot in wet weather.

Target birds

All year: Dipper 90%, Grey Wagtail 70%
Winter: Goosander 90% (early morning)

Other likely species

All year		Winter
Mute Swan	Nuthatch	Fieldfare
Canada Goose	Treecreeper	Redwing
Great Crested Grebe	Thrushes	*Occasional*
Common waterfowl	Pied Wagtail	Mediterranean Gull
Regular gulls	Common finches	Kingfisher
Tits	Siskin	

Recommended route and birding tips

ALTHOUGH THIS is an interesting walk at any time of day, it is best to arrive as early as possible, preferably before other walkers arrive. This is especially true during the winter as the Goosanders that use the lake for roosting fly off as soon as people arrive.

From the recommended car park (P1) follow the surfaced path to the south through the playing fields and then to the right of the children's

play area. Pass to the right of the Boathouse Café and walk around the lake, which holds a variety of waterbirds at all seasons. Now return northwards, following the river upstream until you reach the Llanfrechfa Way road bridge adjacent to where you parked. Continue to follow the river upstream, either by crossing over the road or walking under the river bridge (can be slightly muddy). From just north of the bridge there is a hard-surfaced footpath which passes through some beautiful wooded parkland that is particularly colourful in autumn. The path continues to follow the west bank of the river as far as the Edlogan Way bridge, which is adjacent to Cwmbran railway station. Return to your car by retracing your steps.

To view certain sections of the river it is necessary to leave the surfaced footpath and

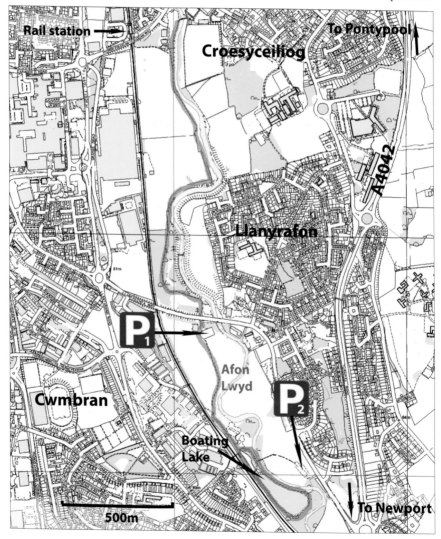

traverse areas where conditions underfoot are more uneven and can become muddy following rain. During the summer months, parts of the river may be screened from view owing to dense vegetation, including Japanese knotweed and Himalayan balsam. When approaching bends in the river, it can be useful to take advantage of any natural cover and, using a telescope, scan the river ahead for Dippers or Grey Wagtails.

During the winter months the playing fields often have flocks of Redwing and Fieldfare, while large numbers of gulls, especially Black-headed Gulls, are frequently present. Check for Mediterranean Gull, which is an occasional visitor.

How to get there

On E edge of Cwmbran

Head north on the A4042 from Newport. At the second roundabout after J25A take the second exit into Llanfrechfa Way. Continue for 1km, then turn left immediately after crossing the Afon Lwyd bridge. Park at P1, adjacent to the playing fields.

Alternatively, there is another large parking area along Llanfrechfa Way (P2), clearly signposted to Cwmbran Boating Lake.

Public transport

Newport-Cwmbran bus services are frequent along Llanfrechfa Way.

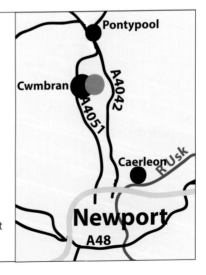

BARGOED WOODLAND Park (Parc Coetir Bargod) is built on the site of three former collieries – Bargoed, Gilfach and Britannia – the last of these closing in 1985. The site once had the highest coal tip in Europe and was immortalized in the L S Lowry painting 'Bargoed' in 1965. Nine years were spent reclaiming the site with 90,000 trees planted. The park is approximately 3km long (north to south) and 400m wide, now cut into two halves by the Bargoed by-pass. The River Rhymney runs through the park and since 2004 its centre line has formed the western boundary of Gwent.

Target birds

All year: Red Kite 5%, Sparrowhawk 50%, Grey Wagtail 90%, Dipper 95%

Spring/summer: Sand Martin 50%

Autumn/winter: Goosander 20%, Kingfisher 25%, Siskin 10%

Other likely species

All year	Spring/summer	Winter
Grey Heron	Moorhen	Fieldfare
Mallard	Common Sandpiper	Redwing
Buzzard	Hirundines	Lesser Redpoll
Green Woodpecker	Skylark	
Great Spotted Woodpecker	Summer warblers	*Occasional*
Common woodland birds	Garden Warbler	Cormorant
Common corvids	Whitethroat	Kestrel
Pied Wagtail	Spotted Flycatcher	Peregrine
Starling	Meadow Pipit	Barn Owl
Common finches		Marsh Tit

Other wildlife
Trout and salmon jumping in Oct/Nov; otters have been recorded.

Recommended route and birding tips

THIS IS a complex walk with numerous deviations that cannot be adequately represented on a map of the scale used here. If, however, you follow the text carefully, using the map as an approximate guide, you will have no difficulty in completing the walk.

Key points

- About 3 miles (5km)
- 11 access points
- Easy, much of route metalled; one or two inclines
- Year-round bird interest
- Network of paths
- Main routes and entrances are navigable by wheelchair but the route between the two sections is not.
- Used by dog walkers, cyclists and horse riders
- Public transport

Southern section – Pengam and Fleur de lis

Park at P1, the main car park. Scan the trees for Great Spotted Woodpecker and look down into the River Rhymney for Dippers and Grey Wagtails. Head north on the metalled path with Lewis School on your left. After approximately 200m there is an S-shaped silver metal bridge on your right. Cross the bridge onto the east bank. From the bridge, scan the river for Dipper, Grey Wagtail and Grey Heron.

Head up the metalled path, looking

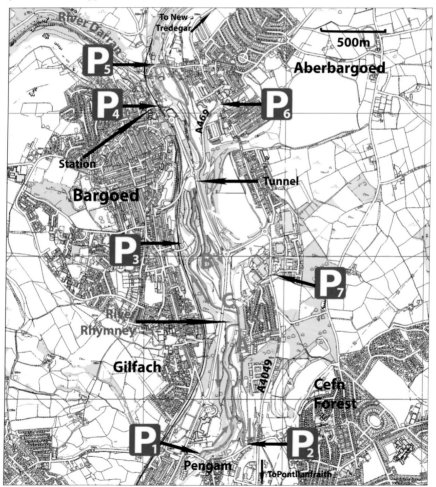

for Treecreeper, tits and warblers in the trees. At the top turn right and head east across the grass (can be muddy) to rejoin a metalled path in front of a small pond where Kingfisher and Moorhen may be seen. Continue south to the gate at Pengam and from there (P2) scan the view back north towards Bargoed for Buzzard, Sparrowhawk or flocks of Jackdaws. Green and Great Spotted Woodpeckers, and Nuthatch could be in the trees and Jays are frequent.

Retrace your steps north and about 100m past the pond you could briefly turn right and walk up the unmetalled slope towards Britannia Industrial Estate. At the top look over the field for Buzzard or woodpeckers, then return to the metalled path. Head north again and after 100m there is a path on the right with steps – look and listen here for Green Woodpecker, then continue north past steps on your left (point A).

At a fork in the path go downhill (left) under the flyover. Look ahead for Grey Heron along the river or on the trees. Briefly walk back along the river bank (unmetalled path) to nearly under the Gwerthonor bridge. Sit and wait as Dipper, Grey Wagtail and Mallard frequent this area. In winter, Goosander can be seen anywhere along the river from late September.

Turn back and rejoin the metalled path. After about 250m, just before the river bends to the right, check the stream on the left for Kingfisher. Continue north to a stretch of rapid water where salmon and trout can be seen jumping in late autumn. Cross the wooden bridge signposted to Bargoed (possibly a bit steep for wheelchairs) and follow the metalled path

left up a slope toward a park exit where there is a map of the park and a statue of three coal miners. This exit is close to Gilfach Halt train station

Return to the wooden bridge and continue north up the west side of the river on an unmetalled path, keeping close to the fence. Goldfinch, Siskin and Lesser Redpoll frequent the alders in winter. Check the Bargoed to Aberbargoed flyover for perched Kestrel, Sparrowhawk or Buzzard watching for prey. In spring and summer, Sand Martins nest in the artificial holes on both sides of the river, and Sparrowhawks can be seen hunting them. Near the flyover there is a small incline (difficult for a wheelchair) to another wooden bridge taking you back to the east bank.

From the bridge check the tunnel to the north and the outlets for Dipper, then head south along an unmetalled path on the east bank of the river where Bullfinches and Goldcrests frequent the buddleia bushes – eventually joining a metalled path near the wooden bridge you crossed earlier. From this point you could take the top route for 50m from the river then turn left heading north on an unmetalled track to the northern half of the park.

Otherwise, continue south, gradually leaving the side of the river. On reaching a small wood (point B), head right around the outside of the copse on a metalled path. Two alternative paths, taking you through the copse, are also possible, all three routes meeting at point C. Beyond the cutting, pass under the flyover and continue following the metalled path south. Check the small pond on your right for waterbirds. Head south past Britannia on your left

41

and check the trees for tits, Nuthatches etc attracted to the gardens.

For those who can, drop down the series of 42 steps at point A and cross the bridge back to the west bank. Follow the metalled track south alongside the river passing a waterworks and weir. Here you might get the best view of Dippers and Grey Wagtails. Keep a look out through the trees for Goosanders resting on the river. This path will take you past Lewis School (on your right) and the S-shaped metal bridge back to the main car park. For those who are unable to go down the steps, continue south on the east side and cross back over the S-shaped bridge to the west side and return to the main car park.

Northern section – between Bargoed & Aberbargoed

Leaving the southern half of the park, step over the road barrier carefully, cross the road to the other side of the roundabout, step over the next road barrier and drop down the track to the west bank of the river. Walk along the path for 300m looking down onto the river and checking for Dippers, then join a metalled path across the stone bridge to the east bank. Follow the path left, signposted to Heol Bedwellty. The man-made river walls here hold good numbers of Sand Martins in the spring/summer.

Continue for about 300m, passing an exercise area on your right, to the confluence of the Rivers Darran and Rhymney where Dippers are often present. Leave the park through narrow gates near P5 and walk left 20m to look over the bridges at the bottom of Aberbargoed hill. Check for Grey Wagtail and Spotted Flycatcher on the trees to the north. Now head back along the road (passing the exit at which you left the park), past the entrance to the ambulance station and continue uphill to a red seat and signpost indicating another entrance to the park. (To the north is Quarry Row and a cycle track to Cwmsyfiog – good for Spotted Flycatcher, Wood Warbler, Cuckoo and Yellowhammer).

Re-enter the park at this point and follow the metalled path between two carved totems; gorse bushes and adjacent private gardens can hold tits and warblers. After about 300m, follow the path back down to the stone bridge and the river. Stay on the east side of the river and join the unmetalled path signposted towards Pengam. Head south for 100m, then up a moderate gradient for 200m back to the roundabout. Cross the roundabout to rejoin the southern half of the park. In summer listen and look for Skylark singing on the tip to your left; at the southern end there is a small pond which often yields Reed Bunting. (The tip is scheduled to be re-developed).

Entering the southern section, walk 100m alongside a meshed wooden fence and descend the unmetalled path down to a seat and a fork in the path. Take either the left hand unmetalled path or the right hand path, both of which will lead you to point B of the southern section walk

For more information please check: The Countryside & Landscape Service on Caerphilly County Borough Council's website.

How to get there

On E edge of Bargoed

Take the A469 to Bargoed or the A4049 to Aberbargoed and follow signs for the park. Use one of the several parking opportunities around the park:

P1 Main car park just west of the River Rhymney (ST153976) with disabled parking.

P2 Limited parking available in front of park gates at the southern end of the park, on A469 off High Street, Pengam (ST157977) east of the river.

P3 Limited parking also between Gilfach Halt train station and the park (ST153992).

P4 Bargoed train station Park & Ride (SO151000), or car park east of Bargoed town (redevelopment pending).

P5 Aberbargoed – at the northern end of the park on the bottom of Bedwellty Road or at Glen View, Chapel Street or Heol Ysgol Newydd (SO154002).

P6 At the bottom of School Street or Heol y Felin off Commercial Street, Aberbargoed (SO153003).

P7 Britannia along Farm View (ST156987).

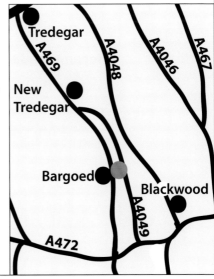

Public transport

By rail: Pengam station is five minutes walk southwest of the park; Gilfach Halt is to the west of the middle of the park and Bargoed train station is near the northern end of the park. See www.traveline.info

By bus: regular services from all neighbouring towns. Information from: Traveline Cymru (0871 200 2233).

43

Key points

- Beacon Hill – 1.7 miles (2.7km)
- Cleddon Bog (long) – 2 miles (3.2km)
- Cleddon Bog (short) – 0.9 miles (1.4km)
- Easy, on well-defined tracks
- Can be wet in places, especially Broad Meend
- Best in June for Woodcock & Nightjar

THESE WALKS take you through mature conifer forests, clear-felled areas, birch woodland, heathland and around a lowland bog, taking in some habitats that are rare in the eastern half of the county. They are worthwhile at any time of year but are most rewarding for birds in the late spring and early summer.

Target birds

All year: Willow Tit 5%, Stonechat 35%, Siskin 25%, Crossbill 50%
June: Woodcock 90%, Nightjar 75%
Spring/summer: Tree Pipit 95%, Linnet 80%, Yellowhammer 20%
Winter: Woodcock 20%, Lesser Redpoll 25%

Other likely species

All year	Thrushes	Wood Warbler
Common raptors	Chaffinch	Whitethroat
Goshawk		
Raven	*Spring/summer*	*Winter*
Tits	Willow Warbler	Winter thrushes
	Chiffchaff	

Recommended route and birding tips

Beacon Hill Walk   SO511053 (NP25 4PR) 1.7miles P1

FROM CAR park P1, take the track to the northeast through the woodland; the track starts near the Wye Valley AONB display board and curves to the right.

Pass through a gate (point A) and continue along the track onto heathland, going slightly downhill. As soon as you go through the gate you are onto an open heath. Much of the Trellech plateau lies on quartz conglomerate and the acid soils were once covered in vast tracts of heather. The heathland was covered with conifers in the 1950s and 1960s but in the early 2000s the Forestry Commission cleared two areas of conifers to re-create heathland – here on Beacon Hill and, just a short distance away, at Broad Meend, by Cleddon Bog. Welsh Mountain and Exmoor ponies graze the area. The Gwent Wildlife Trust now has a management agreement with Natural Resources Wales over both Beacon Hill and Broad Meend.

On reaching a broad cross-track (point B) cross it and continue more or less straight ahead, downhill on a well-marked gravelly path, keeping

a green sign on your right and then a
wire fence on your left. Continue on
the path until another gate is reached; go
through and continue straight, still going
gently downhill, now with a dense conifer
plantation on your left and the heathland
on the right.

As the track bottoms out, you reach a
T-junction (point C). Turn right here
and follow this bridleway until it meets a
substantial track at an oblique angle (point
D). Turn right, slightly uphill. After the
top of the hill, as the road starts to descend,
take a small path to the right (point E)
alongside the heathland's fence. After
about 100m or a little less, you join a broad

track (point F). Turn right on this track,
past the cattle grid and continue across the
centre of the heathland.

After about 500m, you will reach point B
again; turn left to return to the car park.

On Beacon Hill heather and bilberry are
plentiful, as are gorse and birch saplings;
conifers and broad-leaved trees fringe the
heathland. In winter the area can seem
almost devoid of birds, but keep an ear and
eye open for Crossbills, which are common
here and breed in the nearby conifers. Hen
Harrier and Great Grey Shrike have been
seen occasionally in the past.

In the spring and early summer the

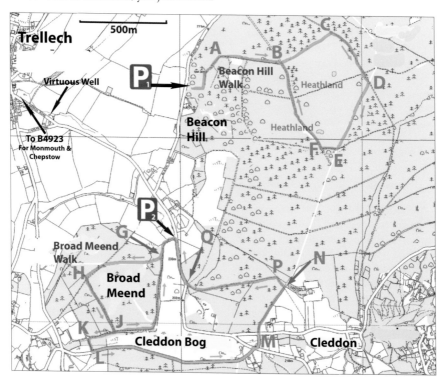

heath is alive with birds. Tree Pipits and Whitethroats are common; Stonechats breed in patches of gorse and a visit at dusk should reveal 'churring' Nightjars. Ravens, Buzzards and Kestrels are often seen and you might just catch a glimpse of a Goshawk – keep an eye on the skylines. Among the Coal, Blue and Great Tits in

the surrounding woodland, watch out for Willow Tits.

This is an area that repays exploration. There are paths around the periphery of the heathland area and across it; all of these are worth walking, if time permits. When exploring, look out for two small ponds where birds often come to drink or bathe.

Cleddon Bog & Broad Meend Heath Walk

Short walk   SO509044   **(NP25 4PS) 0.9 miles   Car park P2**

FROM THE parking area (P2) step around the metal barrier and after about 150m (point G) take a right turn onto a track going uphill. After 100m this brings you out onto the heath, which is to your left. Walk around the heath keeping the wire fence immediately to your left. Follow this path for some 300m then take a stile on your left (point H) immediately before a locked gate. Go gently downhill on a path leading to another stile. There is a pond on your left near the bottom and some good wet boggy areas with *Sphagnum* bog moss.

At the stile, you rejoin your initial track at a more advanced point (J). The same species occur here as on Beacon Hill – breeding Nightjars, Tree Pipits and Stonechats being the main species, as well as Whitethroats. Yellowhammers and Linnets are often seen in the spring and summer, and until a few years ago the area held Gwent's last breeding Turtle Doves.

At this point (J), turn left and walk back to your car keeping the expanse of Cleddon Bog to your right (650m).

Long walk   SO509044   **(NP25 4PS) 2 miles   Car park P2**

ALTERNATIVELY, YOU can turn right at point J and circumnavigate the bog by following the metalled road around it. This is the best lowland bog left in Gwent and it is being conserved. Invading trees are being removed, and grazing reinstated, to keep the area open. Interesting plants such as bog mosses (*Sphagnum*), sundews and bog asphodel grow on the bog, though hummocks of large purple moor grass (*Molinia*), often with standing water between them, make

walking on the bog very difficult.

Having turned right at point J follow the track through a left turn (point K) and then, after 150m, you reach the surfaced road (point L). Turn left along it and continue for about a kilometre, to a T-junction (point M). Turn right and then immediately left; go straight over a small crossroads onto an un-metalled and stony track. Follow this track uphill for 300m. Opposite an iron gate (point N)

46

turn left (way-marked Cotland) and after 75m take an obvious straight track to the left, heading west across open heath. Eventually, after 450m, the path drops down through trees to meet the road (point Q). Turn right and follow this road for about 250m back to the car park.

Whilst no Wood Warblers occur on the heathland or bog, they do breed in the nearby woodlands, usually choosing an area with well-spaced mature oak or larch.

How to get there

About 6 miles S of Monmouth

For the Beacon Hill Walk: at Trellech drive almost through the village and where the B4293 from Monmouth to Chepstow bends sharp right to Llanishen, turn off (going almost straight ahead) and immediately make a left turn onto the small road (Llandogo Road), signed Cleddon. Do not take the road going straight ahead, which goes to Catbrook. Drive out of the village past the Virtuous Well (entry via a kissing gate on the left after about 200m); this is well worth a stop. Continue for about half a mile, then take the first turn left, going uphill and after another half-mile turn right, just past Beacon Hill Farm, into the gravel track for the car park for Beacon Hill. Park here and walk.

For the Cleddon Bog and Broad Meend Heath Walk: after visiting Beacon Hill you can reach the start point of the Cleddon Bog and Broad Meend Heath walk, either by walking, or by driving to the new parking point. On foot, you need to retrace your route, on the metalled road, down to Llandogo Road road again. On reaching it, turn left, walk south along the road for about a third of a mile and, where the fields on your right come to an end, turn right onto a forestry track. If in a car, follow the same route and park at the entrance to the forest, taking care not to block the track (SO509044).

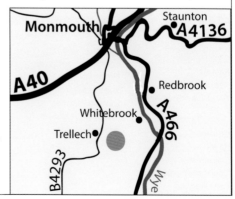

Key points

- 4.5 miles (7.2km)
- Easy walk
- Autumn – spring
- State of tide important
- Telescope recommended
- Wheelchair access along Wales Coast Path
- Bus route fairly close

THIS IS quite an easy coastal walk along the Severn Estuary, from the picnic site at Black Rock to the saltmarsh past Sudbrook near where the Second Severn Crossing reaches Wales. The habitats seen include saltmarsh, mudflats, rocky shore and farmland. A good selection of birds can be seen at any time of year but this area is best during migration, both spring and autumn, and also during the winter especially during a cold spell – even better if there has been snow on the surrounding areas. Being a coastal walk, the state of the tide can be important with high tide usually being best, but unlike most of the estuary, the tide does not go out for miles and birds can be seen at any state of the tide. The walk described is mostly along the footpath on the bank above the saltmarsh and on top of the cliff, but for those feeling a bit more energetic a detour down onto the saltmarsh or onto the rocky shore between Black Rock and Sudbrook can be rewarding.

Target birds

All year: Shelduck 90%, Buzzard 60%, Sparrowhawk 50%, Peregrine 30%, Oystercatcher 60%, Curlew 70%, Redshank 50%

Late summer/autumn: Mediterranean Gull 30%

Winter: Wigeon 90%, Jack Snipe 5%, Snipe 5%

Passage: Whimbrel 60%

Other likely species

All year		*Winter*	Hobby
Pheasant	Common finches	Winter thrushes	Terns (on passage)
Cormorant	Reed Bunting	Brambling	Short-eared Owl
Grey Heron	*Spring*		Redstart
Kestrel	Common Sandpiper	*Passage*	Black Redstart
Regular gulls	Hirundines	Whinchat	Rock Pipit
Great Black-backed Gull	Summer warblers	Wheatear	
Green Woodpecker	Garden Warbler	Spotted Flycatcher	
Common corvids	Lesser Whitethroat	Yellow Wagtail	
Raven	Sedge Warbler	*Occasional*	
Goldcrest	Reed Warbler	Seabirds (during or after persistent strong westerly winds)	
Common passerines		Osprey	
Grey Wagtail		Merlin	

Recommended route and birding tips

MOST OF the route follows the Wales Coast Path, which is fully signposted.

Start the walk at the car park at Black Rock picnic site (P). Have a quick look around the picnic site before you start your walk as many species can be found there, particularly during late summer and autumn when passage migrants can include Spotted Flycatcher and warblers in mixed flocks with tits. From the car park walk for a short distance back down the road until you reach a gate on the right (point A), then follow the Wales Coast Path signs heading east. The trees on either side of the path can be good for warblers during the summer. In winter, the field you walk through is sometimes used by mixed flocks of thrushes and can also be good for birds of prey with Buzzard, Sparrowhawk and Kestrel all reasonably common and quite a good chance of Peregrine.

The saltmarsh is good for Meadow Pipit, Skylark and finches, including Linnet. There is also a small chance of Merlin or Short-eared Owl during the winter, and Hobby during the summer. On the landward side of the seawall is a drainage ditch with a hedge (point B) that is good for birds, including Reed and Sedge Warblers in the summer and finches and Reed Buntings in the winter. After a short walk, go through another gate and walk a short distance to get a good view into Passage Wharf Pill (point C), which often holds small numbers of waders and wildfowl.

Now turn around and walk back along the seawall. For those who don't mind getting a bit muddy, a walk down along the saltmarsh (point D) can give better views of the mudflats and gives the best chance of seeing Snipe and Jack Snipe during the winter. When the gate at the bottom of the field is reached don't go back into the field but follow the path to the left along the marsh (point E), unless it is a big high tide in which case you will have to go back through the field. The short grass here gives the best chance of Rock Pipit, and usually holds the biggest flocks of waterfowl, mostly

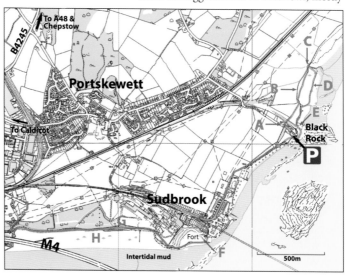

Wigeon and Mallard in winter, but often with Teal and Gadwall.

Unless the tide is very high, you can walk to Sudbrook along the shore (following the red dots on the map), which is rocky and often muddy, and should only be attempted if you are fit, but this route does give the best chance of Mediterranean Gull in late summer and autumn, usually found with Black-headed and Common Gulls between the two stone jetties. For an easier route to Sudbrook, keep following the Wales Coast Path signs. The fields along the path are good for thrushes in winter, and Curlew and Lapwing can sometimes be seen. This is also a good area for warblers including Lesser Whitethroat. When there is a very strong westerly wind, seabirds can sometimes be watched from the cliff top (point F); Kittiwakes are the most common but there is a small chance of almost any sea bird turning up.

In winter the saltmarsh (point H) to the west of Sudbrook can hold big flocks of finches, mostly Chaffinches but usually with good numbers of Greenfinch, Goldfinch and Linnet, and also occasionally Brambling and Black Redstart. The bushes along the top of the saltmarsh and poplar plantation on the right hold finches, tits and warblers. Most of the year part of the former Paper Mill yard (point G) is flooded and this can attract species such as Mallard, Moorhen and Common Sandpiper, with an occasional Water Rail.

The saltmarsh can hold Snipe and Jack Snipe in winter, but both are hard to spot, while Peregrines often hunt over the marsh and under the Second Severn Crossing, and can sometimes be seen sitting on the tops of the pillars. When you reach the gate at the western end of the marsh (point J), turn and retrace your steps to the car park at Black Rock. There are a number of places along the way, especially around the coast at Sudbrook and the picnic site at Black Rock, where a short diversion could be made to lengthen the walk if you wished.

How to get there

On the coast, 3 miles SW of Chepstow

Join the B4245 and head towards Caldicot. At the roundabout between Caldicot Castle and Mitel Business Park turn onto Caldicot Road, which is left if coming from Chepstow and right if coming from Newport. Follow the road right through Portskewett. Near the very end of Portskewett turn right onto Black Rock Road, this is signposted with a Black Rock Lave Net Heritage Fishing sign. Follow Black Rock Road to the end and the car park is on the right (ST512881).

Public transport

The closest bus stop is about half a mile away, at the top of Black Rock Road on Portskewett Main Road, with regular buses from Newport or Chepstow.

THIS IS a walk on the outskirts of Cwmbran through community woodland that has been in local trust ownership since January 2005. The wood, officially known as Coed Gwaun-y-ffeiriad, occupies 100 acres and is actively managed by a group of local residents and supporters.

The walk initially follows the borders of the wood before entering the wood proper, with a plantation of larch and other conifers on the left and mixed deciduous woodland on the right. In spring and early summer there is a good variety of summer migrants, but a reasonable selection of species can be seen at any time of year.

Key points

- **2.5 miles (4km)**
- **Mainly easy on metalled surfaces**
- **Steep early section**
- **Mixed woodland with open heathland**
- **Best in spring/ early summer**
- **Telescope useful**

Target birds

Spring/early summer: Goshawk 5%, Cuckoo 80%, Willow Warbler 90%, Garden Warbler 40%, Whitethroat 50%, Grey Wagtail 50%, Tree Pipit 60%, Linnet 60%, Crossbill 20%

Other likely species

All year	Common woodland birds	*Winter*
Mallard	Pied Wagtail	Winter thrushes
Buzzard		Common finches
Collared Dove	*Spring/summer*	
Great Spotted Woodpecker	Raven	
Common corvids	Hirundines	
	Summer warblers	
	Stonechat	

Recommended route and birding tips

THIS IS a relatively easy walk after a steep 120m ascent from the car park along a metalled track. The majority of the route is along well-defined tracks.

From the car park, go through the kissing gate. Initially the route is steep with bramble, gorse and low trees and bushes on either side. In spring and summer, Whitethroats and Chiffchaffs are regular sightings here, with small Linnet flocks also present. On reaching the ruined foundations of the former mine buildings, with interpretation board (point A), bear

left and continue almost straight ahead, ignoring the wide track on the left.

Continue up through the trees past a disused reservoir on the right. Pied and Grey Wagtails are often in this area, searching the water's edge. Pass through a kissing gate and bear right (way-marked to Pilgrim's Route/Greenmeadow Farm) along the edge of the woodland, keeping the fence line to your right. Continue along the track, keeping alert for Tree Pipit, Treecreeper and woodpecker species.

After about 1km, heathland and the

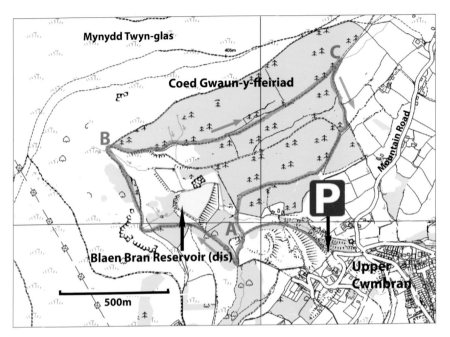

flank of Mynydd Maen open out on your left. Skylarks, Meadow Pipits and Stonechats can be seen and heard here. The track bears right, leading to a metal kissing gate (point B). Go through the kissing gate and enter the woodland along a well-defined track. Initially there are conifers to the left and an open sparsely wooded area to the right. Keep a look out for Crossbill in the conifers, and Wood Warbler and Garden Warbler on your right. Continue along the path for about 1km until you come to a track on the right (point C), immediately after a lay-by-type widening of the track. Take this track, which heads back down towards the reservoir descending through a well-wooded area where tits, thrushes and warblers can be numerous. After about 1km, the path crosses a stream and heads back uphill, where you arrive at the ruined foundations of the old mine that you passed at the start of the walk (point A). Turn left here and return to the car park.

How to get there

2 miles SSW of Pontypool

From Pontypool take the A4042 dual carriageway towards Cwmbran/Newport. Pass a 'McDonalds' and head to Cwmbran. At the next roundabout take the third exit (A4051) (signed Cwmbran) Continue along the A4051 through two roundabouts. At the next roundabout (Aldi store directly ahead) take the third exit, quickly followed by the first exit at the next roundabout (signed Upper Cwmbran). At the next roundabout take the third exit (Maendy Way), continue to the end of the road, turn left, and continue straight for about 0.25 miles. Turn right into Upper Cwmbran Road (signed Upper Cwmbran & Blaen Bran). Continue (passing the Queen Inn on the right) until the road widens out. The car park is straight ahead.

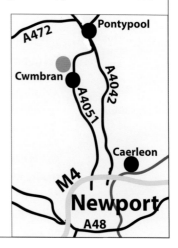

Public transport

By train: regular services run to Cwmbran station from where a short walk will take you to the Town Centre Bus Station.

By bus: regular services from Cardiff, Newport, Blaenavon and Abergavenny stop at Cwmbran Bus Station. From there, the local service to Thornhill will take you to within 800m of the walk start point. Alight at the Playing Fields stop. Cross the road and walk up Upper Cwmbran Road, passing the Queen Inn on the right. The road opens out, the car park/ start of the walk is straight ahead.

Three walks

- **Grouse Walk**
  SO264107
  (NP4 9SR)
  3 miles (5km)
- **Foothills Walk**
  SO278113
  (NP7 9LE)
  5.6 miles
  (9km)
- **Tramroad Walk**
  SO260122
  (NP7 9RY)
  2.5 miles
  (4km)
- **Take mountain precautions** (see p32)

THE BLORENGE is a plateau of upland heath covering an area of about five square kilometres in the Brecon Beacons National Park. Its main flora is heather, bilberry and bracken and its sides are steep slopes covered mostly with bracken, small trees and some rocky screes. The mountain is inhabited by many bird species that are characteristic of upland Wales. The predominant species, Meadow Pipit and Skylark, are present throughout the year, as are Red Grouse, Raven and Buzzard. During the breeding season they are are joined by Stonechat, Whinchat, Wheatear, Cuckoo, Tree Pipit, Willow Warbler, Redstart and Linnet.

Target birds

All walks
All year: Skylark 100%
Spring/summer: Stonechat 75%, Whinchat 90%, Wheatear 90%, Tree Pipit 100%
Foothills and Tramroad walks
Spring/summer: Redstart 90%, Cuckoo 90%
Grouse Walk
All year: Red Grouse 10% (winter), 80% (spring - early morning)

Other likely species

All year	*Summer*	
Buzzard	Willow Warbler	Common woodland birds (Foothills and Tramroad walks)
Raven	Linnet	
Meadow Pipit		

Recommended route and birding tips

THE BLORENGE can be accessed from several starting points, and provides walks of varied lengths and gradients.

Grouse Walk   SO264107   (NP4 9SR)   3 miles   Car park P1 (Foxhunter)

Before leaving the car park (P1), scan the area for Wheatears, which are often visible from here, and then take the path northeast to the highest point of The Blorenge. This is the best route to see or hear Red Grouse, particularly in spring or summer, and ideally in the early morning. The triangulation point at the summit (point A) is very good as an observation point and a quiet wait here can pay dividends. As well

54

as the possibility of spotting Red Grouse, the sight and sound of many Skylarks singing simultaneously is quite uplifting on a spring morning.

Descend from the highest point in a northeasterly direction along the visible footpath. Walk to the right of the brick hut, and carefully approach the edge of the plateau (there is a plunging drop at point B), before following the edge of the escarpment to the right, checking the stony banks immediately below you for Wheatear. Follow the track in a southerly direction through the bracken and take the right track where it forks (point C). This is a very good section to observe Whinchats and Tree Pipits. Turn right at the road (point D) and return to the starting point, pausing at Carn-y-gorfydd car park, to scan over the wall for Stonechats and Whinchats. It is here that the rare Marmora's Warbler was sighted in 2011.

Key points

- 3 miles (5km)
- Circular walk
- Walking boots required
- Several slopes of medium gradient

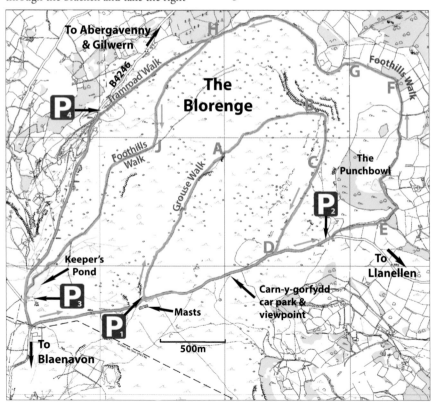

Foothills Walk   SO278113   (NP7 9LE)   5.6 miles   Car park P2

Key points

- 5.6 miles (9km)
- 4 miles (6.5km) if two cars are used, leaving one at Keeper's Pond (P3) SO255107
- Circular walk
- One medium climb of 1km length

HAVING PARKED on the grassy verge just above the cattle grid (P2), take the footpath to the left (north) of the grid, which is signposted 'Llanfoist 3.2km'. Check the conifers close to the road for Siskin. Descend through a gate at a Woodland Trust sign (point E) to the Punchbowl, listening for Blackcap, Chiffchaff and Garden Warbler. Follow the path as it takes you through the Punchbowl and then continues in a northerly direction. After about 1km it gradually turns west adjacent to a small woodland (point F). At a fork in the path above three large trees, take the left fork uphill (point G); continue to the dry-stone wall area, and if you wish, take a rest on the grassy verge whilst looking out for Redstart. The 1km stretch between here and the conifer woodland is excellent for Tree Pipit, Redstart and Cuckoo, particularly to the right of the path.

On approaching the conifer wood, listen for Goldcrest and Coal Tit. At the point where the path abuts the wood (point H), take the bridleway, which is signposted Keeper's Pond, climbing gradually up and to the left of the path. This walk through bracken is very good for Stonechat, Whinchat and Wheatear although the track can become rather overgrown in late summer. When you reach the main path (point J), turn right and continue to Keeper's Pond car park (P3). From here turn left onto the road, and then left again onto the next road, and back to the start point.

Tramroad Walk   SO260122   (NP7 9RY)   2.5 miles   Car park P4

Key points

- 2.5 miles (4km)
- Linear (there and back) walk
- Only slight gradients

FROM YOUR parking place at P4 take the Llanfoist footpath and immediately check the gorse to the right for Whinchat, Stonechat, Linnet and Willow Warbler. Cuckoos often use the trees adjacent to the path as a vantage point. A few hundred metres along the track is a further patch of gorse that should be checked for similar species. Scan and listen for Whinchat, Stonechat and Wheatear to either side of the path as you progress. Listen at the conifer forest for Goldcrest and Coal Tit. The next 1km stretch is very good for Tree Pipit, Redstart, Cuckoo and occasionally Yellowhammer, particularly to the left of the path. The path descends more steeply alongside a dry-stone wall, and looking over it, close to its end, can give excellent views of Redstart on short grass. Finish the walk at the wall's end (above Pen-y-graig

Farm) and return to the start point. An alternative route back can be taken via the bridleway which begins at the conifer wood (point H in the Foothills Walk). If this route is taken, turn right at The Keeper's Pond car park, and walk down the road to the start point.

How to get there

1-2 miles NE of Blaenavon

The B4246 Blaenavon to Abergavenny road runs beside The Blorenge.

For the Grouse Walk: travelling from the south on the B4246, turn right at the top of the hill (at the Torfaen boundary sign) into the unmarked road towards the transmitter masts. Coming from the north, this is a left turn shortly after you pass Keeper's Pond (marked on OS maps as Pen-fford-goch Pond) on your left. Follow this road for just over half a mile and park at the Foxhunter car park, opposite the transmitter masts (P1).

For the Foothills Walk: proceed as for the Grouse Walk but drive past the transmitter masts for a further mile and park on the grassy verge just above the cattle grid at P2. There is alternative parking at the viewpoint just up the hill.

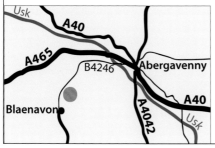

For the Tramroad Walk: travelling from the south, pass Keeper's Pond and drive a further mile. Park on the verge by a prominent tree on the left (west) side of the road opposite a two-armed fingerpost (P4), where there is room for two to three cars. There is alternative parking in lay-bys both up and down the road. The walk starts on the east of the road at a footpath sign marked 'Llanfoist 3.5km'.

Key points

- 2.2 miles (3.5 km)
- Moderate; some steeper sections
- Partly on open access land
- Best in spring/ summer
- Walking boots recommended
- Former industrial landscape
- Some off-road motor cycle activity
- Public transport

THIS WALK takes you through a former industrial landscape now characterised by widespread colonisation of gorse and other scrub. Beyond the disturbed areas the walk opens out to the more typical habitat of Gwent's western valleys – heathland, grassland, ancient woodland and ffridd. The remnants of built features scattered throughout this area provide additional attractions for those who enjoy supplementing their walks with an interest in industrial archaeology. A springtime visit is often the most productive, but a walk at any time of year can produce an interesting species list.

Target birds

Spring/summer: Cuckoo 40%, Whitethroat 50%, Ring Ouzel 10%, Redstart 50%, Wheatear 60%, Pied Flycatcher 10%, Tree Pipit 40%, Linnet 60%, Lesser Redpoll 40%, Yellowhammer 60%, Reed Bunting 60%

Other likely species

All year	*Spring/summer*	*Occasional*
Common raptors	Peregrine	Grey Heron
Stock Dove	Summer warblers	Red Kite
Tawny Owl		Merlin
Woodpeckers	*Winter*	Hobby
Common corvids	Woodcock	Red Grouse
Raven	Winter thrushes	Grey Partridge
Goldcrest	Common finches	Little Owl
Meadow Pipit	Siskin	Dipper
	Brambling	

Recommended route and birding tips

STARTING FROM your parking place at the Big Arch, proceed through the arch structure and go straight ahead through the metal kissing gate. Here the landscape opens out into an area of grassland surrounded by vegetated coal tips to the north and a railway embankment (now cycleway) to the east. Kestrels are known to have bred within some of the structures in this area and species such as Jackdaw, Redstart, Great Tit, Swallow and Pied Wagtail also take advantage of the many built features. Whitethroat, Blackcap, Willow Warbler and Chiffchaff are also commonly found in the dense scrub that characterise the boundary features here.

Passing between the two derelict former National Coal Board buildings (point A), the footpath climbs steeply for about 100m. At the crown of the slope good views of the setting of this former industrial landscape can be achieved. (NB in wet conditions, there is an alternative path passing to the left of and then behind the derelict buildings).

Here the true extent of the gorse scrub can be appreciated and a visit during the spring when the plants are in flower is recommended. It is at this point that those with knowledge of bird song will be able to identify the songs of Yellowhammer, Stonechat, Lesser Redpoll and Linnet. Other species frequently encountered will include Song Thrush, Blackbird, Whitethroat, Dunnock, Wren, Willow Warbler and Meadow Pipit. Where the plateau of colliery spoil remains unvegetated, Lapwings have been recorded.

Continuing along the path, the terrain moderates for easier walking. Take a left turn at the electricity poles (point B) and make the short climb up to Farm Road (there is a Jehovah's Witness building on your left at the top of the slope). Turn right onto Farm Road and walk a short distance until there is a road off to the left. Take the left turn and walk uphill for a short distance. The road turns to the left and the landscape once again opens up to consist of ponds,

spoil tips, rough grassland and scattered trees (point C). Walk past the yard and building on your left, and after a short climb take a path on your right, which begins adjacent to a stile on the left side of the road. This location (point D) can be good for Little Owl and, in winter, mixed finch flocks.

After about 50m go over a stile and walk west along Cwm Sychan, with fine views across the valley. Initially the footpath passes through grazed fields with some large beech trees as boundary features. Further on, the path is close to typical ffridd habitat with frequent Tree Pipits, Meadow Pipits and Skylarks; Whinchats are also present where bracken dominates. At the western end of the valley you will reach a dam.

The valley here is characterised by a disused pond with a large stone dam, and surrounded by sheep-grazed grassland and ffridd habitat. The best time to visit is in springtime when Wheatears may be joined by one or more passage Ring Ouzels to feed in the short, grazed grassland. The marshy areas are good for Reed Bunting and, occasionally, Snipe. Raptors have featured in the past with Merlin and more commonly Peregrine and Red Kite.

Turn right here and cross to the north end of the dam (point E), then turn right (east)

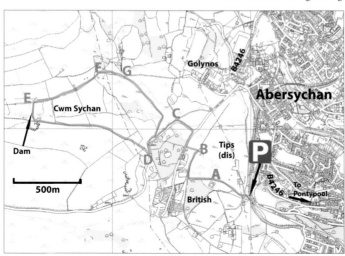

through sheep-grazed fields flanked with berry-laden hawthorn trees. The trees in this area support winter thrushes and are also ideal for the occasional passage Ring Ouzel.

As you cross a stile you will see a large red-bricked former colliery engine house (point F). Once again the habitat here is a mixture of coal spoil, grassland and heathland. At this point look out for Whitethroat, Pied Wagtail and breeding Long-tailed Tit. The familiar 'walking stick' dropping of the Green Woodpecker is worth looking for on the many anthills that are present here.

Keeping the engine house on your right, descend the track for about 200m until you come to a fork (point G), and take the right (less well-defined) path. You are now descending towards the yard and building

you passed earlier, and the pathway follows a former industrial track that drops steeply and is flanked by some large spoil tips to the east. This area is known as The British Heath and supports Tree Pipit, Whinchat, Stonechat, Linnet and Whitethroat during spring and summer. In winter flocks of Fieldfare and Redwing can be encountered. Woodcocks are often flushed from the more scrubby areas. A small, mature beech woodland to the east of the track supports Wood Warbler and other typical woodland birds such as Nuthatch, Treecreeper, Green Woodpecker and Redstart on its outer edge.

Step carefully over the small brook, pass the spoil heaps and rejoin the surfaced road (between points C and D). Turn left and walk down to Farm Road, then retrace your steps to the Big Arch, returning along the same footpath as on your outward journey.

How to get there

3 miles NW of Pontypool

Leaving the A4042 at the Pontypool roundabout, take the A427 towards Pontypool. At the roundabout take the second exit onto the A4043 signed Big Pit Blaenavon. Follow the A4043 via several roundabouts and through Pontnewynydd. Before traffic lights in Abersychan turn left onto Union Street (B4246). Continue for half a mile before arriving at Big Arch, The British. The Big Arch is a former railway bridge/tunnel on the left hand side of the road at a point where the main road turns sharply right. The Big Arch is used by occasional road traffic but there is space to park on the left in front of it.

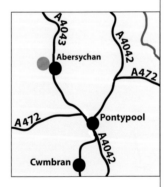

Alternatively, from Brynmawr, exit the A465 at Brynmawr roundabout and follow the signs to Blaenavon and from there, the A4043 to Abersychan and Pontypool. Just after traffic lights in Abersychan, turn right onto Union Street (B4246) and continue as above.

Public transport

Buses serve Talywain (not Sundays), from where it is a short walk to the Big Arch.

WE HAVE used the title Brynmawr Ponds to cover two former industrial lakes – Dunlop Semtex Pond and Machine Pond. The walk takes you through the urban fringe of Brynmawr following readily accessible paths around both of the ponds. Much of the habitat is typical of that found in the South Wales valleys, including wetland, scrub, acid grassland and open water. The walk is circular, commencing in a supermarket car park before proceeding to more open managed parkland. It can be rewarding throughout the year, though be prepared for bracing weather during the depths of winter. The year-round presence of water birds and the accessible nature of the lakes make this a good walk for beginners getting to grips with the seasonal plumage variations of wildfowl. Spring and autumn can produce an unexpected wader or passerine on passage.

Key points

- About 1.2 miles (2 km)
- Easy walking mostly on metalled surface
- Good all-year birding
- Challenging weather during winter
- Facilities in supermarket
- Main route wheelchair friendly
- Accessible by public transport

Target birds

All year: Tufted Duck 100%, Great Crested Grebe 70%, Little Grebe 70%, Coot 100%, regular gulls 80%, Stonechat 40%, Skylark 50%, Reed Bunting 50%

Winter: Gadwall 20%, Pochard 70%, Goldeneye 40%, Goosander 60%, Water Rail 10%

Other likely species

All year	Grey Wagtail	*Winter*
Mute Swan	Pied Wagtail	Wigeon
Canada Goose	Goldfinch	Teal
Cormorant	Linnet	Winter thrushes
Grey Heron		Common finches
Red Kite	*Spring/summer*	
Common waterfowl	Lapwing	*Occasional*
Herring Gull	Common Sandpiper	Smew
Lesser Black-backed Gull	Hirundines	Passage waders
	Summer warblers	Common Tern
Meadow Pipit	Whinchat	Common Gull

Recommended route and birding tips

This is an easy walk, though with some inclines, and follows metalled wheelchair-accessible surfaces although it is possibly a little steep for some wheelchairs at points C and D. Adjacent

61

habitats can be accessed if desired but this will often involve more of a ramble on uneven ground.

An observation area at the southern end of the Lakeside Retail Park car park gives good views of the Dunlop Semtex Pond (DSP) but with some restriction at the eastern corner owing to waterside vegetation. The car park itself can also be useful for viewing Lesser Black-backed and Herring Gulls during spring and early summer, when a nearby factory unit supports a thriving colony of breeding birds.

Leaving the car park, follow the path to the left of the Willow Tree pub, over a small bridge with wooden sides, and on to the outskirts of a housing estate (point A). At

this point the path splits in three directions. Take the left hand route, which follows the edge of the lake. After approximately 100m the path opens out into a semi-circular viewing area (point B) and offers fine all-round views. During the autumn and winter months the lake supports a moderate population of wildfowl. Historically, flocks of over one hundred Tufted Duck and Pochard have been recorded, along with similar numbers of Coot. Canada Goose is now present all year together with Mallard, Mute Swan, Great Crested Grebe, Little Grebe and Moorhen. A regular wildfowl counter will also infrequently record Teal, Wigeon, Gadwall, Goosander, Goldeneye, and Water Rail. Rarities can occur and have included Smew and Scaup.

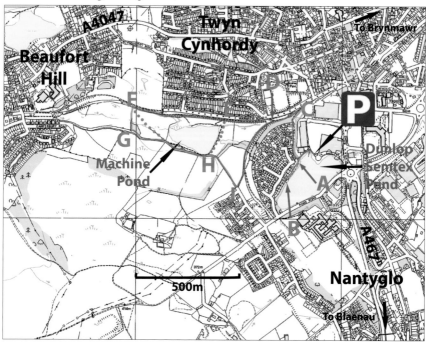

During the breeding season some wildfowl remain to breed, notably Tufted Duck, Great Crested Grebe and Little Grebe. During the passage months of spring and autumn, Common Sandpiper, Sand Martin, Common Tern and Sedge Warbler often occur.

From the viewing area, retrace your footsteps back to the bridge (point A). Now take the footpath due north that runs to the left of an inlet stream between the rear of the retail park and the housing estate. This green corridor has produced Water Rail feeding alongside the stream and Lesser Redpoll and Siskin in the developing alder carr. After about 200m the path climbs steeply for a short distance to a T-junction (point C). At this point, good elevated views of the retail park with DSP beyond are obtainable. Here, during spring and summer, better views of the gull colony are offered, with nests and immature birds clearly visible.

Take the sharp left turn. The path now leads to another former industrial lake known to birders as Machine Pond, which is part of Parc Nant-y-Waun. The lake and its surroundings have been developed as a managed parkland environment with good walking and fishing facilities, and wheelchair-friendly cycle paths. Although smaller than the nearby DSP the assemblage of wildfowl is often the same, although this site, with its extensive reed margins to the north, is often better for species such as Teal, Gadwall and Snipe.

Dunlop Semtex Pond in late summer   *Dave Brassey*

63

Goldeneye is also more frequent here.

Where the path begins to curve round to the left (point D), follow the narrower path that forks to the right and takes you onto a higher, broad path that leads due west above the north bank of the lake. At point E it is possible to take a narrow path along the northern edge of the lake that rejoins the main path a little further on (not recommended for wheelchairs). On the western side of the lake a steep adjacent field has supported breeding Lapwings. In the spring, singing Skylarks and Meadow Pipits are also characteristic here. Proceed through a small wooded area, where winter thrushes and finches can be found, while in spring you may be rewarded with an early singing Chiffchaff or Willow Warbler.

200m beyond the lake (point F) take a left turn that leads over a large footbridge and crosses an area of open water and marshland. This is a good vantage point from which to view the pond. In the adjacent habitat Reed Bunting is a frequent breeding bird. Stonechats and Whinchats are also present in summer.

Continue across the bridge and after a short distance turn left (point G) onto a broad metalled path which leads eastwards back to the lake and along its south bank. At point H you can take a narrower path along the east bank of the lake, leading back to point E, but the recommended route continues along the main path through young woodland and scrub habitats. After about 250m you reach the corner of a housing estate (point J) where you turn left through a kissing gate. Continue northwards, looking and listening for Willow Warblers, Blackcaps and other woodland birds, and watching out for over-flying Brambling, Red Kite or Peregrine. Rejoin your outward path at point D and return to the car park.

How to get there

Outskirts of Brynmawr

Head north towards Brynmawr on the A467, and at the Brynmawr roundabout follow the signs for Town Centre. At the second roundabout take the first exit left. Continue to the next roundabout taking 2nd exit into the Lakeside Retail Park. The walk starts at the far end of the shops that are on your right as you enter the car park.

Public transport

Lakeside Retail Park is a five-minute walk from Brynmawr Bus Station. There are no rail services to Brynmawr.

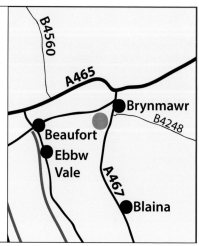

THIS IS a fairly long, linear walk on which you return by retracing your outward route. It follows the lower Usk Valley, passing the Celtic Manor Resort Golf Course with associated lakes and pools, and approaching close to the River Usk in places. It passes through, or close to, a variety of other habitats, including woodland and farmland, so birdlife is always varied and there is interest in all seasons. The basic walk is along the Bulmore Road, but with an optional diversion up a steep footpath. There is no public access to the golf course but the lakes can be viewed from the road, or more distantly from the footpath diversion. The lakes are most rewarding in winter and at first light before golfing activity has started. There is no access to riverside fields or river bank, but the river is visible from the road at several points and in winter holds Goosander, Wigeon and Teal, with Green Sandpiper regular on the lower stretches.

Key points

- About 4.5 miles (7km)
- Easy walk on metalled road
- All-year birding interest
- Best at first light
- Wheelchair access along road
- Telescope essential
- Road traffic very light
- Public transport

Target birds

All year: Great Crested Grebe 90%
Winter: Goosander 90%, Wigeon 90%
Autumn/spring: Green Sandpiper 40%

Other likely species

All year		Spring/summer/autumn
Cormorant	Thrushes	
Mute Swan	Reed Bunting	Common Sandpiper
Canada Goose	*Winter*	Reed Warbler
Tufted Duck	Little Grebe	*Occasional*
Common waterfowl	Teal	Barnacle Goose
Buzzard	Pochard	Brent Goose
Tits	Common Sandpiper	Goldeneye
Skylark	Winter thrushes	Barn Owl

Recommended route and birding tips

FROM YOUR parking place, walk back along the road towards Caerleon. After about 100m there is a pair of locked metal gates on the left with a walk-thru stile to the left. Pass through the stile and proceed up the steep lane till you reach a derelict farm on the left. Turn right at the yellow way-marked sign, and after a few strides you will reach an open area with

65

commanding views over the Usk Valley, golf course and lakes (point A). From here, use your telescope for a preliminary scan of the lakes for birds of interest. Now retrace your steps to the road and continue towards Caerleon.

You will soon reach the golf course and see the lakes on your right. Fairly good views over the pools can be obtained through gaps in the hedge and at gateways; viewing is easier in winter when there is less foliage. Tufted Ducks and Great Crested Grebes are present all year and breed; in the case of the grebes, up to three pairs have bred in recent years. In winter Goosanders are likely, but generally early in the morning before golfing activity gets underway.

About 2km from your parking place, a long stretch of the river can be viewed from Little Bulmore (point B) and during the winter months Goosanders are usually present here. After a further 900m (point C), the confluence of the Afon Lwyd and the River Usk can be viewed, though with some difficulty, between trees. During the winter a number of ducks including Wigeon, Teal and Mallard can be seen and Green Sandpiper is a regular occurrence on these lower stretches of the river. Continue for another 500m and turn right opposite the Bell Inn into Isca Road. Walk to the far end of the road for excellent views of the river (point D) where Green Sandpiper may again be seen. Complete the walk by retracing your steps to your parking spot.

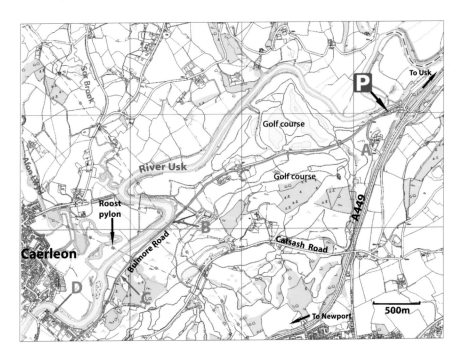

How to get there

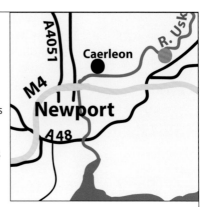

About 2 miles E of Caerleon

From Caerleon take the B4596 to Newport and after crossing the bridge over the River Usk, turn immediately left into New Road (signed to Christchurch). After just 300 metres turn left again onto Bulmore Road. This is a single-track road with passing spaces but carries very little traffic. After about two miles you pass under a footbridge over the road, and soon afterwards the road straightens and widens greatly (ST374920), allowing safe roadside parking. Pull your nearside wheels onto the left hand verge.

Public transport

Bus services run frequently between Newport bus station and Caerleon, stopping at Caerleon bridge near the Ship Inn. From the bus stop, walk along Lulworth Road and Isca Road to reach Bulmore Road and walk the route in reverse.

Key points

- Distance 1.3 miles (2km)
- Easy
- Some paths usable by wheelchairs
- Facilities close by in Abergavenny
- High disturbance levels
- Public transport

THIS WALK is close to the centre of Abergavenny. The Castle Meadows are used intensively by dog-walkers, and the disturbance level is extremely high at all times of the day, including late summer evenings. A visit at first light from May to August offers the best chance of a quiet time. The meadows comprise improved grassland, which is grazed by horses and cattle in summer to late autumn. There is easy access from Byfield Lane car park, by Linda Vista Gardens, and the route is negotiable by wheelchair, with a hard-surfaced path along the river. There are several other access points, which are harder to locate. It is not far from either the Abergavenny Bus Station or the railway station. The mature gardens and orchards close to the meadows hold a variety of bird species, as also do the hills surrounding the town. Beware paragliders landing unexpectedly!

Target birds

All year: Goosander 60%, Sparrowhawk 30%, Kingfisher 50%, Dipper 80%

Spring/summer: Hobby 30%, Common Sandpiper 90%, Sand Martin 100%

Other likely species

All year
Mallard
Cormorant
Grey Heron
Buzzard
Moorhen
Regular gulls
Tawny Owl
Green Woodpecker
Great Spotted Woodpecker
Common corvids
Tits
Nuthatch
Grey Wagtail

Pied Wagtail
Common finches
Reed Bunting

Spring/summer
Hobby
Hirundines
Summer warblers
Spotted Flycatcher

Winter
Little Grebe
Water Rail
Snipe
Winter thrushes
Meadow Pipit

Lesser Redpoll
Siskin

Passage
Little Ringed Plover
Stonechat
Wheatear

Occasional
Lesser Spotted Woodpecker

Recommended route and birding tips

THIS IS an easy, level walk, and most birds can be seen easily with binoculars. The concrete track can have standing water in wet conditions. Once or twice a year the river can flood the entire area to a depth of several feet but it drains away very quickly, and the sandy ground does not hold water long.

Exit the car park in the southwest corner (disabled access) below the Linda Vista Gardens. The trees attract common garden and woodland birds. You can cross the meadows straight to the river following an established track, or continue along the hedge to the road bridge, with orchards and gardens to your right. At the bridge (point A) there is disabled access. Stop for a few minutes here, as Dippers are often seen near the bridge, and it is a good spot to see Kingfisher and Common Sandpiper too. There is a very deep pool below the bridge where salmon gather in the autumn before running up-river. Otters have been sighted here, while on summer evenings, daubenton's bats can be seen hunting over the water surface, and noctule bats fly high overhead.

Follow the hard-surface path along the length of the river and look out for Goosander, Common Sandpiper and Grey Wagtail. Watch the sky overhead for raptors. There is also a good track nearer the water's edge for most of the way.

At point B, 500m along the river from the bridge, there is a large shingle bank (a designated SSSI), which is becoming increasingly vegetated as willow becomes established. You can walk out on this when water levels permit, and lampreys can be seen here. Common Sandpipers have bred here in the past. The large sand-cliff opposite had a strong colony of Sand Martins until it was destroyed by erosion early in 2013; fortunately it was already showing good signs of recovery later in the year. Kingfishers have also nested here some years. In harsh winters, this is a good spot for Water Rail and Snipe. The alders and willows are good for Siskin and Lesser Redpoll in winter, while in summer you will find warblers and

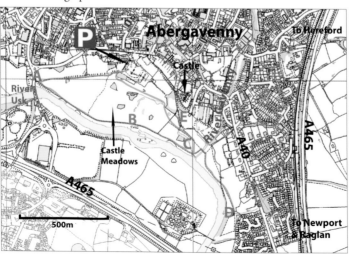

Reed Buntings here. Little Egrets do not nest anywhere locally, but single birds can often be seen in winter. During migration, Meadow Pipit, Stonechat, Wheatear and Little Ringed Plover pass through, and even Osprey has been sighted.

In 300m there is a footbridge across a ditch. About 30m further on there is a larger bridge across the Gavenny stream (point C) - this is another good spot for Water Rail in winter. The path leads on along the river to two smaller fields with a gate between, where there are mature oaks. This can be a good spot for Lesser Spotted Woodpecker, plus Tawny Owl, Spotted Flycatcher and Bullfinch, attracted by the old fruit trees in nearby gardens. In winter, Redwing, Fieldfare and other thrushes occur, while in the autumn, Goldfinches come for the thistle heads in the unmown areas. At the end of the second field (point D), turn and retrace your steps to the bridge.

Instead of turning left at the end of the bridge to follow the river bank, walk straight ahead, parallel to the hedge on your right. Then either cross a level bridge across a ditch and carry on to your access point to the meadows, or keep right and leave by a gate (point E) below the castle. Once through the gate, bear left up a steepish path (the dotted red line on the map), keep straight on, and you are back in Tudor Street, where there are public toilets, and the access to the car parks. This road is parallel to the main shopping street, which has abundant coffee shops and cafes.

How to get there

S of Abergavenny town centre

From Merthyr, leave the A465 at the Town Centre turn-off (A4143), and turn left by Waitrose supermarket. Cross the river, take the second exit at a roundabout, up a slight rise and take the first turning right (Tudor Street); just past the Job-Centre on your left is a turning on the right down to the car park. This car park is free except on Tuesdays (Market Day – very busy). Other car parks are not free.

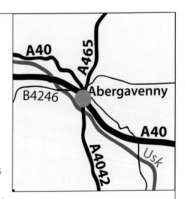

From Brecon, pass the hospital, and take the third exit at the roundabout, first exit at the next roundabout, up a slight rise and take the first turning right, as above.

From Newport or Monmouth, take the A465 towards Merthyr. Take the first exit marked Abergavenny A4143 (following signs to Abergavenny), which leads to the Waitrose supermarket roundabout and joins the route from Merthyr.

THIS WALK takes in an easy circuit of approximately 2.5 miles (4 km) in an elevated area of mixed pasture and arable farmland typical of central Gwent. The River Usk lies immediately to the west of the suggested route, while Clytha Park and Clytha Castle, an eighteenth century folly, lie to the northwest. The walk starts at a popular country inn, crossing fields and following quiet lanes flanked by large deep hedges. Areas of woodland, both young and mature, lie along the walk and the area is criss-crossed by additional routes that can be incorporated by the walker.

This is a walk best suited to the spring or summer when about 35-40 species can be expected, including a number of red-listed farmland birds.

Key points

- 2.5 miles (4km)
- Easy walking on quiet lanes and footpaths; several stiles
- Best in spring/ summer
- Cattle likely to be encountered
- Facilities at Clytha Arms

Target birds

All year: Lapwing 80%, Stock Dove 80%, Little Owl 50%, Lesser Spotted Woodpecker 5%, Marsh Tit 30%, Skylark 90%, Linnet 90%, Yellowhammer 90%

Spring/summer: Hobby 30%, Spotted Flycatcher 80%, Redstart 50%, Yellow Wagtail 20%

Other likely species

All year	Nuthatch	*Winter*
Mallard	Treecreeper	Winter thrushes
Red-legged Partridge	House Sparrow	Common finches
Grey Heron	Pied Wagtail	Siskin
Common raptors	Grey Wagtail	Lesser Redpoll
Raven	Bullfinch	
Moorhen		*Occasional*
Tawny Owl	*Spring/summer*	Goshawk
Green Woodpecker	Hirundines	Red Kite
Great Spotted Woodpecker	Summer warblers	Curlew
	Garden Warbler	Barn Owl
	Whitethroat	

Recommended route and birding tips

THE STARTING point for this walk is The Clytha Arms pub. From the car park, take the tarmac road to the main road, which should be crossed carefully, and then ascend a set of stone steps opposite the pub. Pass through the gate and over the stile, and after a short distance, turn right to cross another stile. Turn left and walk up the field with the hedge to

71

your left (if you are following an OS map this is the most easterly of three marked footpaths leading from the stile). Clytha Castle can be seen clearly to your right.

The path leads to a cottage with a stile to the left of it, cross it and continue uphill to a gate. Go through the gate, and follow the footpath which runs diagonally to the far top corner, to the left of the large trees. To your left is an area of woodland called 'New Covert', the edges of which are worth scanning for Spotted Flycatcher and Redstart. At the next stile turn right to meet a narrow lane (point A). From here there are far-reaching views north towards Ysgyryd Fawr – check for raptors, as Kestrels are occasionally seen, Buzzards are common and Red Kite increasingly so.

Take the centre lane past Twyn Farm and then turn right past Twyn Cottage. Little Owls regularly nest in the outbuildings here, as do colonies of Swallows and House Sparrows. There is a sizeable overgrown pond that is easily overlooked adjacent to Twyn Cottage (point B) where Mallard and Moorhen both breed. Grey Wagtail is often seen here, as are numerous tits, finches, warblers and thrushes. Unsurprisingly, Sparrowhawks visit here on occasion. As you follow the lane up a slight gradient, look and listen out for Yellowhammer and Linnet calling from the tops of taller hedges and telephone wires.

Follow the lane down a dip past a few houses where Great Spotted and Green Woodpeckers often put in an appearance. The lane leads to a T-junction where you should turn right. There is woodland either side of you here, in which Jay, Marsh Tit, Blackcap, Garden Warbler and Bullfinch can be seen among other species. Pass Pen-yr-heol, a smallholding, and carry on uphill for a short way to point C where there are good views from this elevated position. Lapwing and Skylark regularly breed nearby and can be easily seen and heard. Curlews are occasional breeders and the hedges here hold good numbers of Whitethroats most years. Retrace your steps downhill and take the grassy track to your left, immediately next to Pen-yr-heol. Yellowhammer

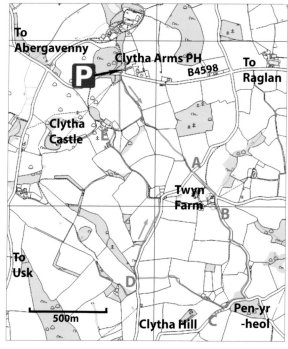

and Linnet frequent this locality and there are good views across the fields, which can produce Stock Dove and Red-legged Partridge as well as the more common Wood Pigeon and Pheasant.

At the end of the track there is a stile to the left; cross it, head right and go through a gate into the next field by way of a track behind the house. Follow the left hand hedge until you meet another gate (nearby stile is overgrown), pass through it and aim ahead to the left of the large trees. Follow the path to a lane (point D) whilst keeping an eye and ear open for the Skylarks that breed here and Yellow Wagtails feeding among the livestock.

Turn right and follow the lane past a small stand of Scots pine in which Coal Tit and Goldcrest may be found. As you approach a house on a sharp right bend, look out for a stile on the left. Cross the stile and keep the hedge to your right;

pass through the gap in the hedge down to the large open field below. With the hedge to your right, pass through the gap with the large trees and continue downhill toward the outbuildings/stables (point E). This footpath gives good views northwest towards The Blorenge – again, look out for raptors and Raven. The buildings hold good numbers of breeding Swallows and House Martins, which in turn attract the occasional speculative visit from Hobby during the summer.

Exit this field via the gate and follow the track downhill. At the first junction, turn right along a grassy track into a large open field. Cross diagonally through the field, aiming for the larger trees. Cross the stile in the corner and turn left towards the road – the Clytha Arms is straight ahead. Along this final leg you will pass mature beech, lime, oak and sweet chestnut trees that attract Spotted Flycatcher in summer and numerous finches in winter.

How to get there

About 7 miles SE of Abergavenny

The walk start point is The Clytha Arms, a dog-friendly pub/restaurant where birdwatchers can park. This is situated on the old Abergavenny to Raglan road.

If approaching from the A449, exit at Raglan and follow the A40 to the first roundabout, then take the fourth exit marked Clytha – the pub is on your right after about 3 miles.

From the A465/A4042 roundabout at Abergavenny, initially follow signs for A40 to Midlands and Monmouth, and then follow signs for the B4598, signed Usk and Raglan, (taking care not to join the A40). The pub is on your left after about 6 miles.

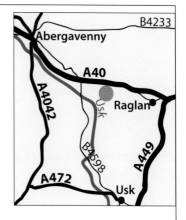

Key points

- Southern path: 5 miles (8km) return
- Northern loop: 4.4 miles (7km) circular walk
- Combined walks: 6.2 miles (10km)
- Steep climb, reasonable fitness required
- Walking boots essential
- Best in spring/ summer
- Take mountain precautions (see p32)
- Dangerous to stray from track
- Telescope useful

This is a walk through the uplands of northwest Gwent in an area that is typical of the coalfield area of the county. The walk skirts plantations, bogs, lakes and streams, together with old farms, before climbing on to the Coity Mountain itself, reaching heights of over 500m. The views from the summit are spectacular. The final section overlaps the Waun Afon Bog Walk (Walk 50).

A visit in spring or summer will produce the most species, but autumn passage can produce some interesting sightings. Winter can be bleak on the tops, with little to see, but there is always a chance of something unusual, whilst the lower levels can always be productive. A total of over 30 species should be easily possible at any time of the year.

Target birds

All year: Reed Bunting 50%
Spring/summer: Grasshopper Warbler 30%, Ring Ouzel 10% (during passage), Redstart 40%, Whinchat 50%, Stonechat 50%, Wheatear 70%, Tree Pipit 50%

Other likely species

All year	Common woodland birds	Hirundines
Common raptors		Summer warblers
Peregrine	Grey Wagtail	Whitethroat
Red Kite	Pied Wagtail	Meadow Pipit
Red Grouse	Common finches	
Grey Partridge		*Winter*
Pheasant	*Spring/summer*	Hen Harrier
Green Woodpecker	Hobby	Merlin
Great Spotted Woodpecker	Lapwing	Barn Owl
Common corvids	Curlew	Long-eared Owl
Raven	Snipe	Short-eared Owl
	Cuckoo	Winter thrushes
	Skylark	Brambling

Recommended routes and birding tips

From the car park at Whistle Road, Garn-yr-erw, follow the metalled road southwest. On the left is a plantation (point A), which in spring and summer can hold Chiffchaff, Willow Warbler, Blackcap and Garden Warbler. On the right is a wet area that can hold Grasshopper Warbler and Sedge Warbler. Keep an eye on the sky for raptors, including Kestrel, Sparrowhawk and Buzzard, and also Peregrine. After approximately 300m the road passes over the railway line and the Whistle Inn is on the left. Look out for common birds in this area, together with Stonechat. Shortly after this, the metalled road becomes a track (point B) and passes the ruins of Field Farm on the right hand side. Look for Little Owls on the old buildings and Redstarts and Wheatears along the dry-stone walls. Watching at dusk may produce a Barn Owl and, on summer evenings, the sound of drumming Snipe may be heard. On the left are some semi-improved fields: Grey Partridge can occasionally be seen here.

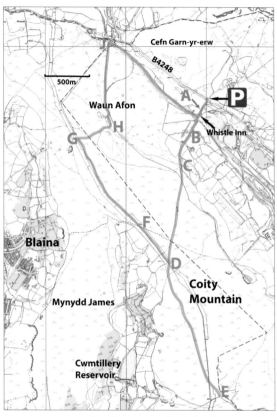

Shortly, the track begins to rise to a steep ascent (point C). Cross over the stile and follow the obvious track towards the summit. After a short distance, the track crosses a metalled road and heads upwards. Meadow Pipits and Skylarks can been seen here, together with Whinchats in spring and summer. After passing an old quarry below the path on the left, the top is soon reached.

Continue along the track until you approach a dry-stone wall where a crossroads is reached (point D). Keep a sharp lookout, since Hen Harrier and Merlin are sometimes seen, particularly at spring and autumn passage periods. Hobbies may also be seen during spring and summer, crossing from one valley to the next, or hawking for dragonflies on the moorland pools. Red Kites are fairly regular all year round, whilst Short-eared Owls may be seen during late winter, particularly in late afternoon.

At the crossroads in the path, there are two options.

Southern path

Turn left and head south.

The chances of finding Red Grouse increase as the path leads to the south. Large stands of mature heather are to be found either side of the path and the grouse are to be found here. All the typical moorland species can be encountered. Head south as far as you wish (toward point E), then turn and retrace your steps.

Northern loop

Turn right at point D and head north.

This option allows for a circular walk, but is not so productive in terms of finding Red Grouse, although several other species may be encountered.

The path follows a dry-stone wall, where Redstarts and Wheatears may be seen, and when it forks, take the wider track to the right (point F). After about 1km, the path skirts a small disused quarry on the left, where Wheatears can be seen in spring and summer. Ring Ouzel on passage can occasionally be found here in mid-April. Keep looking out for raptors.

The path then begins to descend. After about 300m a round metal post (point

G) is found on the right hand side of the track. From just beyond this point take the broad track on the right hand side, and descend to join an unclassified metalled road (point H). There are several remnant patches of heather here, which can hold a few pairs of Red Grouse. Short-eared Owls also hunt here in winter, particularly in late afternoon and Hen Harrier can be present during passage and also in winter. Follow the metalled road north towards the B4248.

Shortly after passing through a gate and barrier (point J) and before reaching the B4248, turn sharp right through another gate and follow the old railway track south. Initially the track is metalled but it forks right after a short while onto a grassy surface between two banks. Look for Whinchats, Stonechats, Reed Buntings and Grasshopper Warblers along the track. After approximately 1km, the track rejoins the road at the Whistle Inn. Turn left here and follow the road back to the car park.

How to get there

1-2 miles NW of Blaenavon

Leave Blaenavon on the B4248 signposted Brynmawr. After about 1.25 miles, enter the village of Garn-yr-erw. Shortly after leaving the village turn left onto an unclassified road signposted to the Whistle Inn and immediately turn left again into a car park.

Public transport

Regular bus service between Blaenavon and Brynmawr.

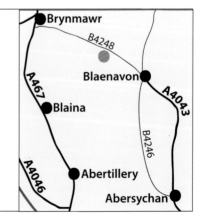

THIS WALK takes you across the Gwent Levels to the seawall, south of the village of Undy in the southeast of the county. The walk is on level terrain with about half a dozen gates/stiles to cross, but can be very muddy in places after prolonged periods of rain. Birding interest varies greatly with the time of the year but is potentially good at any season. To maximise the number of waders and waterfowl seen, it is best to visit at high tide, but great care must be taken not to disturb roosting flocks.

Target birds

All year: Shelduck 80%, Oystercatcher 80%, Curlew 90%, Redshank 70%

Winter: Wigeon 90%, Little Egret 80%, Spoonbill 5%, Merlin 30%, Grey Plover 30%, Dunlin 90%, Snipe 50%, Turnstone 40%, Short-eared Owl 70%, Snow Bunting 10%

Summer: Hobby 50%, Lapwing 90%, Cuckoo 40%, Wheatear 60%

Other likely species

Spring/summer	*Autumn/winter*	*Passage*
Red-legged Partridge	Brent Goose	Ringed Plover
Peregrine	Teal	Common Sandpiper
Avocet	Pintail	Greenshank
Willow Warbler	Black-tailed Godwit	Redstart
Whitethroat	Bar-tailed Godwit	Whinchat
Lesser Whitethroat	Stonechat	Whimbrel
Garden Warbler	Water Pipit	Yellow Wagtail
Sedge Warbler	Brambling	
Reed Warbler		

Key points

- **4 miles (6.5km)**
- **Flat terrain**
- **Parts can be very muddy**
- **All year interest**
- **Best at high tide for waders & wildfowl**
- *Disturbance to roosting wader flocks must be avoided*
- **Telescope essential**

Recommended route and birding tips

THE WALK begins at St Mary's Church, Undy, from where an impressive rookery can be seen behind the derelict farm opposite. In the early part of the walk you can see the flat landscape of the Levels reclaimed from the sea many years ago. The hedgerows along this part of the walk are good places to see more common species such as Dunnock, Collared Dove, Robin, Blackbird and Wren.

From the car park, with your back to the church and facing the derelict farm, turn right along the road. Follow the road for about 150m to a junction (point A) where you bear right into a lane signposted as Cycle Route 4 and

77

with 'no through road' signs after about 20m. Continue along this winding lane, ignoring any side roads or tracks, passing Brook House on your left and eventually reaching a T-junction (point B) where you go right into another winding lane. After about 300m you will see on your right a wide metal gate with a smaller one next to it (point C). Pass through the small gate and check the culvert on your left, which is a favourite haunt for both Pied and Grey Wagtails. Almost immediately pass through another gate on your right to enter a field; turn left, keeping the small brick building and the hedge on your left. On the far side of the hedge there is a large reen known as Collister Pill and the raised walk on which

you are standing is known as the seawall reen bank. On the lower land to your right, keep your eyes peeled for Red-legged Partridge, Grey Heron, Little Egret and Meadow Pipit. To your left, on the other side of the Pill, the ploughed fields are ideal habitat for Lapwing. Keeping the fence and Pill on your left, continue along the raised bank till it opens into a broad field with a large tree, which is a good spot for owls. Shortly afterwards you will see a stile and bridge crossing the Pill. Ignore this bridge and continue following the Pill until your way is barred by a locked gate; you will see another bridge over the Pill on your left with a stile at each end (point D). Cross the bridge through the two stiles. This is a

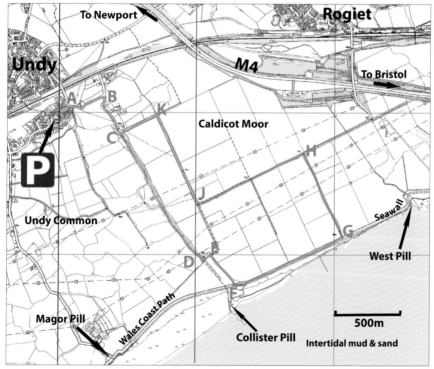

good spot to see Whitethroat, and Willow and Garden Warblers. Cross the field towards the gate at the other side, but turn right at point E before reaching the gate, following the hedge to the seawall, which is clearly visible.

Just before reaching the seawall (point F) you will cross another bridge with a hedgerow on your left that may hold Linnet, Goldfinch, Song Thrush, and Lesser and Common Whitethroats. Before climbing the seawall please be aware that the area beyond the wall is a haven for all types of waders and wildfowl, so care must be taken not to disturb the flocks. Carefully look over the wall – when the tide is in, the saltmarsh grassland acts as a high-tide roost for many species including Grey Plover, Shelduck, Black and Bar-tailed Godwits, Dunlin, Curlew, Whimbrel, Avocet and Little Egret. After viewing the grassland (and the mudflats, if the tide is out), continue eastwards towards the Second Severn Crossing. Please note that if the tide is in, you must continue your walk behind the seawall to avoid disturbing

roosting waders The ditch on your left serves to protect the adjacent farmland against the very high tides that sometimes spill over the seawall.

Continue along the track for about 800m towards an avenue of trees on your left (point G), where you cross a cattle grid, pass through barriers and head north up the avenue of trees. This part of the walk occasionally holds rare migrants that have included Yellow-browed Warbler. The marshy fields either side hold both Snipe and Lapwing. This lane continues through a sheep enclosure, which can be very muddy after wet weather, towards another T-junction. The pylons around you are favourite viewing platforms for Peregrine, Hobby, Buzzard and Merlin. Turning left at the T-junction (point H), continue along the stony track for 800m, reaching another T-junction (point J), where you turn right towards the motorway. After 700m you reach another junction (point K) where you bear left back towards the first gate you passed through (point C). Retrace your steps along the lanes to the church car park.

How to get there

3-4 miles E of Newport

Leave the M4 at J 23A and follow the signs for Magor village on the B4245. Continue through Magor into Undy. Look out for a high footbridge over the railway line on your right; after passing the footbridge take the next right turn at the crossroads (just before the pedestrian crossing lights) into a road called The Causeway. Proceed over the railway bridge, passing playing fields on your left, and take the next left turning at a small crossroads. Continue along this road until you reach St Mary's Church. Park in the church car park.

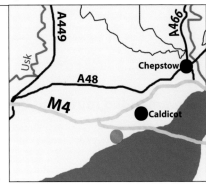

Key points

- 2.7 miles (4.3km)
- A shorter route provides views of both lakes
- Moderately strenuous
- Stout footwear/ wellingtons required
- Telescope recommended
- Toilets by car park
- Free parking at site
- Wheelchair accessible beside lower lake

IN A remarkable feat of engineering, a pipeline delivers water from high in the Black Mountains to the upper Cwmtillery Lake, a reservoir that feeds the domestic supply of the South Wales valleys. Whilst this lake is private, the smaller lower lake is the centrepiece of a popular public park. The walk encompassing both lakes and the valley above them will take a minimum of two hours but a much shorter route will provide views of the lakes and area between them. Habitat is very varied, comprising lakes, woodland, stream, scrub, fields and uplands.

Target birds

All year: Little Grebe 90%, Tufted Duck 90%, Dipper 60%
Autumn/winter: Goldeneye 30%, Pochard 80%, Goosander 50%, Kingfisher 30%

Other likely species

All year
Canada Goose
Greylag Goose
Gadwall
Teal
Common waterfowl
Grey Heron
Cormorant
Common raptors
Red Kite
Goshawk
Regular gulls
Barn Owl
Green Woodpecker
Skylark

Grey Wagtail
Pied Wagtail
Common woodland birds
Siskin
Linnet
Bullfinch
Yellowhammer
Reed Bunting

Spring/summer
Hobby
Common Sandpiper
Cuckoo
Hirundines

Chats
Summer warblers
Garden Warbler
Whitethroat
Redstart
Tree Pipit

Winter
Snipe
Water Rail
Winter thrushes
Brambling

Passage
Osprey
Curlew

Recommended route and birding tips

From the car park follow the path round the west side of the lower lake, looking in particular for Little Grebes, which breed here, with Kingfisher and Water Rail possible in winter. Continue north on the path alongside the stream that flows between the lakes, where Dipper and Grey Wagtail are possible. The scrubby plantations hold Bullfinches and, in summer, several species of warbler. Cross the footbridge over the stream and re-join the road, then head up the valley to the water treatment plant and the northern lake, which is private but viewable from the path. Cormorant and Grey Heron are regular whilst a passing Osprey is a tantalising possibility in autumn.

Scan the upper slopes of the valley for passing raptors and Ravens. Chats may be present on the moorland slopes.

If short of time, return at this point along the road to the car park. Otherwise, continue on the public footpath above the east side of the lake to the woods, following the power line across the middle of the meadow. Once in the woods, follow the footpath, turning sharp left at the obvious sign (point A) (beyond here the track is for private access only). The woods may hold Tree Pipit and Redstart in summer, with Brambling in winter. At point B, ford a minor stream and then cross the Tyleri, following the path round the boggy bowl. A public bridleway leads all the way back to the start of the walk over grassy slopes – the landscaped remnants of mining spoil tips. For the very adventurous, another bridleway heads on to the moor at the head of the valley with the possibility of associated upland birds.

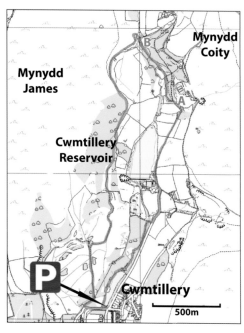

How to get there

Immediately N of Cwmtillery

Leave the A467 in Abertillery at the traffic lights (signposted Town Centre/Cwmtillery), bear right onto Castle Street then, almost immediately, left onto Alma Street (signposted Town Centre/Cwmtillery); after 200m join Gladstone Street before almost immediately bearing left back onto Alma Street at the junction with Foundry Bridge. Continue on Alma Street for another 200m at which point bear left to stay on Alma Street. Continue on Alma Street (which becomes Gwern Berthi Road) for about 1 mile, at which point it bears round to the right. After a further 100m the lower pond of Cwmtillery Lakes will appear on your left. Just beyond the pond turn left into Cwmtyleri and park on the left. Parking is free.

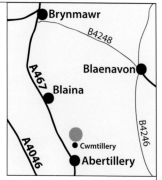

Key points

- 1.5 miles (2.5km)
- Moderate walk on variable surfaces
- Some steeper sections
- Walking boots recommended
- Open access land
- Good all-year birding
- Disabled access restricted to Local Nature Reserve
- Car park locked between 8pm and 8am
- Public transport

THIS WALK takes you through a Local Nature Reserve and into the wider post-industrial landscape of the uplands around Garn-yr-erw, near Blaenavon, which is now designated as a World Heritage Site. It is a circular walk that takes in lakes and ponds, wildflower-rich grasslands, heathland and marshy grassland. It can be rewarding at any time of year and can produce over 30 species of birds on a good day. The weather can be a touch unforgiving during the winter months, so to birdwatch comfortably, the best seasons are spring and summer. The bird assemblage is typical for the Gwent uplands, but can produce a rarity especially during passage months.

Target birds

All year: Red Kite 40%, Skylark 100%, Stonechat 50%, Meadow Pipit 100%

Spring/summer: Red Grouse 30%, Lapwing 50%, Grasshopper Warbler 40%, Whinchat 20%, Reed Bunting 60%

Winter: Goosander 40%, Wigeon 20%, Teal 20%, Tufted Duck 70%, Pochard 40%, Short-eared Owl 20%

Other likely species

All year	*Spring/summer*	
Canada Goose	Snipe	Sedge Warbler
Common waterfowl	Cuckoo	Ring Ouzel
Cormorant	Hirundines	
Grey Heron	Summer warblers	*Occasional*
Little Grebe	Wheatear	Hen Harrier
Common raptors	Grasshopper Warbler	Little Ringed Plover
Peregrine	Short-eared Owl	Golden Plover
Regular gulls		Jack Snipe
Common finches	*Passage*	Green Sandpiper
	Common Sandpiper	Redshank
	Sand Martin	Kingfisher

Recommended route and birding tips

THE FIRST section of the walk, in Garn Lakes Local Nature Reserve, is mostly on improved surfaces, but when it enters the wider landscape it uses unsurfaced public rights of way.

From the car park there are good views of the southern lake, which during winter months supports moderate numbers of Goosander, Wigeon and other commoner wildfowl; Kingfisher has also been recorded here.

Leaving the car park, turn right (northwards) and follow the easily accessible pathway around the lake. As the walk meanders through grassland, streams and alder copses, look out for Bullfinch, Siskin, Lesser Redpoll and Grey Wagtail. After about 150m, just before the bridge, take the uphill path to the right. The walk opens out at the northern lake with views of the Coity Mountain to the left and the post-industrial landscape of Garn-yr-erw to the right. The lake here is characterised by expansive margins of emergent vegetation. This habitat provides excellent breeding opportunities for commoner wildfowl such as Coot, Canada Goose, Little Grebe, Mallard and Moorhen. During passage

months, Lapwing, Common Sandpiper, Sedge Warbler and Sand Martin are all commonly encountered. In winter the main interest is wildfowl with small numbers of Teal, Wigeon, Pochard and Tufted Duck present on most visits. Other birds recorded during the winter include Short-eared Owl and Jack Snipe. Lesser Black-backed, Herring and Black-headed Gulls are also regularly present.

Take a right fork onto a narrow track and leave the Garn Lakes park through its northern exit (point A). Carefully cross the main Blaenavon to Brynmawr Road. Walk around the barrier and through a gate onto a metalled former colliery road into the wider Open Access landscape of Cefn Garn-yr-erw. The habitat here is more typical of the uplands of northwest Gwent.

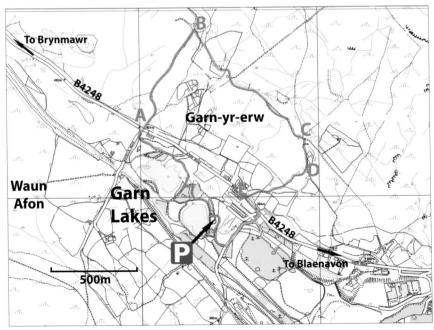

Birds in this area are more numerous and at their best during spring and summer. The atmospheric and characteristic song of Skylarks is prominent here. Look out for Wheatears and Stonechats in suitable locations as you climb the slope. The plateau of re-graded colliery spoil is now one of the few remaining breeding sites for Lapwing in Gwent. Other wading birds include Snipe and the occasional Golden Plover on passage. Also listen out for distant calling Red Grouse at this point.

At the point where the track divides, close to the crown of the slope (point B) turn acutely right, heading for the Hills Pit chimney in the distance. Here, impressive views of the industrial landscape can be seen. At this point Skylarks, Meadow Pipits and Wheatears are frequent. Here, too, Snipe display and raptors such as Buzzard, Red Kite and Peregrine are frequent. Heading south through spoil tips and remnants of stone walls, the walk passes a number of ponds. These ponds are worth a look for dragonflies and damselflies, and the scrubby fringes support breeding Reed Buntings and reeling Grasshopper Warblers. With the distinctive landmark of Hills Pit chimney now getting closer, the sheep-grazed grassland and open aspects provide rich feeding opportunities for Meadow Pipits and hirundines in late summer.

During winter, this landscape with its berry-laden hawthorn trees can support impressive flocks of winter thrushes that often include a late or early Ring Ouzel.

At Hills Pit (point C) the walk turns to the right and drops down past the chimney back towards the village of Garn-yr-erw. Sheltered between the spoil tips, stands of gorse and hawthorn support breeding Lesser Redpolls, Linnets and Stonechats, while other less typical breeding birds include Blackbird and Chaffinch.

When the track diverges take the right fork way-marked Human Endeavour. Here the walk follows a well-worn track through a field gate (point D) back to the Blaenavon-Brynmawr road. In winter months a large flock of Jackdaws roost in the mature trees surrounding the small settlement of Garn-yr-erw. Starlings and House Sparrows are also frequent, along with House Martins and Swallows during summer. Once again, taking care when crossing the road (point E), turn left towards the main entrance of Garn Lakes Local Nature Reserve, with its stone wall entrance feature.

Following the metalled road through the reserve and passing a small, planted copse to the south, the habitat opens out into wetland with developing stands of *Phragmites* reeds. It is worth checking here for wading birds, as Lapwing, Snipe, Redshank, Little Ringed Plover and Green Sandpiper have all occurred. Breeding birds such as Reed Bunting and Mallard are frequent, with Skylark and Meadow Pipit on the drier parts. Cuckoo, Kestrel and Sparrowhawk are frequently recorded as fly-overs.

Returning to the metalled road towards the main car park, the hedgerows and grasslands are home to many commoner birds. During spring this area is alive with birdsong of summer visitors – namely Willow Warbler, Chiffchaff and Blackcap. Finches are also commonplace with frequent Goldfinches, Greenfinches and Chaffinches.

How to get there

One mile NW of Blaenavon

Leave Blaenavon on the B4248 signposted Brynmawr. Follow the brown 'duck' signage for about a mile to Garn Lakes Local Nature Reserve. Alternatively take the B4248 south from Brynmawr, and drive for about 3 miles, again following the brown 'duck' signage.

Public transport

Regular bus service between Blaenavon and Brynmawr.

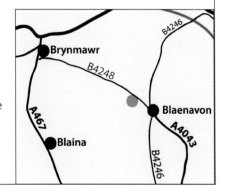

Key points

- 0.9 miles (1.4km) (to reservoir & back)
- 2.2 miles (3.5km) (complete circuit)
- 2.6 miles (4.2km) (to dam & back)
- Terrain is rough in places
- Stout footwear recommended
- Take mountain precautions on complete circuit (p32)
- Keep strictly to paths in breeding season
- Good place for a short visit
- Very exposed in bad weather
- Limited parking

GARNLYDAN RESERVOIR is not a site that holds a wide range of species or even exceptional numbers of any one particular species. So you might wonder why this site is worth a visit. Over the years a number of birders have adopted it as their 'patch', and their regular visits have produced some surprising species. Habitats at the site are limited to open moorland and open water, although there is a large adjacent area of coniferous woodland, which is home to the expected range of species associated with this habitat, including Crossbill, Long-eared Owl and Goshawk.

Target birds

All year: Red Grouse 20%, Red Kite 60%, Snipe 80%, Raven 75%, Skylark 90%

Summer: Grasshopper Warbler (easy in evenings)

Winter: Goosander 75%, Hen Harrier 20%

Other likely species

All year
Buzzard
Kestrel
Peregrine
Regular gulls
Carrion Crow

Spring/summer
Little Ringed Plover
Common Sandpiper
Swallow
Whinchat

Stonechat
Wheatear
Common garden birds
Meadow Pipit
Reed Bunting

Winter
Merlin
Wigeon
Mallard
Siskin

Lesser Redpoll
Common Crossbill

Passage
Hirundines
Waders (occasional)
Terns (occasional)

Recommended route and birding tips

THE WALK starts off in our neighbouring county, Brecknockshire, but quickly brings you back into Gwent, taking you through open moorland and past several small quarries. The path initially leads to a larger quarry and a shallow pool, which occasionally attracts passing waders. From there, a hard track leads you down to the reservoir. Walk to your right to continue around the reservoir in an anticlockwise direction. When you reach the dam wall you are recommended to turn back and retrace your outward route to the car park. However, it is possible to continue beyond the dam and cross the northern edge of the reservoir via sheep tracks – but great care and good footwear are required. Outside the breeding season, when ground-nesting birds have gone, you can take other tracks to explore more open grassland and moorland, and a few small copses of evergreens.

The initial walk to the reservoir should produce Wheatears in good numbers. Garnlydan Reservoir is often one of the first sites at which this harbinger of spring appears, and several pairs stay to breed in the loose rocks next to the paths. Spring is also when other upland species are most visible, Skylark and Meadow Pipit being the most obvious. The wet areas of moorland are home to Reed Bunting and even Grasshopper Warbler, which can in some years breed in good numbers. Dusk from late April is usually the best time to listen for the Grasshopper Warbler's distinctive reeling song. Another strange sound of the spring

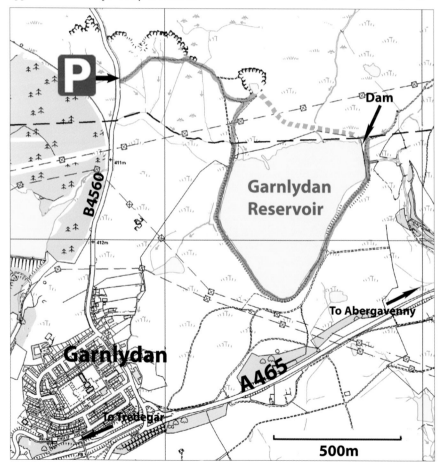

is the 'drumming' display of the Snipe that breed on the adjacent moorland. Evening/night-time visits in calm weather should allow you to hear this distinctive sound.

Summer is a quiet time, though some of the breeding waders can be seen around the shallow edges of the reservoir. Little Ringed Plovers, Common Sandpipers and the very occasional pair of Curlews breed, though the latter species has been steadily decreasing in northwest Gwent in recent years. In years gone by, other upland waders such as Dunlin bred just over the border in Brecknockshire and occasionally visited the reservoir but the species has now disappeared from the site. The same can be said for Golden Plover, though the occasional bird turns up on spring and autumn passage.

Late summer sees the start of passage and affords your best chance of something unusual at the site. Bad weather during August can often force migrating waders and terns to stop off to rest at the reservoir. Common, Arctic and Black Terns have all been seen during this month, as have Greenshank, Oystercatcher and even Spotted Redshank, though the latter has only ever been noted once. Migrating Marsh Harriers have also occurred at this time of year. Other rarities to have been found in recent

years are Wryneck and a Pomarine Skua, which was brought down by thick fog and stayed a few hours to rest.

Autumn sees the arrival of the first of the wintering wildfowl. The reservoir is the only site in northwest Gwent that hosts a small wintering flock of Wigeon. By winter, Goldeneye and Tufted Duck can also be seen. Autumn and winter are the seasons when you have the best chance of seeing a Red Grouse that has wandered over the border from the heather moorland in Brecknockshire.

A mid-winter visit can be worthwhile as Garnlydan Reservoir hosts a good number of Goosanders, which feed on local rivers and come back to the reservoir to roost in the evenings. Up to 20 have been seen in the past. There also used to be a large gull roost, though this has been absent in the past few winters. Raptors, too, are easiest to see in winter with Hen Harrier being your target species. Look out for these on the open moorland or going to roost in nearby forestry in the evenings; they can often be quite elusive. Merlin, Peregrine and Red Kite along with more common raptors such as Buzzard and Kestrel are all present on site during the winter.

How to get there

1-2 miles NW of Brynmawr

Garnlydan Reservoir is situated north of the A465 Heads of the Valleys Road. Turn off the dual carriageway onto the B4560 to Llangynidr. Start your walk from the lay-by alongside the B4560 on the right as you head out of Gwent into Powys. The lay-by is about 300m past the 'Welcome to Powys' sign. The track then goes east towards the reservoir.

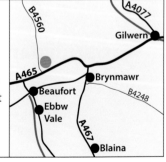

THE RIVER Usk at Gobion (properly known as Llanvihangel Gobion) is one of the best birding sites in the county, with a wide range of species, and is of interest at any time of year. The riverine habitat is diverse and includes shingle, earth banks, oxbow lakes (old and new), river meadows and woodland, and is bordered by scrub, farmed pasture and arable areas. This attracts a wide range of breeding and wintering species, and there is also a good spring and autumn passage, which is likely to produce the greatest variety of birds. Characteristic riverine species such as Dipper and Kingfisher are present all year, with uncommon breeders such as Hobby and Yellow Wagtail arriving in the spring. The spring and autumn passages bring waders, whilst wildfowl arrive in the winter. This is the best site in the county to observe Green Sandpiper, which is present all year. Two walks are described, the Oxbow Lake Walk and the Green Sandpiper Walk.

Key points

- Oxbow Lake Walk: 2.5 miles (4km)
- Green Sandpiper Walk: 2.5 miles (4km)
- Easy
- Best Green Sandpiper site in Gwent
- All-year interest
- Can be wet and muddy
- Parking very limited
- Telescope useful
- Public transport

Target birds

All year: Green Sandpiper 80%, Kingfisher 40%, Lesser Spotted Woodpecker 10%, Dipper 90% (winter), 50% (summer), Grey Wagtail 80%

Spring/summer: Hobby 40%, Little Ringed Plover 50%, Curlew 30% (hearing), 10% (seeing), Common Sandpiper 90%, Sand Martin 100%, Reed Bunting 70%

Winter: Siskin 50%, Lesser Redpoll 10%

Other likely species

All year	Common woodland birds	*Spring/autumn passage*	Tufted Duck
Mute Swan			Merlin
Canada Goose	Pied Wagtail	Mandarin Duck	Water Rail
Goosander	Meadow Pipit	Garganey	Winter thrushes
Common waterfowl	Common finches	Little Egret	
Little Grebe	Reed Bunting	Greenshank	*Occasional*
Buzzard		Redshank	Osprey
Sparrowhawk	*Spring/summer*	'Blue-headed' Wagtail	Water Pipit
Peregrine	Spotted Flycatcher		
Green Woodpecker	Hirundines	*Winter*	*Other wildlife*
Great Spotted Woodpecker	Summer warblers	Teal	Otter
	Yellow Wagtail	Pintail	

89

Recommended route and birding tips

Oxbow Lake Walk	SO348091/348088 (NP7 9BG) 2.5 mls P1/P2

The nearside path (to the north of the bridge) is signposted as the Usk Valley Walk and takes a route away from the riverside to begin with. Cross the field and pass through the gate, then turn right along the hedgerow, checking for finches and thrushes. When you reach a house (point A), bear obliquely left across the field following the way-mark. Approach the fence stealthily, as beyond is a large oxbow lake, which you can scan for wildfowl (mainly Mallard, Teal and Tufted Duck), Snipe, other waders and, in the winter, Water Rail. Grey Herons are common here and Hobbies can be seen taking dragonflies in summer. Keep the oxbow on your left and pass through a couple of kissing gates to a large arable field (point B). This field is normally left as stubble after harvesting and is worth scanning for Meadow Pipit and Skylark, whilst a row of alders alongside the fence can attract mixed flocks of Lesser

Redpoll and Siskin. Continue following the footpath, checking the fields for flocks of Fieldfare and Redwing in the winter, until a way-mark, tucked away on your left by a gate (point C), shows the right of way across the field to the river. These flocks sometimes attract hunting Merlin or Peregrine. This nearside riverbank usually holds a Sand Martin colony, which can provide quite a spectacle in summer, particularly when Hobbies hunt for this agile bird. The river is quite open here and is worth scanning in both directions, as is the large shingle bank opposite, which can hide waders such as Common and Green Sandpipers as well as Grey and Pied Wagtails. Ospreys, which pass through on passage, sometimes stay here for a few days, plunge-diving into the water at this point, as do the resident Kingfishers. Continue on the path and just before the next gate (point D), scan the pool parallel to the tree line on

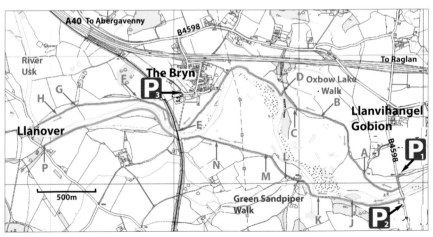

the right. Pass through the gate, climb up the bank and from the highest point, scan the river in both directions – a telescope can be useful here. The long stretch of gently flowing water upstream usually holds Little Grebe and otter can occasionally be seen. After passing through the next gate, scan the trees in the pond to your right for thrushes and woodpeckers. (If you have parked at The Bryn village, follow either of two footpaths signed Riverside and Llanellen respectively, and you will join the river in this area). Continue up the river until the railway bridge is reached (point E). Unfortunately, it is not possible to follow a circular route (returning south of the river) as the railway bridge has no footway. So you can either return to the starting point, or walk under the bridge and continue on the Usk Valley Walk for about 1km to a point opposite Llanover Church.

For this second option, go through the first field and on to a stile at the end of a barbed wire fence on your left (point F). The route then crosses the field at an oblique angle, but take care here as the field is large and there are no intermediate way-marks. The next stile is by a metal gate in the far fence-line (point G). Cross this stile and go through the gate next to the WW2 pillbox on your right (point H). Turn immediately left along the fence to the river. Dippers breed in this area and superb views of both adults and juveniles can be had in the spring. The bridge ahead is private so you should now retrace your steps to the start point.

Green Sandpiper Walk   SO348091/348088 (NP7 9BG) 2.5 mls P1/P2

FROM YOUR parking place cross carefully to the south side of Pant-y-Goitre bridge. Go through the 'stepthru' stile by the wooden finger post and take the path upstream, scanning the far bank for Common and Green Sandpipers, Dippers and Wagtails. When the woodland (point J) is reached check the brambles for Bullfinch. Around this point there is an area on the right consisting of a series of channels and sandy ground, covered in trees and scrub that can hold Woodcock in the winter. Continue to a point just before the second stile (point K), where the river takes a right turn, and scan the river and floodplain.

Take care over the next section, which can be slippery in wet weather and is close to the riverbank. Cross the bridge (point L) and continue upstream checking the scrub alongside the derelict building. Lesser Spotted Woodpeckers have been seen here and Spotted Flycatchers are sometimes present during the summer. Just beyond the barn, scan the wood to the south (left), as in spring it holds a heronry and the huge nests are sometimes visible from here. Cross a stile (point M) and note the oxbow lake to your right. This is probably the most reliable site for Green Sandpiper, and a careful approach can sometimes allow a short view before the bird emits its musical call and flies towards the river, showing its white rump and dark wings.

Return to the hedgerow on your left as there is no access to the river bank at this point, and continue to a point about 100m beyond the last of a small row of trees. At

91

this point (N) a small pond can be observed to your right (a small tree in the middle can be seen above the dip in the ground) – this regularly holds Green Sandpiper. Continue along the hedgerow to the railway bridge.

At this point either return to the start point or continue alongside the river for a further 1km upstream to Llanover. In the latter case, cross a stile on the left hand side and then bear right through a large metal gate and cross underneath the railway line. Retrace your steps from point P as there is no riverside footpath beyond this.

How to get there

4 miles SE of Abergavenny

Take the B4598 from the roundabout south of Abergavenny towards Usk and Clytha. After just over three miles, turn right towards Usk (still on the B4598) at the junction near the Steel Horse Café (formerly the Charthouse Restaurant). Pant-y-Goitre bridge is reached in just under 0.5 miles; park either on the verge in a lane on the left hand side just before the bridge (P1), or cross the bridge and park in the wide farm access on the right hand side (P2). This gateway is commonly used for parking, but please heed the instruction on the gate not to obstruct the access.

Alternatively: for the Oxbow Lake Walk, it is possible to park at P3 (see map) near the church in the village named The Bryn (SO330096, NP7 9AP), and join the walk at point E on the map. In this case, turn right off the B4598 at an earlier junction signposted to The Bryn.

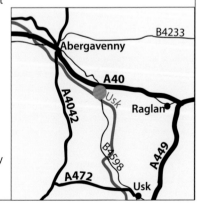

Public transport

A regular bus service runs from Abergavenny Bus Station to Monmouth, stopping at The Bryn village and the B4598 turn-off to Usk.

THIS IS an easy walk on level ground through Goetre* House Wood, a local reserve owned by the Gwent Ornithological Society. As the western boundary of the wood adjoins the Monmouthshire and Brecon Canal the walk can extend along the canal towpath, and this is the route recommended here. You can find a good variety of birds at any time of year and the ground flora, in particular wild daffodils and bluebells, is an attractive feature in spring. The best time for birds is when the woodland migrants are breeding, and both Pied and Spotted Flycatchers are regularly seen here. Woodpeckers are also regular breeding species. Lesser Spotted are seen and heard in the wood and they also nest in alders along the canal towpath.

Key points

- About 3 miles (5km)
- Possible to shelter under bridges
- Walking boots recommended in wet weather
- Facilities (toilets, shop, pub) in Penperlleni
- Free car parking
- Public transport

Target birds

All year: Buzzard 100%, Sparrowhawk 20%, Moorhen 100%, Tawny Owl 20%, Green Woodpecker 50%, Great Spotted Woodpecker 80%, Lesser Spotted Woodpecker 5%, Marsh Tit 10%, Jay 50%, Bullfinch 20%

Spring/summer: Little Grebe 20%, Hobby 10%, Pied Flycatcher 80%, Spotted Flycatcher 50%, Blackcap 100%

Winter: Woodcock 5%, Lesser Redpoll 20%

Other likely species

All year	Starling	Swift
Mallard	Thrushes	Kingfisher
Grey Heron	Robin	Swallow
Stock Dove	Dunnock	House Martin
Common corvids	House Sparrow	Redstart
Raven	Pied Wagtail	Summer warblers
Tits	Common finches	
Nuthatch		*Winter*
Wren	*Spring/summer*	Winter thrushes
	Hobby	Siskin

Recommended route and birding tips

FROM THE car park, cross the A4042 carefully (fast traffic) and walk up the lane opposite (Parc-y-Brain Road). Birds seen and heard from the lane include Raven, Rook, Jackdaw, Dunnock, Greenfinch, Blue Tit, Great Tit, Swallows nesting in the farm barn and House Martins nesting on the house to the right. The wood is about 320m along this road and is accessed through a small gate on the left (point A). Before leaving the road look to your right – at the bottom of the field

93

is a pond that is worth checking as Grey Herons often feed here and Little Grebes attempt to nest. Go through the pedestrian gate into the field. After about 20m there is an interpretation board showing a map and information on the birds that can be seen. Follow the footpath through the wood to the canal.

Walking along the path through the wood, you will find a variety of woodland species according to season. In the summer months there is a good chance of seeing Spotted Flycatcher, often sitting on a bare branch of an oak tree, then flying up to catch insects and returning to the same branch. Pied Flycatchers use the numerous nest boxes scattered throughout the wood and can often be seen from the path. Blue Tits and Great Tits also use the nest boxes, as do Nuthatches. Not all of the boxes are for birds – the Gwent bat group has erected a number and these are regularly used by the two species of pipistrelle.

As well as mature oak, beech and ash, there is an extensive understorey of bramble, which can be breeding habitat for Blackcap, Long-tailed Tit and Song Thrush. Coal Tits are also seen and an occasional Marsh Tit. Jackdaws nest in the larger trees and Tawny Owls are regular breeders. Although a Kestrel box has been erected, this species seems to have disappeared from the area, as have other species such as Little Owl, Yellowhammer and Skylark. Reports of sightings of these once common species would be welcome.

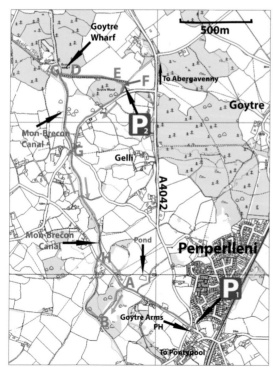

Turn right when you reach the canal (point B). You can see into the wood from the towpath until you pass the boundary and reach Parc-y-Brain Farm. Mallard and Moorhen breed on the canal and Kingfisher can often be seen, particularly in late summer. Proceed along the towpath until you reach Goetre Wharf basin. This is where, in winter, you are likely to see Lesser Redpoll and Siskin.

At Goetre Wharf take the path to the right just after the aqueduct (point C), signed Goytre Hall Wood. It is steep downhill but there are handrails for support. At the bottom of the slope turn left through the gate (point D) and follow the bridleway until you come to a gate into a wood (point E). Rather oddly, the finger post directs you to 'car park'. Follow the path until you come out at a small car park and picnic site (point F). Leave the car park and turn right onto the lane. Proceed along the lane past Saron Chapel, rejoining the towpath at bridge

74 (point G). Leave the canal at bridge 72 (point H) and walk back down the lane to Goetre village and your car.

The spellings Goytre and Goetre are both correct and used according to custom and practice. Goetre means wood town from the Welsh words Coed (wood) and Tref (town). Goytre is the anglicised spelling.

How to get there

About 3 miles NE of Pontypool

Driving on the A4042 road from Pontypool to Abergavenny, turn right at Penperlleni, and then turn immediately left into the public car park opposite the Goytre Arms pub. Parking is also possible at P2 (SO317062) where the recommended route can be joined half way round.

Public transport

Hourly buses between Abergavenny, Pontypool and Cwmbran stop at Penperlleni.

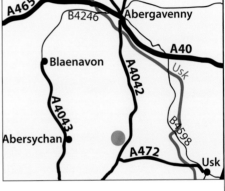

Goetre House Wood

Keith Roylance

95

Key points

- Very short walk
- Very weather and tide dependent
- Access to sea-watching point requires care
- Best in spring and late summer/ autumn
- Telescope essential
- Birds may be distant and difficult to identify

THIS IS the primary site in Gwent for observing seabirds that find themselves in the Severn Estuary, usually as a result of a sustained period of strong winds. High tides during or immediately following gales from the southwest or west regularly produce a range of species rarely seen elsewhere in the county. That said, the birds' occurrence is unpredictable and, when they are seen, they are often distant and rarely present for more than a few minutes. Regular visits during suitable weather and watches of several hours are required if you want to see seabirds in Gwent. Whilst the birds can be observed from the easily accessible seawall, access to the favoured sea-watching point requires a clamber up and down the seawall.

Target birds

All year: Rock Pipit 20%

Spring/autumn/winter: Common Scoter 10%, Fulmar 25%, Manx Shearwater 20%, Storm Petrel 10%, Gannet 75%, Turnstone 50%, Great Skua 10%, Arctic Skua 20%, Kittiwake 50%, Common Tern 10%, Arctic Tern 20%, less regularly occurring seabirds

Other likely species

All year	Whimbrel	Purple Sandpiper
Shelduck	Curlew	Pomarine Skua
Cormorant	Redshank	Long-tailed Skua
Oystercatcher	Regular gulls	Sabine's Gull
Spring/autumn/	Great Black-backed Gull	Little Gull
winter		Mediterranean Gull
Ringed Plover	Sandwich Tern	Little Tern
Knot	*Occasional*	Black Tern
Sanderling	Great Northern Diver	Guillemot
Dunlin	Leach's Petrel	Razorbill

Recommended route and birding tips

SHOULD YOU wish to see lots of seabirds, or seabirds up close, or properly rare seabirds, get in your car, jump on the M4 and visit any one of the many seabird havens or headlands elsewhere in the UK. However, if you want to see seabirds in Gwent this is the place to try.

Wait for a period of strong, ideally sustained, winds from

the southwest or west, either in spring or, more likely, autumn. In addition to your standard binoculars and notebook, pack clothing suitable for the weather, a telescope and something to eat and drink to keep your spirits up. Most regular visitors also bring some form of 'sit mat' – the top of the seawall was not built for comfort. Arrive an hour or two (or three if really keen) before high tide, and plan to stay until an hour or so (dependent on bird activity) after high tide.

On arrival, the hedgerows and trees should be being lashed by the gale and, as you climb the steps onto the seawall, the roar of the wind in the leaves should combine with a raging estuary to form a furious accompaniment as you turn right and trudge, shoulders hunched, hand on hat, along the wall (point A) towards the point. Just before the path on top of the seawall terminates at the house (point B), carefully climb down the seawall onto the foreshore via the, somewhat rudimentary, step. Unless you enjoy bashing your telescope against concrete, you may find it easier to place it on the seawall, clamber down and then retrieve it. Pass the private 'slipway' on your right, climb back up the sea-defences to the base of the concrete seawall and proceed, carefully, along the narrow 'path'. Sit at a point (C) as far along as possible whilst retaining shelter from the wind and avoiding any spray from the incoming tide. If all that scrambling sounds a bit much, try watching from the top of the seawall in the lee of the house; your view won't be as good but you should be sheltered from the elements and you won't have broken any bones.

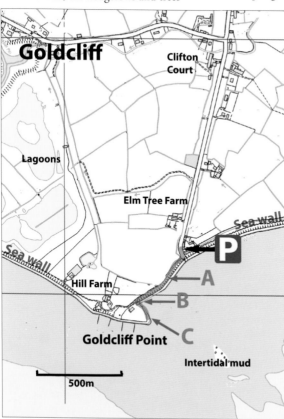

Once comfortably atop your 'sit-mat', back to the wall, telescope set, take your bins and get a feel for (a) the distances over which you'll be scanning, and (b)

the apparent size of the passing gulls to give you a measure against which to compare less easily identified species. If other birders are present, try to familiarise yourself with the obvious features on the far side (e.g. the naval college, caravan park, Clevedon Pier etc.) as any directions to passing birds will be based on their position in relation to these landmarks.

A reasonable search strategy is to slowly scan back and fore between about ESE and SSW, alternating every so often between binoculars and telescope. Usually, birds will be moving up-channel on the rising tide and down-channel (often involving the same individuals) as the water subsides. Most birds pass the Point in mid-channel or beyond, seemingly preferring to remain over the deep-water channel on the Somerset side of the estuary.

At this distance the identification process is heavily dependent on 'jizz', an appreciation of which is only really gained via experience. If you are new to the game do not necessarily try to name every passing dot – some defy any categorisation (bird sp.?!) whilst 'auk sp.', 'Commic tern' and 'skua sp.' are entries that grace all the regulars' notebooks. On the other hand, birds will pass by very close in, even directly overhead, and can easily be missed, so do check with the naked eye every now and again.

Finally, remember distant House Martins skimming the estuary are not storm petrels, and that rakish, dark-looking thing dashing after the Kittiwake is just as likely to be a first-winter gull as a skua. Beyond that it is mostly down to perseverance and luck – you will likely need both.

How to get there

About 5 miles SE of Newport

If travelling on the M4 from the west, exit at J28 and take the third exit at the roundabout onto the Southern Distributor Road (A48). Follow this for approximately 4 miles until, at the sixth roundabout, take the second exit onto Queensway Meadows. If travelling on the M4 from the east, exit at J24 and take the first exit at the roundabout onto the Southern Distributor Road/Ringland Way (A48). Follow this for approximately 2.5 miles until, at the fourth roundabout, take the first exit onto Queensway Meadows, at the next roundabout take the third exit onto Meadows Road. Stay on this road (as it becomes Nash Road then Goldcliff Road) for 3.7 miles. At the point where the road bends sharply to the left take the right turn (caution: this junction is on a blind bend) and follow the minor road 0.5 miles to the seawall. Park at the end of the minor road, avoiding the local residents' gateways.

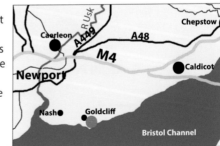

THIS LARGE site immediately south of the A4048, three miles west of the town of Risca, is part of the Sirhowy Valley Country Park. It is readily accessible by car or public transport, and offers a range of walks with a good variety of birds. The walk recommended below is fairly strenuous and will take about 2.5 hours, allowing for time spent birdwatching, but shorter routes are easily planned. The habitat is steep hillside with broad-leaved woodland, mainly of sessile oak and birch with some ancient beeches, and also includes conifer plantation, much of which is Scots pine. Some paths lead up to high pasture with beech copses. On parts of the lower slopes there is a traditionally managed farm with cattle grazing and pig enclosures. The large number of tracks and footpaths enable the planning of short, medium and longer walks, on steep or flat terrain. The lowest track (a former railway line) is fine for wheelchairs but is the least interesting from a birding standpoint.

Key points

- 3.5 miles (5.6km)
- Often strenuous
- Best in spring/ summer
- Excellent for Wood Warbler
- Walking boots recommended
- Adjacent walk on former rail track suitable for wheelchairs
- Free parking

Target birds

All year: Kingfisher 20%, Grey Wagtail 80%, Dipper 20%

April-June: Cuckoo 30%, Wood Warbler 100%, Garden Warbler 60%, Redstart 80%, Pied Flycatcher 20%, Tree Pipit 90%, Siskin 100%, Crossbill (erratic); in the case of the summer visitors the percentages apply only after arrival dates

Other likely species

All year		*Spring/summer*
Red Kite	Raven	Swallow
Sparrowhawk	Nuthatch	House Martin
Tawny Owl	Treecreeper	Summer warblers
Green Woodpecker	Goldcrest	Whitethroat
Great Spotted Woodpecker	Common finches	Spotted Flycatcher
Common corvids		Linnet
		Meadow Pipit

Recommended route and birding tips

STARTING AT the Pont Lawrence Rees car park, walk onto the adjacent bridge over the river and linger there for a while to see Grey Wagtails that usually breed nearby. With luck you may also find a Dipper here or see a Kingfisher flash by along the river. After crossing the bridge, take the stepped path straight ahead, and then turn right, following the metalled road that climbs to the Ynys Hywel Activity Centre (closed at the time of writing). Along this steep slog you should expect an abundance of birdsong, often including Blackcap, Garden Warbler, Chiffchaff, Willow Warbler, Robin, Wren and Blackbird. Also listen out for thin *piu piu* calls of Siskins as they flit around the treetops.

On reaching the Ynys Hywel Centre, pass the small storage building on your left and then turn left up steps and onward onto a steep stepped path leading directly up the hillside. At the top of the steps (before entering the forest) turn left onto a smaller level path that passes in front of the camping barn. You will soon have pasture

with scattered trees and copses to your left, and woodland to your right. Listen out for Redstart song from the trees on the left but locating the bird among the foliage can be surprisingly difficult. In March and April, Nuthatch calls will be frequent from this point on. The path climbs after a while and ends at a forestry road that is signposted Sirhowy Valley Walk (point A).

Turn left along this track and continue for about 500m, listening to Willow Warbler and Chiffchaff song, before taking a path on the right signposted Sirhowy Valley Walk. At this point you enter the Graig Goch wood and there is a welcome sign that gives information on wildlife of the area. Continue up this path, with the Ynys Hywel farm on your left, for 250m, ignoring the first path to the right, which is a dead end, till you reach the second path on the right, which is marked by a finger

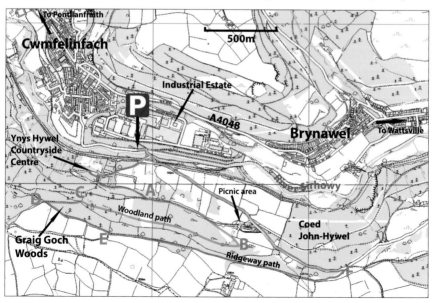

post with a Redstart picture (point B). This sharp turn takes you onto the 'woodland path' marked on the map. Along here you are bound to hear the song of Wood Warblers, sometimes five or six singing males, and they are typically easy to see. Unfortunately this is no longer true for Pied Flycatcher, which used to be a certainty but has become scarce in recent years. After about 500m the beech and birch woodland gives way to Scots pine plantation and the dominant songs become those of the Goldcrest and Coal Tit. The trees are well spaced, making Wood Warblers even easier to see as they flit among the trunks.

On reaching a wet area with short boardwalks spanning ditches (point C) you have a decision to make – whether to go up or down. The recommended route is to keep straight ahead for a few metres and then follow a short steep scramble to the left that soon lessens into a gradual climb and takes you to point D. However, the first few metres are difficult and you may prefer to shorten the walk by taking the stepped path on the right down to the forestry road, turn right again and return to point (A) from where you can retrace your outward route to the car park. Assuming you stick to the longer walk, continue up the path into an area of open beech woodland where you reach a T-junction with a wide, rough track (point D). Turn sharp left up this track (the route to the right again returns you to the forestry road) and look out for Crossbills in the pines, though being an irruptive species they are not present every year. Another point of interest is the large number of beeches on the right of the path where numerous trunks sprout from horizontal sections at

their bases, showing that they once formed part of a layered hedge.

Join the Ridgeway path at point E and continue eastward (left) with woodland on your left and pasture with beech copses on your right. Scan the hawthorns along the hedge lines for Redstart and listen for Tree Pipits that sing from the tops of the beeches. Cuckoos are frequent here in spring and sightings of Stonechats are possible. Continue for about 1.5km (ignoring the marked path leading downhill on the left, which would take you back to point A) until you reach a metalled road that slopes down steeply to the left (point F). Follow the metalled road without deviation back to the car park, continuing

to look out for birds such as Tree Pipit, Siskin, and woodpeckers, among others.

Possible extensions to the walk

The recommended walk described here can profitably be extended either east or west.

101

Eastward from point F, the path forks, with both Ridgeway and Sirhowy Valley Walks following the right fork, which rises steeply. Take the left fork which follows a level course and eventually leads you through open habitat where Whinchat and Stonechat are likely to be seen, together with Meadow and Tree Pipits. After about 2.5km take the metalled road on the left which leads steeply downhill and soon crosses the forestry road. Turn left along this road to return to the junction by the Ynys Hywel Farm and picnic area.

To explore westward, start from point A and follow the forestry road as it winds up to the moorland summit of Mynydd y Grug, emerging onto the Ridgeway path. Spend some time exploring the dry-stone walls on the northern and western edges of

the moorland where breeding Wheatears can reliably be found. From the northwest corner of the moorland there is a track that leads to a ruined farm (Pen-y-rhiw) where breeding Redstarts are always found. Return along the Ridgeway path, descending back to the car park at either point E or F.

For visitors using wheelchairs or those with lower fitness levels, the former railway track through the Sirhowy Valley Country Park (starting from the Pont Lawrence Rees bridge) offers an interesting and extensive walk to the east, with a good variety of species including Chiffchaff, Willow Warbler, Garden Warbler and Blackcap but lacking the upland species found on the steeper walks.

How to get there

3 miles W of Risca

By car, take the A4048 to the small town of Cwmfelinfach. Toward the east side of town turn south down Islwyn Street, follow this road down to the river, and then alongside the river until you reach a narrow bridge over the river, and park on the right just before you reach the bridge (in the Pont Lawrence Rees car park). The picnic area (see map) also has a car park, but this is open only when staff are working at the adjacent Ynys Hywel Farm (usually around 9.00am to 4.00pm).

Public transport

Take the number 56 bus that runs a frequent service between Newport and Blackwood/ Tredegar via Cwmfelinfach (alternate buses go through to Tredegar and display this route sign).

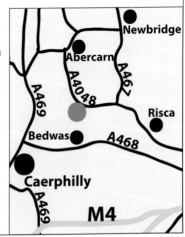

IGHMEADOW WOODS (also known as Redding's Inclosure) are situated just to the east of Monmouth. They form a compact block, detached from the main Forest of Dean woodlands, and are owned and managed by the Forestry Commission (FC). The eastern part is in Gloucestershire, and the western part in Gwent. The whole block is managed from the FC's office at Coleford (rather than by Natural Resources Wales which manages all other former FC land in Gwent). The walk suggested stays in the Gwent section, but many other tracks and paths can be explored once you are familiar with the area. Because of the deep valleys, and the number of tracks and paths, it is possible to get disorientated and move further away from your intended destination than towards it.

Highmeadow Woods are predominantly broad-leaved (oak and beech high forest, with some larch mixed in); there are also mature blocks of evergreen trees (mainly Douglas fir) and areas that have been clear-felled and are at various stages of regeneration. The area has a number of evocative names, such as the Hearkening Rocks, Suck Stone and Headless Hill, which can fire the imagination to explore further.

Key points

- **4.2 miles (6.7km)**
- **Moderate**
- **Mostly good forest roads**
- **Walking boots advisable**
- **Good chance of Hawfinch**
- **Keep to described route as easy to get lost**
- **Deer and wild boar are possible**
- **Keep dogs under control in spring**

Target birds

All year	Hawfinch	Wood Warbler
Goshawk	Siskin	Pied Flycatcher
Peregrine	Lesser Redpoll	Spotted Flycatcher
Woodcock	Crossbill	
Lesser Spotted Woodpecker		*Winter*
	Spring/summer	Redwing
Firecrest	Tree Pipit	Fieldfare
	Redstart	Brambling

Other wildlife

It is also worth keeping a look out for mammals as this is a good area for fallow deer, though numbers have been reduced (culled) in recent years, and occasionally a muntjac can be seen. At the time of writing, this is likely to be the only location in Gwent where wild boar can be encountered. In the spring, when there are young present, it is advisable to keep dogs under control or they may provoke an attack from the protecting sows.

103

Recommended route and birding tips

THROUGHOUT YOUR walk, look out and listen for forest birds, which may be encountered anywhere. If you are familiar with the call, behaviour and flight of Hawfinches, there is a very high chance (70-80%) of seeing them.

From the car park, proceed past the barrier, keeping to the forest road, and after about 350m you will reach a junction (point A); turn left (the other track will be the one you will return along). After a further 700m, there is another junction (point B) where you take the right fork

(straight on). Continue to follow this forest road as it descends into the valley, with sharp bends to the right and then to the left, until after 2km you reach a crossroads of well-defined tracks (point C).

Turn right; after a while this track begins to climb gently, and the gravel surface gradually deteriorates into a grassy ride. At the time of checking this route, there had been some recent timber extraction along the track, and it was quite muddy, but this should soon recover to a grassy surface. After nearly 1km from the crossroads, you

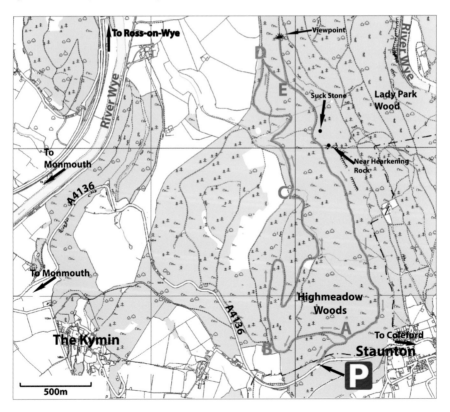

will become aware of a field bordering the wood edge on your left, and after a further 300m you will come to a track cutting back sharply uphill on the right (point D).

Take this track, which was also muddy from timber extraction, but when it has dried out it will have a better stoned substrate than the one you have just left. There will be a high deer fence on your left, and an area of regeneration following felling in 2010/2011. This will be the steepest climb of the walk but after about 200m you will reach a better quality forest road (point E).

If you make a short detour to the left, you will soon reach a viewpoint that looks over the Wye Gorge and the Doward beyond (an ancient hill fort now managed by the Woodland Trust). On the near side of the Gorge is a woodland reserve (Lady Park Wood), an area that has not had management interference, in order that the natural processes in mature woodland can

be researched. Our return route however is the right hand track, and after 2km you will arrive back at the first junction (point A) not far from the car park.

The return route has a number of areas recently clear-felled, from which you have extensive views, and you should linger to look for soaring raptors or overflying smaller birds. On the way back you will also pass below the Suck Stone and Near Hearkening Rock, with steep pathways off the forest road for you to explore. The county boundary runs parallel to the forest road at the top of the ridge to your left, and beyond it are more steep-sided valleys to explore at a future date.

This is an excellent area for looking for the usual range of woodland birds, and given the mix of broad-leaved and coniferous high forest, as well as young plantations and recently felled scrubby areas, provides opportunities for finding a wide range of species.

How to get there

3 miles E of Monmouth

Leave Monmouth on the A466 going east across the river towards Chepstow. A short distance over the Wye river bridge, take the left fork at the mini-roundabout onto the A4136 Coleford road. Follow this winding road for 2.75 miles until a 'Forest of Dean/Gloucestershire' road sign and lay-by are reached on the left hand side. Immediately after the lay-by, park in the wide mouth of a forest access road on the left hand side (SO541125). Take care not to block access for forestry vehicles.

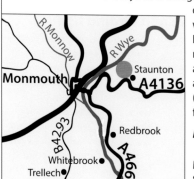

Public transport

The regular bus service which plies between Monmouth and Coleford stops close by, at Staunton.

THE PROMINENT hill just west of Monmouth is covered with a mix of broad-leaved woodland with some wonderful old yew trees and conifer plantations; it is known as King's Wood or The Hendre Woods. The hill is criss-crossed with forest tracks and paths, and the Offa's Dyke footpath runs up from Monmouth, goes over the hill and drops down to cross the Worthybrook to Hendre road. Expect a broad range of woodland birds. There is all-year interest but May to July is the best season.

Key points

- About 3 miles (5km)
- Some moderately steep sections
- Best in spring/summer
- Good selection of woodland and woodland edge birds

Target birds

All year: Goshawk 5%, Woodcock 5% (at dusk), Marsh Tit 50%, Siskin 90%, Crossbill 80%, Yellowhammer 75%

Spring/summer: Nightjar 50% (at dusk), Tree Pipit 90%, Yellow Wagtail 60%

Winter/early spring: Goshawk 50%, Hawfinch 10% (higher if you know the calls)

Winter: Lesser Redpoll 80%

Other likely species

All year
Common raptors
Tawny Owl
Green Woodpecker
Great Spotted Woodpecker
Common corvids
Raven

Common woodland birds
Siskin
Yellowhammer

Spring/summer
Hobby
Cuckoo
Summer warblers

Wood Warbler (some years)
Garden Warbler
Lesser Whitethroat
Whitethroat
Redstart (some years)

Winter
Winter thrushes

Recommended route and birding tips

WALK RIGHT (north) along the track past the converted barn. Take the blue horseshoe way-marked bridleway through the gate, and then through a second way-marked gate into the wood (Note: the track shown following the edge of the wood on OS maps no longer exists). Continue uphill on the bridleway until you reach a T-junction (point A). Ignore the small footpath opposite with a horseshoe way-mark and turn left. Follow this broad track as it descends, winding through larches and conifers to reach a large track (Offa's Dyke Path) at a T-junction (point B). Turn right and in less than 50m turn left (point C), and follow this broad track down through conifers. This is a good spot for Crossbill and flocks of both Siskin and Lesser Redpoll in the winter. To the right is a large clear-felled area, planted up again. This is a sure spot to hear and see Tree Pipit in the spring and summer.

Near the bottom of the hill, past a small pond on your left, take a right turn (point D) into the clear-felled area. Continue on this track. To your left you will eventually see an old tower. Continue on the track around bends and downhill until you see the sign for Offa's Dyke footpath on your right (point E). Follow this path up through the woodland until, after a view across the clear-fell, you meet the broad track again (point F). Go straight over and follow the Offa's Dyke track down out of the woodland.

In this open country and woodland edge habitat look out for Whitethroat, Lesser Whitethroat, Yellow Wagtail and Yellowhammer in spring and summer. In

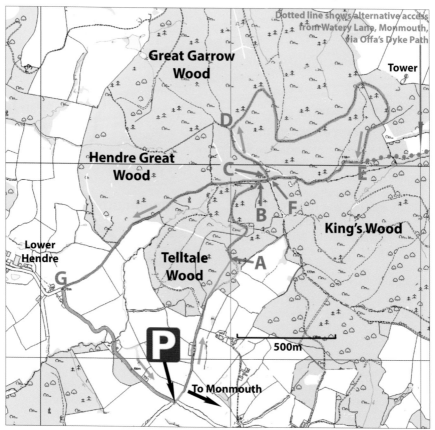

late winter to early spring keep a lookout to your left for displaying Goshawks over Telltale Wood. Continue till you reach the minor road (point G). Turn left past a farm and walk down over a small stream to

return to your car.

There are many other tracks in the northern block of woodland – Panterris, Milburn, Garrow Woods – all of which are worth exploring.

How to get there

About 3 miles W of Monmouth

The walk starts on the small road that runs from Wonastow to The Hendre. From Monmouth take the Wonastow Road to the southwest; shortly after passing Wonastow village, take the right fork to The Hendre. Continue along this road for about one mile until you reach signs for bridleways to your left and right. On the left is a track that takes you to Treowen and on the right a track that goes up to the hill. Park here.

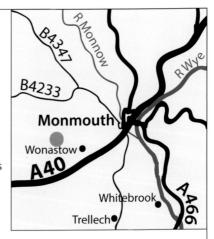

Alternatively, you can walk up into King's Wood along the Offa's Dyke footpath from Monmouth. Leave Monmouth on the B4233 to Rockfield. Just beyond the Fire Station turn left onto Watery Lane and park near the end of this dead-end road at SO491130. Enter the arable fields to your right and follow the way-marked Offa's Dyke Path along the edge of a small wooded dingle, listening and looking for Yellow Wagtails in the breeding season and Yellowhammers. After about 2km you enter the wood and will soon join the recommended route at point E on the map.

THIS CIRCULAR walk through ancient broad-leaved and conifer woodland, taking in Lasgarn Wood, Cwm Lasgarn and returning along Waterworks Road, is a little over half a mile north of the village of Abersychan. It can be productive at any time of year but spring and summer are always the most interesting and on a good day between 25 and 30 species can be recorded. The walk has some initial steep inclines with gentler terrain following the route of an old limestone quarry tramroad.

Target birds

All year: Buzzard 90%, Tawny Owl 10%, Goldcrest 50%, Dipper 60%, Siskin 50%, Lesser Redpoll 50%, Crossbill 30%

Spring/summer: Wood Warbler 60%, Garden Warbler 30%, Spotted Flycatcher 5%, Redstart 60%, Pied Flycatcher 50%

Winter: Brambling 10%

Other likely species

All year	Skylark	Garden Warbler
Sparrowhawk	Thrushes	Wheatear
Green Woodpecker	Meadow Pipit	*Winter*
Great Spotted Woodpecker	Common finches	Winter thrushes
Tits	*Spring/summer*	Woodcock
Marsh Tit	Cuckoo	*Occasional*
Willow Tit	Hirundines	Red Kite
	Whitethroat	Firecrest

Key points

- 1.5 miles (2.7km)
- Mostly moderate
- Some steeper sections
- Walking boots recommended
- All-year interest; spring and summer best
- Public transport

Recommended route and birding tips

AT THE parking place listen for Dipper, Grey Wagtail and the occasional Kingfisher, all of which frequent the nearby Afon Lwyd. Hirundines including Sand Martin are common at this point as well. Spotted Flycatcher can also be seen close to the Rising Sun Bridge.

Entering the wood near to the interpretation board (point A), the walk climbs steeply for around 3-400m and can be quite challenging. Here Wood Warblers are frequently noted in full song during spring, and in daytime it is not unusual to find a Tawny Owl roosting against the trunk of one of the many mature beech trees. Other typical woodland birds include Great Spotted Woodpecker, Treecreeper, Nuthatch, Marsh and Willow Tits and Chiffchaff. At a point where the terrain

109

levels and the path branches (B), take a left turn onto a bridleway at the wooden post, heading north – from this point the walk takes a noticeably easier route following an old tramroad; note the round holes drilled in the stonework that once secured the rail track. Here the deciduous wood thins into mixed woodland, with recent felling of larches providing some diversity, and ideal Nightjar habitat. The remaining conifer woodland can support moderate (sometimes high) numbers of Siskin, Lesser Redpoll, Coal Tit, Goldcrest and Crossbill. Raptors such as Buzzard, Sparrowhawk and Red Kite take advantage of the open space created by woodland management operations.

Proceeding north, the footpath continues through mature woodland. Where the

density of tree cover lessens and scrub increases, Redstart, Garden Warbler and Blackcap are common. After a kilometre (point C) take a left turning at a signpost, following the bridleway downhill through mature conifer woodland from where Woodcocks are often flushed. A short distance beyond, the walk enters a further area of mature beech woodland (point D) where Wood Warbler, Redstart and Pied Flycatcher all breed. In winter flocks of Bramblings and Chaffinches feed on a good beech mast crop.

Continue through the woodland and follow the path around the side of the now disused reservoir to emerge onto Waterworks Road (point E). The disused reservoir is worth a careful look as Common Sandpiper and Kingfisher have

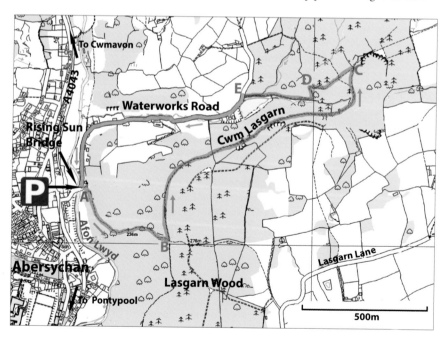

occurred there. Occasionally, Goshawk is seen overhead, and the deep grunt of Ravens is heard. Where the farmland and hedgerow border the road, Firecrest has been recorded. Turn left and follow the road downhill where finches, including Bullfinch and Greenfinch, are often well represented. After 700m the road takes you back to your starting point.

How to get there

About 4 miles N of Pontypool

From Pontypool take the A4043 northwards and follow the road to Abersychan. Continue through the village centre towards Blaenavon for approximately half a mile. Passing a redbrick primary school (Victoria Village) on the left, take the first turning right onto Waterworks Road towards the Rising Sun Bridge. Directly over the bridge, park in the shadow of the mature woodland close to a way-marked public right of way sign.

From Blaenavon take the A4043 south to Pontypool. Follow the road for approximately 4 miles to Abersychan, then turn left on to Waterworks Road towards the Rising Sun Bridge. Directly over the bridge, park in the shadow of the mature woodland close to a way-marked public right of way sign.

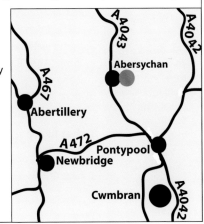

Public transport

There is a regular bus service between Pontypool and Blaenavon, with bus stops at approximately SO270042 and SO270044.

Three walks

- Pettingale Hide Walk 1.1 miles (1.8km) moderate
- The Sor Bay Walk 1.5 miles (2.4km) easy
- The Green Pool Walk 1.2 miles (1.9km) easy

Key points

- 3.8 miles (6.1km) to cover all walks
- Moderately steep hill on Pettingale walk
- Paths can be very muddy
- Permit needed for Sor Bay & Green Pool
- Public access to the dam and Pettingale
- SSSI for wintering wildfowl
- Telescope essential
- Very limited wheelchair access

THIS IS a series of short walks around the largest inland water in Gwent. The second two walks listed on the left involve entering the reservoir grounds, for which a permit is required (see under Key points). The reservoir has an area of 174 hectares, consisting mainly of open water, but with reedbeds and willow carr. Adjacent habitats include broad-leaved woodland, hedgerows, scrub, hay meadows, agricultural land and marsh. There are six birdwatching hides at the site and also a bird feeding station. The site is designated as an SSSI for wintering wildfowl, but a visit any time of the year can be productive. The winter gull roost is impressive and can attract rare species, whilst Ospreys are regular in the passage months.

The northern, shallower end is the best area for wintering wildfowl and breeding birds, but the deeper water of the southern end near the dam attracts wildfowl which can include rare grebes and divers in winter. The Pettingale hide on the western shore is the best site from which to observe the winter gull roost in late afternoon.

Target birds

All year: Great Crested Grebe 100%, Little Grebe 60%, Water Rail 20%, Kingfisher 80%

Summer: Hobby 20%, Common Sandpiper 60%, Sedge Warbler 100%, Reed Warbler 100%

Autumn passage: Osprey 10%, Little Ringed Plover 30%, Golden Plover 10%, Black Tern 20%, Common Tern 30%, Arctic Tern 20%

Winter: Wigeon 100%, Teal 20%, Pochard 50%, Tufted Duck 30%, Goosander 60%, Lapwing 20%, Jack Snipe 10%, Snipe 100%

Other likely species

All year		
Mute Swan	Cormorant	Stock Dove
Canada Goose	Little Egret	Little Owl
Common waterfowl	Grey Heron	3 woodpecker species
Red-legged Partridge	Common raptors	Common woodland birds
Pheasant	Peregrine	
	Regular gulls	

112

Raven	Whitethroat	Redstart
Marsh Tit	Stonechat	Wheatear
Lesser Redpoll	Spotted Flycatcher	Yellow Wagtail
Crossbill	Pied Flycatcher	*Occasional*
Yellowhammer	*Winter*	Whooper Swan
Reed Bunting	Bewick's Swan	Range of duck species
Spring/summer	Shelduck	Great Northern Diver
Cuckoo	Winter thrushes	Slavonian Grebe
Hirundines	Brambling	Black-necked Grebe
Summer warblers	*Passage*	Range of wader species
Wood Warbler	Curlew	Scarce/rare gulls
Garden Warbler	Redshank	

Recommended route and birding tips

The Dam   SO325985 (NP4 0TA)   Car park P1

A WINTER VISIT is best started at the dam, and for those visiting for the first time, the view from here offers a good introduction to the reservoir topography. Park in the pull-off half way across (P1) and scan from here. Birds in winter include a selection of wildfowl, particularly diving ducks, and may include rarities such as Slavonian Grebe and divers. More than 30 species can be seen from this point. This is not a formal parking area so you should stay close to your vehicle while here.

Pettingale Hide Walk   ST321992 (NP4 0SS)   1.1 miles   Car park P2

FROM P1, drive west along the dam, follow the road along the reservoir edge and up a hill, and after a sharp left bend the car park is on the right, just before the Water Treatment Works (P2). The Pettingale hide is 900m from here. Walk out of the car park back onto the main road and turn immediately left down a track that quickly narrows into a path. Follow this path downhill, skirting the top edge of the wood. A selection of common woodland species can be found here, with Wood Warblers sometimes present in spring.

At the end of the wood, go through a metal kissing gate into an open field. Views of the reservoir can be obtained here. Walk down the field to a stile at the far bottom (northeastern) corner. The Pettingale hide is just over this stile. This hide is most productive during late afternoon in winter, when gulls come in to roost. Check the gull flock carefully for Mediterranean and Iceland Gulls. The hide also gives good views over the southern part of the reservoir, so a wide range of birds can be seen.

Northern end	SO332007 (NP4 0TG) 2.7 miles Car park P3

The following two walks require a birdwatching permit obtainable from the Rangers' office about 100m uphill from the east side of the dam. Park in the anglers' car park (P3), inside the gate (SO333008). From here, two options are available.

Sor Bay Walk	1.5 miles

From the car park (P3), turn right (westwards) along the path just before the buildings. Almost immediately, the bird feeding station and hide will be reached. A selection of passerine birds can be seen here. Walk approximately 400m further

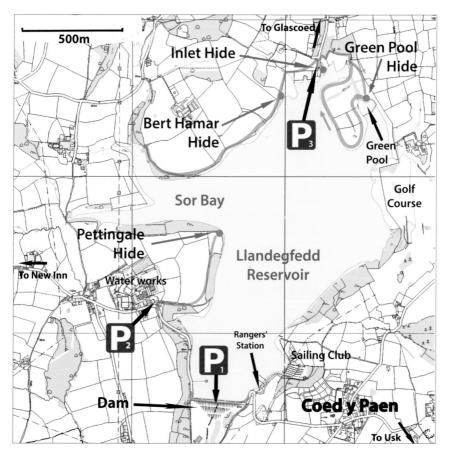

114

along the path to reach the Bert Hamar hide. Scan from here to observe wildfowl and, in winter, birds such as Goosanders and gulls coming in to roost during late afternoon. Look on to the adjacent agricultural land to the west in winter: flocks of Lapwing and small numbers of Golden Plover may be present.

Walking a further 800m will bring you into Sor Bay, which can hold good numbers of wildfowl and occasional rarities such as Slavonian Grebe, while a heronry can be seen on the opposite bank. Take care not to disturb roosting birds. This part of the walk can become very overgrown in summer. Retrace your steps to the car park.

The Green Pool Walk   1.2 miles

From the car park (P3) turn left (eastwards) through the gate. The first hide is just 40m ahead, slightly to the right. Enter the hide and scan the inlet area of the reservoir. In winter, a selection of wildfowl can be seen, including occasional Bewick's Swans. During summer, Great Crested Grebes breed in this area and Sedge and Reed Warblers may be seen.

Leaving the hide, continue northwards along the path and around the reservoir inlet. The area can be very wet at times. After passing the Prioress Mill pumping station river outlet, keep straight ahead with the fence on your left. The path crosses a hay meadow where Lapwings and Yellow Wagtails used to breed. Turn south and follow the path to the Green Pool hide, which you can see in the trees ahead. From the hide, situated at the end of a small pool, look and listen for Water Rails, which breed here. Little Grebes also breed, while Snipe and occasionally Jack Snipe are present in winter. Sedge and Reed Warblers are present in summer.

Leave the hide and turn left along a muddy track-cum-boardwalk between a double line of trees. Tawny Owls can be seen and heard here at dusk. On emerging into a field, turn left and walk alongside the wire fence until you reach the reservoir shoreline: look for waders during passage periods. Common Sandpipers are regular during the summer. The larger mature trees occasionally hold Lesser Spotted Woodpecker and Pied Flycatcher, while flocks of thrushes can be seen on the open ground and along the hedgerows in winter. You will soon pass the Island hide on your right, but this tends not to be very productive.

Proceed slowly around the shoreline, taking care not to disturb feeding Wigeon and other species in winter. Scan the reservoir at regular intervals: Osprey may be seen fishing during early spring and autumn. In winter, Peregrines may be seen overhead, whilst Hobbies may be present in summer. Ravens, Buzzards and Sparrowhawks are regular and Red Kites are sometimes seen. Look for waders during spring and autumn, particularly if reservoir levels are low and areas of mud are exposed. Little Egrets may also be seen. Follow the shoreline back to the reservoir inlet and return to the car park.

How to get there

About 3 miles E of Pontypool

Follow the A4042 Newport to Abergavenny road. South of Pontypool follow the signs from the roundabout to New Inn. After entering the village, turn right onto Jerusalem Lane, signposted Llandegfedd Reservoir.

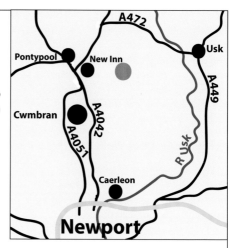

To reach Pettingale Point and the dam, turn right 400 m along Jerusalem Lane into Sluvad Road and continue for about one mile until the Water Treatment Works is reached – park just past here (P2) for the Pettingale Hide. The reservoir dam is a further half-mile along this road (P1).

To reach the northern shore, turn right in New Inn onto Jerusalem Lane, but ignore the right hand turn signposted Llandegfedd Reservoir and carry straight on along the unclassified road. After about 2.6 miles, turn right at a crossroads in Glascoed village, following a 'no through road' sign. After approx. 500m, the anglers' car park (P3) will be reached.

THIS SUPERB area in the foothills of the Black Mountains, offers excellent opportunities for birding owing to its unspoilt woodland and moorland. It is easily accessible from Abergavenny or Hereford, being just off of the main A465. The walk takes in the Afon Honddu and the valley slopes to the south and west. It requires a moderate level of fitness due to the uphill sections of woodland walking.

Target birds

All year: Red Grouse 5%, Goshawk 5%, Red Kite 30%, Merlin 10%, Dipper 90%, Lesser Spotted Woodpecker 10%, Lesser Redpoll 70%, Crossbill 60%

Spring/summer: Hobby 20%, Cuckoo 80%, Redstart 80%, Stonechat 70%, Pied Flycatcher 60%, Tree Pipit 40%, Yellowhammer 60%

Autumn/winter: Redwing 90%, Fieldfare 90%

Other likely species

All year	Goldcrest	Bullfinch
Common raptors	Meadow Pipit	
Green Woodpecker	Grey Wagtail	*Spring/summer*
Common woodland birds	Siskin	Hirundines
	Linnet	Summer warblers

Key points

- 3.5 miles (5.6km)
- Slightly shorter option available
- Moderate to strenuous
- Many divergent paths – OS map useful
- Sturdy footwear
- Facilities at Queen's Head pub
- Free car park (or nominal charge at Queen's Head pub)

Recommended route and birding tips

STARTING AT the forestry entrance car park, walk around the barrier and follow the track into the forest. You will now have woodland on your right and heavy tree cover on your left. Listen out here for Goldcrest and tit flocks and also Bullfinch; you may be lucky and see Crossbill.

After about 300m you will come to two ill-defined paths (point A), one on your left that turns back at an acute angle and climbs, and one on your right that goes forward and down – take the one on the right. You are now in woodland with a steep bank sloping down to the right; stay on this path descending all the way. Here look out for Chiffchaff, Wood Warbler and Blackcap; scan the skyline and you may also see Red Kite.

Keep going until you come to the fence and follow the path that runs alongside it, keeping the fence on your right. Ahead you will see a stile – cross it and go straight on, heading towards the farm building (point B). Just as you reach the farm turn acutely to the right, following the farm track down to the road (point C).

When you reach the road turn round and scan the ridge behind you for raptors – Goshawk is possible. Cross to the stile opposite, follow the path past the building and down to the river, bearing left as you reach the river, and cross the footbridge. Pause here for a while and look out for Dipper, Grey Wagtail and sometimes Kingfisher.

Now follow the path uphill through the field, keeping the fence on your left. Continue until you reach the stile at the road (point D); cross the stile and turn left following the road uphill. When you reach

the junction (point E), with the church (which is worth a quick look) in front of you, turn left. Now follow the road going downhill, making sure not to deviate.

You will shortly come to a road bridge across the river where you have another opportunity to observe Dipper and Grey Wagtail. Follow the lane, which goes past farm buildings, and then go uphill to the junction (point F). Scan the ridge ahead for raptors then turn left and follow the road; after about 25m you will see a stile on your right. Cross the stile and go straight ahead uphill heading towards the trees (walk through the tree line bordering the fence line).

When you reach the fence line, turn right. Keep walking straight ahead with the

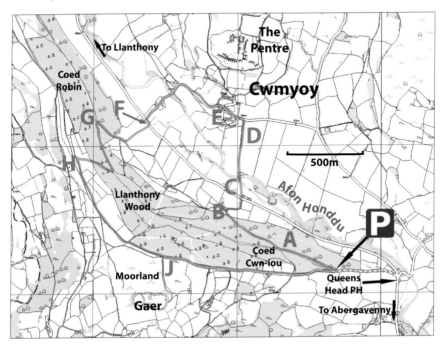

fence to your left. Do not deviate from this path. After about 100m you will come to a stile with a small cast iron gate at the side of it; cross this stile into the woods (ignore an earlier gate on your left).

After crossing the stile, follow the path through the woods for about 200m. Here, look out for all three species of woodpecker, and listen for Goldcrest. When you reach the wide forestry track (point G), turn left. Follow this track for about 400m until you come to a path on your left (way-marked Llanthony Road) – ignore this but take the next one just past this on the right, signposted Gaer Ridge (** see shorter option below). Keep on this path climbing uphill for about 150m until you come to a small wooden gate. Go through this gate and bear left, heading uphill towards the trees at the fence line. When you reach the trees keep the fence on your left and head for the gate. Go through the gate and turn

left, following the mountain track (point H).

As you walk, check the moorland on the right for Meadow Pipit and Skylark – you may also see Stonechat. Pause for ten minutes or so anywhere between points H and J, and once more scan for raptors – Peregrine has been seen on the rock face beyond the church at Cwmyoy and Red Kite is a possibility. Continue for about 800m, keeping an eye on the stone wall on your left, where you may also see Wheatear and Redstart, until you reach the gate (point J). Go through it onto the track that will return you to your start point.

** If you wish to make the walk less strenuous, you can at this point continue along the main forest track back to the car park instead of taking the Gaer Ridge path. This avoids the climb to the ridge and shortens the walk a little.

How to get there

About 7 miles N of Abergavenny

From Abergavenny take the A465 towards Hereford for about six miles. When you reach Llanvihangel Crucorney, take the slip road, which is signposted Skirrid Inn. At the pub take the turning directly beside it, signposted Cwmyoy 3 miles. Follow the road downhill bearing left at the bottom, going under the railway bridge for about 1.5 miles until you come to the Queen's Head. Just as you pass the pub there is a turning left that goes steeply uphill – your start point car park is about 300m up this hill. There is alternative parking at the Queen's Head walkers' car park situated opposite the pub at the bottom of the steep lane; there is a nominal charge to park here – please pay at the pub.

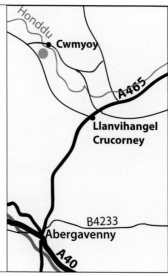

Key points

- Main walk 3.1 miles (5km)
- Extension 1.7 miles (2.7km)
- Easy
- Can be wet and muddy
- All-year interest, best in spring/ summer
- Cattle with calves may be encountered.
- Free car park
- Public transport to 1km from start

LANWENARTH IS the first notable birdwatching site on the River Usk after it enters the county. It consists principally of riverine habitat, including a floodplain, islands, shingle, tree lines, scrub and farmland. If time allows, a damp field and conifer woodland can also be explored. Llanwenarth provides the chance to see river species such as Dipper, Kingfisher and Grey Wagtail all year around, but it really blossoms in the spring and summer when migrants such as Common Sandpiper, Sand Martin and warblers arrive, together with Kestrel, Lesser Spotted Woodpecker and sometimes Hobby.

Target birds

All year: Goosander 90%, Little Owl 30%, Kingfisher 40%, Lesser Spotted Woodpecker 10%, Dipper 100% (winter), 50% (summer), Grey Wagtail 80%

Spring/summer: Kestrel 50%, Hobby 20%, Curlew 30% (hearing), 10% (seeing), Common Sandpiper 90%, Sand Martin 100%, Garden Warbler 70%

Autumn passage: Green Sandpiper 30%

Winter: Siskin 50%, Lesser Redpoll 10%

Other likely species

All year	Great Spotted Woodpecker	*Winter*
Little Grebe		Little Egret
Grey Heron	Pied Wagtail	Teal
Mallard	Treecreeper	Winter thrushes
Red Kite		
Buzzard	*Summer*	*Occasional*
Sparrowhawk	Goldcrest	Osprey
Tawny Owl	Chiffchaff	Water Rail
Moorhen	Blackcap	Snipe
Green Woodpecker	Lesser Whitethroat	Stonechat
	Spotted Flycatcher	

Recommended route and birding tips

Main walk	3.1 miles

EXPLORE THE churchyard first. Goldcrests, Greenfinches and winter thrushes can be found here, particularly in the yew trees. In spring, take a look over the back wall as Curlews are sometimes present in the field. Spotted

Flycatchers can sometimes be seen in the summer, often using gravestones as perches. Turn right after leaving the churchyard and cross the stile on the left side of the road, adjacent to an ancient black poplar. Cross the field and just prior to the next stile (point A), scan the triangular hole and eaves of the barn to your right for Little Owl. Cross the stile and walk to the river.

At this point (B) turn right, and walking upstream check the shingle on your left for Dipper and Grey Wagtail. Just before the island is the former site of a chain ferry (the winding gear is still visible on the far bank) which allowed parishioners to cross the river on a punt-like boat to reach Llanwenarth Church. The island is now overgrown with scrub but provides a nesting site for Common Sandpiper. It is worth keeping an eye on the river's surface beyond the island as otters have been present at this point recently. Always be vigilant for the high-pitched sibilant call of Kingfishers as they fly along the river. Follow the river to the next stile, which is about 30m from the river bank.

Turn left and immediately cross the next stile. Follow the hedge line tight to the left and look carefully down the steep river bank (point C), as Dipper or Kingfisher can sometimes be seen at the base of the bank. Walk across the field for about 100m to a descent to the flood plain (point D). Approach this point stealthily and carefully view the area below, particularly if there is floodwater lying. The end of the island furthest upstream provides an area of slack current where Mallard and Goosanders congregate. Descend the slope and walk across the flood plain. The bank of the river here houses the nest holes of a large Sand Martin colony, which provides a tremendous spectacle. The willows normally hold good numbers

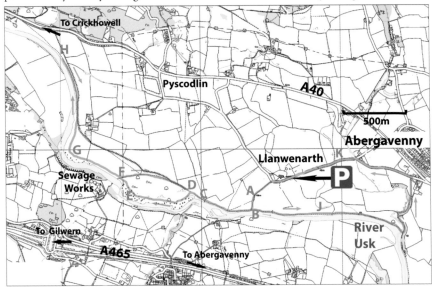

121

The River Usk at Llanwenarth *Jonathan Baker*

of Treecreepers, and the alders are worth checking for Siskins or Lesser Redpolls in winter.

Beyond the island the river slows and noctule bats can sometimes be observed feeding on warm evenings in late September. Continue until you reach an area of scrub (point E), which provides habitat for breeding Garden Warblers and Blackcaps. Where the scrub thins, walk through to the river and check the shingle and river bank. Return to the field and continue until another stile (point F) is reached. Scan the river upstream from here, as the current is very slow at this point and Little Grebe can sometimes be observed.

Cross this stile and walk on to the next stile. At this point the river becomes very rough (point G) with many rocks and rapids present. This is a good spot to observe

Dippers, except in the spring when they mainly leave the river for breeding territories on smaller tributaries. After the river calms there is an area of scrub on the bank that is worth checking for warblers in spring or summer. Views of Mallard, Moorhen or Goosander can normally be obtained on this stretch, with Green Woodpecker often present in the trees on the far bank. Stop where the river bends left (point H) and retrace your steps to the flood plain (point F). Then follow its left hand edge or the central tree line, which marks a previous course of the river, and can sometimes turn up additional species. Continue to the point where you first reached the river (point D).

At this point either return to your starting point or explore further by extending your walk around a loop to the east.

Extension walk   1.7 miles

CROSS THE stile and carry on down the river. This section of the river has a uniformly slow pace with little shingle and most riverine birds are much scarcer, although Moorhen, Little Grebe and Goosander are still present. The latter species can often be seen trailing ducklings in June. The hedges to the left may contain Lesser Whitethroat so it is worth listening for the rattle of their call. Continue across stiles and a bridge until you reach a point where there are about five trees in the centre of the field to the left, standing on the edge of a ditch (point J). These trees are used by Lesser and Great Spotted Woodpeckers so are worth viewing from the river. Cross a second bridge and view the shingle on a river island, as it often holds Goosanders.

Turn left and enter the conifer woodland, listening and looking for Goldcrest and Coal Tit. Cross the stile at the end of the wood and walk on to the road. The farm on the right is usually a good place to observe hirundines. Turn left at the road and then view the large overgrown garden on your right; it frequently holds warblers, which can include Common and Lesser Whitethroats. Continue along the road until you cross a small brook. At this point (K) scan the field on your right – it is often damp and may harbour Snipe, Mallard, Grey Heron, Lapwing and occasionally Little Egret. Continue along the road to return to your starting point.

How to get there

Immediately W of Abergavenny

Leaving Abergavenny on the A40 to Brecon, pass Nevill Hall Hospital and, after about 200m, take an unsigned left turn into a lane. Continue to Llanwenarth where you can park opposite St Peter's Church.Public transport

Bus stops at Nevill Hall Hospital or Pyscodlyn Farm can be reached by services from Abergavenny Bus Station. Both stops are about 1km from the start of the walk.

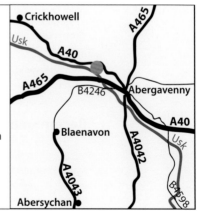

Key points

- 4.2 miles (6.7km)
- Easy walk, on metalled surface
- Fields/ woods along route are strictly private
- Good year-round birding
- Wheelchair accessible only along the road

THIS IS a walk through countryside typical of northeast Monmouthshire, through the Monnow valley among low, rounded hills with a mixture of woodland, pasture and arable in roughly equal proportions. This return walk skirts Osbaston and enters open countryside alongside the river. It is a good walk at any time of year – one that will reveal between 30 and 45 species, depending on the weather and time spent – and is best undertaken slowly, in dry weather. The birding is interesting, though rarely spectacular. Spring and autumn bring some passage, although, as is generally the case, this is unpredictable.

Target birds

All year: Mandarin Duck 30%, Sparrowhawk 60%, Buzzard 100%, Peregrine 30%, Tawny Owl 10%, Lesser Spotted Woodpecker 5%, Marsh Tit 80%, Dipper 60%, Yellowhammer 90%

Spring/summer: Goshawk 20%, Hobby 30%

Winter: Goosander 30%

Other likely species

All year		Winter
Canada Goose	Tits	Winter thrushes
Mallard	Thrushes	Finches (up to eight species)
Cormorant	Grey Wagtail	Meadow Pipit
Grey Heron	Pied Wagtail	
Little Grebe	Common finches	*Passage*
Kestrel	Reed Bunting	Lesser Whitethroat
Stock Dove	*Spring/summer*	Grasshopper Warbler
Kingfisher	Cuckoo	Wheatear
Green Woodpecker	Hirundines	Pied Flycatcher
Great Spotted Woodpecker	Summer warblers	*Occasional*
Common corvids	Whitethroat	Red Kite
Raven	Spotted Flycatcher	Regular gulls
		Lesser Spotted Woodpecker

Recommended route and birding tips

THIS IS an easy walk; there are no steep hills and it is mostly on a metalled road – indeed, it can be made entirely on a metalled surface if so desired.

On leaving the car, double back, take the first right, pass behind the school and proceed alongside the river (point A). Pass the main weir (500m, point B); continue for 100m by the river then follow the path to the right, uphill past a house, to rejoin the road. Turn left onto it and head north; note that Gwent ends (and Herefordshire begins) at point F.

Viewing from the road is generally straightforward, but note that there is no access to any of the fields, woods or the river banks; nonetheless, a good deal of the river may be viewed from a number of vantage points along the road.

The first 700m of the walk passes Osbaston. The main interest here is along the River Monnow. Dipper, Kingfisher and Grey Wagtail are often seen near the remains of the old mill race or at the weir.

After about 700m, one enters more open country, with pastures and the river bank to the left, and arable fields stretching uphill to the right. At point C, scan the skyline, especially to the east (right) for soaring corvids and raptors. Of the latter, Buzzard is virtually guaranteed and Sparrowhawks frequently hunt over the fields; both species breed nearby. In spring, six species of raptor have been seen in a morning from this point. Also in spring and summer, there is a small Sand Martin colony near here; though this is out of sight of the road, the birds often hunt over the surrounding fields.

Raven is usually seen and heard here. Mallard and Mandarin Duck may also be found anywhere along the river, though most frequently at point D, and Grey Heron and Cormorant roost in riverside alders. Little Grebes breed nearby and can usually be seen somewhere along the river. Kingfisher is rather less frequent, but listening for the distinctive high-pitched whistle may help locate one.

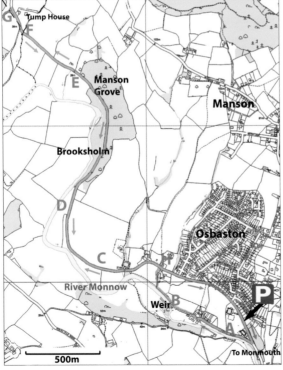

Finches and thrushes may be found almost anywhere, especially in autumn and winter when large numbers may be present. Yellowhammers and, less often, Reed Buntings can be found in the thick hedgerows, which in summer hold numerous breeding Whitethroats.

After 1.5km, the road enters woodland, composed of mainly alder and ash with an underlying scrub layer between the road and the river. On the

125

slopes above the road there are plantations of larches, mixed ash, oak and spruce woodland with an outgrown hazel coppice understorey in the deciduous areas. Occasionally a Lesser Spotted Woodpecker may be found in the alders, though this elusive species can never be guaranteed. Marsh Tits breed here and are usually seen in the denser vegetation along the road, though they can be silent for long periods and are then difficult to find. Great, Blue and Coal Tit, as well as Long-tailed Tit, are all relatively common.

In spring and summer, warblers, especially Blackcap and Chiffchaff, are abundant in the woods, with all of the commoner woodland passerines well represented. Passage warblers in spring include Lesser Whitethroat, Willow Warbler and an occasional Grasshopper Warbler, while Pied Flycatcher and Wheatear have also appeared.

In winter, flocks of Goldfinch, Siskin and, less commonly, Lesser Redpoll, are to be seen in the taller alder trees; Linnet flocks feed in the open fields. Goosander might be seen anywhere along the river. Both of the larger woodpecker species are common, though the Green prefers the pasture areas; there are up to four pairs of Green in this part of the valley and they are among the noisier residents.

After 2km, one emerges from the woods to sweeping views across the valley to the left (west); this is point E on the map. Here it is always worth scanning carefully for a few minutes. In summer and autumn, Spotted Flycatcher is often found in this area, as is Bullfinch all year round.

From this point onwards the well-grown hedges produce many finches, thrushes and other small passerines, while Kestrel is more likely here.

As one approaches the 3km distance, the road climbs a short but steep hill, past Tump House (point F) on the right. At the top of the hill, on the left (point G) is a drive entry and from here one may scan back down the valley to the south, to Monmouth and beyond. Yellowhammer is commonly seen here, as are Stock Dove and innumerable Woodpigeons, with frequent sightings of Buzzard, Sparrowhawk and Raven. In winter, Stock Dove flocks may reach 150 or more.

Keep an eye on the skyline to the east; raptors occur and may include Peregrine, Red Kite or Goshawk. Raven is common as are large mixed corvid flocks.

Return to the parking point by retracing your route, keeping straight and not leaving the road at point H. Keep an alert eye open through all the key habitats on the way back; much can change in an hour and on this walk, new birds are just as often found on the return leg!

How to get there

Immediately NW of Monmouth

Leave the A40 dual carriageway at the only roundabout, for Monmouth centre. At the traffic lights, turn right and, in 240m, turn left into a narrow downhill road. After 400m, a school is reached on the left; one may park here where the road is much wider; take care, for it is busy.

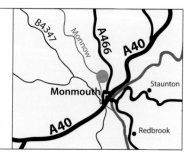

MAGOR MARSH, a Gwent Wildlife Trust reserve, is a wonderful remnant of wetland on the Gwent Levels much of which was purchased in 1963 thanks to the foresight of the newly formed Monmouthshire Naturalists' Trust and in particular to the efforts of Pat Humphreys and Barbara Thorne. The reserve has open water, small reedbeds, willow carr and woodland, sedge beds, wet pastures and reens (ditches). In recent years more pastures and meadows have been secured by the Trust to the west of the 60-acre core area of Magor Reserve. Whilst you may not see any rarities on your visit, you will see an array of wetland and woodland birds and there is always the chance of something more unusual. In 1981 a study by Chris Jones produced 82 bird species in one year.

Since the reserve was established early in the 1960s a number of rare birds have appeared. None are rarer than the American Bittern which appeared in late October 1981 and remained until early in 1982, the first 'twitchable' American Bittern in Britain. Donations from birders went towards the purchase of two flower-rich hay meadows on the western edge of the reserve.

Key points

- **0.8 miles (1.3km)**
- **Very short**
- **Flat but marshy**
- **Boots recommended**
- **Wheelchair access – see** *Best walks for disabled access*
- **Telescope useful**
- **Water voles reintroduced**
- **Cattle present in autumn and winter**
- **No dogs allowed**
- **The Derek Upton Centre is open only for special events**
- **No seats in the hide**
- **Public transport**

Target birds

All year: Little Grebe 75%, Little Egret 40%, Water Rail 50%, Reed Bunting 75%, Cetti's Warbler 80%

Spring/summer: Hobby 10%, Marsh Tit 40%, Reed Warbler 90%, Sedge Warbler 80%, Grasshopper Warbler 20% (heard)

Winter: Teal 75%, Snipe 80%, Kingfisher 75%

Other likely species

All year	Great Spotted Woodpecker	Swallow	Siskin
Grey Heron		Chiffchaff	Lesser Redpoll
Mute Swan	Tits	Blackcap	Tree Sparrow
Mallard	Nuthatch	Whitethroat	
Coot	Treecreeper		*Occasional*
Moorhen	Bullfinch	*Winter*	Stonechat
Common raptors	Tree Sparrow	Gadwall	Whinchat
Green Sandpiper (passage)		Shoveler	Grey Wagtail
	Spring/summer	Winter thrushes	Meadow Pipit
	Sand Martin		

127

Recommended route and birding tips

FROM THE car park, walk over the bridge into the reserve. Follow the boardwalk across the fields and eventually to the hide at the pond. As you walk you may see or hear Reed Buntings, while the explosive song of Cetti's Warbler can be heard throughout the year; the first record of Cetti's was in 1995. Occasionally in the summer a Hobby visits the reserve to hunt for the abundant dragonflies. Marsh Tits are also sometimes heard or seen in the spring and early summer months when, too, you may be lucky enough to hear Grasshopper Warblers reeling. Snipe may be flushed from the wet fields especially in the winter months although the high count of 233 on 10 March 1981 has not been repeated in recent years. Siskins and Lesser

Redpolls are always possible in the winter months too.

From the hide at the pond enjoy the tranquillity (sitting on the seat you have brought) and await something of interest. Little Grebe, Mute Swan and Mallard are regular whilst Little Egret and Grey Heron often put in an appearance. Listen out for Reed and Sedge Warblers during the spring and summer in the surrounding reedbeds and also the grunts and shrieks of Water Rails. In the summer Swallows and Sand Martins are often seen over the reserve, especially around the lake, and an artificial cliff has been built to try to encourage nesting by the Sand Martins and perhaps a Kingfisher. Green Sandpipers occasionally turn up by the pond. In the

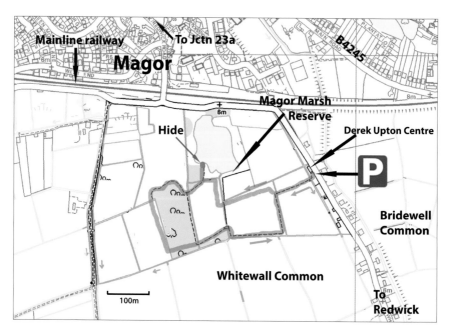

winter, ducks other than Mallard may include Teal, Gadwall and Shoveler and in spring it is worth looking out for Garganey; this small duck bred in 1965 and 1969 with a pair seen in 1970, and single adults were observed in several subsequent years. Breeding has occurred more recently at Newport Wetlands Reserve so there is always the possibility of a pair nesting again at Magor.

Other paths (some muddy) and boardwalks take you west to the two hay meadows by the Blackwall Reen and then back along the southern side of the reserve to the car park. There is more GWT reserve land to the west – comprising flower-rich hay meadows and rushy pastures with scrapes. Snipe and Lapwing may be found here in the winter months.

How to get there

About 5 miles E of Newport

Leave the M4 at J23A and follow the signs for Magor village on the B4245. In Magor village turn right following the signs to Redwick and take another turn right, past the ruins of the Old Priory and over the bridge above the main London to Newport railway line. Immediately over the bridge turn left and continue around the bend for 300-400m. On the right you will see a gate into a car park by the Whitewall Reen. The Gwent Wildlife Trust Reserves booklet provides excellent details of how to reach the reserve and includes a map of the reserve.

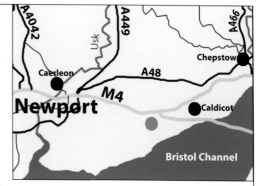

129

LARGELY OVERLYING carboniferous limestone, this woodland complex comprising The Minnetts, Thicket Wood, Slade Wood, Hardwick Plantation, Ifton Great Wood and Rogiet Brake is best known for its rich botanical and entomological treasures. The suggested walk leads first through fields with views towards the Severn Estuary to the south. The next, and major, part of the route passes through mixed woodland of various stages but, currently, few clear-fell areas. The final part of the route along Minnetts Lane passes once more through farmland.

Over the years birdlife has changed with woodland management and is, today, typical of a semi-mature woodland. Compared with past times, habitat diversity at The Minnetts is now poor owing to a lack of clear-felling to create open, scrubby areas. In the past (1950s-1970s) clear felling provided habitat for Tree Pipit, Grasshopper Warbler and Nightjar, all of which used to breed but now appear to have gone. On a walk through this area during the spring/summer expect to see about 30-35 bird species.

Key points

- 2.8 miles (4.5km)
- Generally easy
- Can be very muddy in places
- All year interest
- Good botanical interest
- Working forest – some paths may be unavailable at times
- Wheelchair access along Minnetts Lane only

Target birds

All year: Buzzard 95%, Sparrowhawk 30%, Green Woodpecker 30%, Stock Dove 20%, Tawny Owl 10%, Hawfinch 5%

Spring/summer: Woodcock (at dusk) 20%, Hobby 10%, Red-legged Partridge 10%

Autumn: Spotted Flycatcher 30%, Pied Flycatcher 30%

Other likely species

All year		
Red-legged Partridge	Common finches	Garden Warbler
Peregrine	Lesser Redpoll	Lesser Whitethroat
Kestrel	Crossbill	Summer warblers
Common corvids	*Spring/summer*	*Winter*
Raven	Shelduck (breeding)	Winter thrushes
Common woodland birds	Mallard (breeding)	Brambling
Marsh Tit	Cuckoo	*Passage*
Starling	Hirundines	Redstart
	Grasshopper Warbler	Wood Warbler

Recommended route and birding tips

FROM THE parked car walk up Windmill Lane to a point close to the old ruined windmill. From here follow the footpath to the right, along the edge of the field. Listen out for Curlews calling from the fields to the west. On reaching the woodland (point A) cross the stile on your left that leads through the part of Minnetts Wood called Rogiett Brake. Follow the path straight ahead, ignoring the junction to the right after about10m, and take the right fork (point B) after about 50 metres. At the next junction (point C) turn right (following the yellow way-mark arrow), walk as far as the fence (point D) (Ifton Quarry boundary) and bear left along it. After about 150m turn left (point E) at a right-angle to the fence (ignore the yellow way-mark arrow, which points straight

ahead). Along this stretch you pass through an area of numerous wood ant nests, so keep an eye open for both sight and sign of Green Woodpecker activity. Continue through the forest on this northerly route until reaching the main forestry track (point F), which links Highmoor Hill to the top of Minnetts Lane. Now turn left to walk in a westerly direction along the track, soon to arrive at a relatively high point from which there are views to the south and west. Owing to the proximity of the Severn Estuary, such birds as gulls (Black-headed, Common, Herring and Lesser Black-backed), Curlew and Whimbrel sometimes pass over, the Whimbrel at times of passage (typically May, August and September).

Another feature of this woodland is its breeding Mallards and Shelducks, the latter

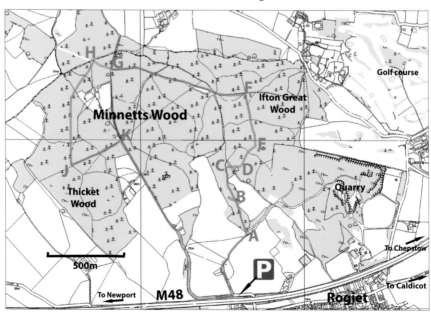

walking their ducklings down to the Severn Estuary – a very hazardous journey. Both of these ducks are mostly seen along this track during the spring but only an early morning visit is likely to be productive. In late summer and early autumn various summer migrants pass through the area on their way south. These include Spotted Flycatcher, Pied Flycatcher, Redstart and Wood Warbler. If you have a botanical interest, take note during spring and summer of the limestone flora along this stretch, which includes marjoram (wild oregano), yellow wort and red bartsia among others.

On reaching the Forestry Commission barrier (point G), the main track now turns sharply to the left (Minnetts Lane) and this can be taken to walk back to the car. The suggested route, however, follows straight on along a newly stoned track (currently rather rough). After a short distance (about 110m) take a path to the left (point H),

skirting the land belonging to the property known as 'The Minnetts'. Along this path, during the summer months, the split stones of the wild cherry may be found, and, with luck, the Hawfinches that split them may be seen. (After a prolonged period of wet weather, this path may flood or become extremely difficult owing to mud, in which case retrace your steps to the top of Minnets Lane and return to your car from there).

At the next junction (point J) turn left along the broad track (towards the east). On reaching the barrier (point K) turn right down Minnetts Lane to return to your car.

Apart from the route described here, there is a network of paths leading to all parts of the woodland, so a whole day may be spent here. This is particularly true if your interests include all aspects of natural history.

How to get there

About 1 mile W of Caldicot

Leave the M4 motorway at Junction 23 and take the B4245 to Magor and Undy. On leaving Undy the road passes under the M4, goes through Llanfihangel Rogiet and on to Rogiet. Once in Rogiet, take the first road to the left (opposite the sign to Severn Tunnel Railway Station) – this is Minnetts Lane. This lane also passes under a motorway

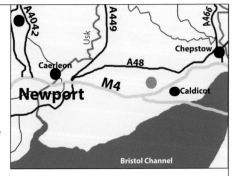

(the M48) and leads around to the left. Park on the grassy verge a short distance along this lane. From here the first turn to the right is Windmill Lane – the first leg of your walk into Minnetts Wood. Alternatively, you can park a single car opposite the entrance to Windmill Lane, but large farm vehicles turn in and out of the lane so take care not to cause any obstruction.

THIS WALK covers two sites of quite different character – The Moorings and a flooded field near Caerleon. Owing to their fairly close proximity, both can easily be covered in the same visit.

The Moorings is an area of rough, marshy grassland and *Phragmites* reedbed, some six hectares in extent, surrounded on three sides by a loop of the tidal River Usk and on the remaining side by a housing estate. The extensive reedbed, which, apart from those on the coast, is probably the largest expanse of *Phragmites* along the River Usk, holds a good population of Reed Warblers in summer. During winter, the wet areas usually hold Snipe. The Caerleon flooded field lies about a kilometre southeast of The Moorings, on the north bank of the River Usk, bounded on the other sides by farmland and a golf course; it holds a variety of wildfowl and also gulls, among which Mediterranean Gull is not unusual. Both sites involve a fairly short walk and can be productive at any time of the year, although there are more birds during winter and the spring and autumn passage periods. The Moorings is popular for dog walking so, to avoid disturbance, visits are best timed for first light.

Two walks

- The Moorings Walk: 1 mile (1.6km)
- Flooded Field Walk: 1 mile (1.6km)

Key points

- Short walks
- The Moorings can be very wet
- Wellington boots recommended
- Telescope useful at The Moorings; essential at flooded field
- Early morning best to avoid disturbance

Target birds

Summer: Reed Warbler 100%, Reed Bunting 100%

Autumn/winter/spring: Wigeon 90%, Teal 90%, Goosander 80%, Lapwing 90%, Snipe 70%, Common Sandpiper 60%, Green Sandpiper 60%, Redshank 90%, Cetti's Warbler 70%, Stonechat 60%

Autumn/winter: Mediterranean Gull 20%

Other likely species

All year	Winter	
Mute Swan	Shoveler	Curlew Sandpiper
Canada Goose	Water Rail	Dunlin
Grey Heron	Meadow Pipit	Ruff
Buzzard	Skylark	Black-tailed Godwit
Regular gulls		Jack Snipe
Kingfisher	*Occasional*	Spotted Redshank
	Little Ringed Plover	Greenshank
	Little Stint	Bearded Tit

133

Recommended route and birding tips

The Moorings Walk	1 mile

ARRIVE EARLY to avoid disturbance from other walkers, and preferably when the tide is fairly high, as this reduces the area of exposed mud and renders the birds much easier to pick out. There are two paths: one follows the riverbank closely, while the other skirts the eastern edge of the *Phragmites* reedbed and joins the riverbank path after about 400m (point A). Ideally, walk out on one footpath and return on the other.

From your car, walk into Chichester Close and after 25m turn right onto an open grassed play area from where you can see the start of the paths across the marsh. Cross the grassed area and take the less obvious path (from the far right corner) that runs near the river's edge. Take care along this path as the bank is actively eroding and collapses often occur, particularly at high tide.

During winter high tides, Redshank and Lapwing are usually present in moderate numbers, roosting on the opposite side of

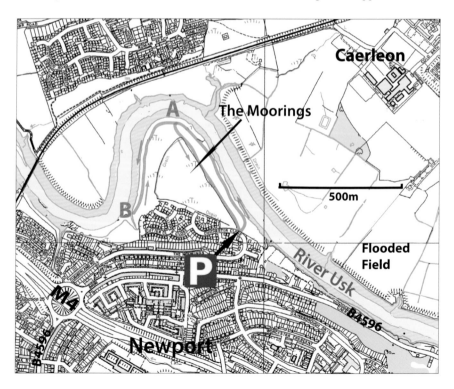

the river. About 400m into the walk there is a large inlet on the other side of the river that often holds Wigeon, Mallard, Teal, and also waders. Along this stretch of the path, which is generally wet, you are likely to flush Snipe quite frequently in winter, and occasionally a Jack Snipe too. The riverbank between the large inlet and the next smaller inlet to the west, is a favoured area for Common Sandpipers and Green Sandpipers, either over-wintering or on passage. The final section of river as far as the inlet at Clipper Close (point B) often has Goosanders during the winter, while other ducks are regular and include an occasional Shoveler.

From point B, return by the same footpath because the route close to the reedbed can be hard going due to long grass tangled with flood debris. However, during autumn and winter a detour into this area can flush additional Snipe. On reaching a point level with the large inlet on the opposite bank, take the footpath to the right (point A), which takes a straight route back to the play area following the eastern edge of the *Phragmites*. Along this stretch, during spring and summer months, you should see Reed Buntings, and you will hear the repetitive, grating song of Reed Warblers – a little 'pishing' is likely to bring some of the latter into view. Water Rail and Cetti's Warbler occur regularly during winter months.

The Flooded Field Walk   1 mile

The flooded field lies on the north side of the River Usk. However, its situation – surrounded by farmland and a golf course – means that access from that side of the river is very restricted. The field is best viewed, therefore, from the B4596 road to the south – this also has the advantage that the sun will be at your back. However, you will be viewing birds from a distance of at least 180m, so a telescope is essential. The field is usually flooded from October to April but the extent of the water depends on the recent rainfall levels. High tide is always the best time to visit, as many birds from the river will move onto the site during the high-water period.

From your car, parked near the play area, walk back up the hill (about 300m) to the B4596 Caerleon Road. Turn left and walk 500m to a point that gives commanding views over the flooded field. The field can be viewed, using a telescope, from the pavement, but closer, although restricted, views may be obtained down a lane that leads to a row of housing.

A good range of birds can be seen at any time of the year. Kingfisher is possible at any season, while during winter, Mallard, Teal, Wigeon, and Shoveler are all regular, and Bewick's Swan and Greylag Goose more occasional. From autumn and throughout winter, Common, Lesser Black-backed, Black-headed and Herring Gulls are present, with combined counts reaching several hundred, while a careful search will regularly turn up Mediterranean Gull among them. Common and Green Sandpipers are usual from autumn through to spring, and a variety of other waders has occurred on passage. Unusual birds during migration include Little Stint, Spotted Redshank and Greenshank.

135

How to get there

Between Newport and Caerleon

Leave Newport on the B4596 signposted to Caerleon, and after passing the roundabout over the M4, take the second turning on the left into a road called The Moorings. Follow the road as it bends to the right and then to the left, and park in the small pull-off to the right just before you pass the Chichester Close signs.

Public transport

The Moorings and the Flooded Field are served by buses that run frequently between Newport and Caerleon.

Reedbeds at The Moorings

Al Venables

THIS IS a walk in a typical upland area of northwest Gwent which, as well as covering open moorland, also includes mixed woodland and farmland. The route commences at Capel Newydd, on the Llanover road out of Blaenavon, traverses a section of the Blaenavon Community Woodland and then crosses the open moor of Mynydd Garnclochdy. It then drops down into more woodland above Cwm y Nant, before ascending across farmland and rejoining the Llanover road to the east of the starting point.

This is a good walk at any time of the year and, as other walkers are rarely encountered, there is the feeling of 'getting away from it all'. The moorland should be avoided in bad weather, as it is easy to get disorientated without map and compass. With the mix of habitats, a good variety of birds may be seen, although the high ground can be barren early in the year until migrants return. Some 30 - 35 species may be possible.

Key points

- **3.5 miles (5.5km)**
- **Moderate; some steep gradients**
- **One strenuous climb of 150m**
- **Varied year-round birding**
- **Take mountain precautions (see p32)**
- **Walking boots required**
- **Can be wet and muddy in places**
- **Open moorland very exposed; appropriate clothing required**
- **Moorland and Cwm y Nant woodland designated as 'Open access land'.**
- **Wheelchair access only on Llanover road section**
- **Short detour to good pub**

Target birds

Spring/summer: Spotted Flycatcher 20%, Redstart 20%, Whinchat 40%, Stonechat 50%, Crossbill 20%

Other likely species

All year
Common raptors
Woodpigeon
Green Woodpecker
Great Spotted Woodpecker
Common corvids
Raven
Goldcrest
Skylark

Nuthatch
Treecreeper
Common woodland birds
Meadow Pipit
Common finches
Siskin

Spring/summer
Cuckoo
Swallow

House Martin
Wheatear
Chiffchaff
Willow Warbler
Tree Pipit
Linnet

Occasional
Red Grouse
Red Kite
Peregrine

Recommended route and birding tips

CAPEL NEWYDD was a Chapel-of-Ease attached to Llanover Church, and served the surrounding rural area before the establishment of the ironworks and Blaenavon town. It was demolished in the late 19th century and its position is marked with an iron cross just below the parking bays; the outline is still visible.

137

Enter the woodland to the rear of the right hand parking bay. This is an area of mixed deciduous and coniferous woodland, high above the valley of the Afon Lwyd, with glorious views in both directions along the valley and to Coity Mountain opposite. Part of the path meanders along the rim of a disused quarry; although fenced off, care should still be exercised.

Listen out for the metallic *jip-jip* call, indicating the presence of Crossbills and in summer, the distinctive *zzit* of the Spotted Flycatcher. Various tits and Nuthatch are also usually present. The wood ends after about 600m, with an area of ancient, contorted beech trees and a stile that gives access to the moorland of Mynydd Garnclochdy.

After crossing the stile turn left and walk alongside the wall until it ends and continue for a further 25m across the moorland in the same easterly direction (the path can be indistinct at this point, especially in late summer when bracken can be shoulder high), until you join a broad bridleway. The bridleway is a medieval packhorse trail, which was the original route for teams of mules carrying pig iron from Blaenavon ironworks down to Newport. Turn right (south) along the path for 600m to reach a 'crossroads' of tracks marked with wooden finger posts (point A). Take the left track up and over the moorland ridge in a roughly easterly direction.

On this upland area of heather, whinberry, bracken and rocky outcrops, look out for Skylarks and Meadow Pipits, and in the summer time, Stonechats and Whinchats bobbing amongst the bracken.

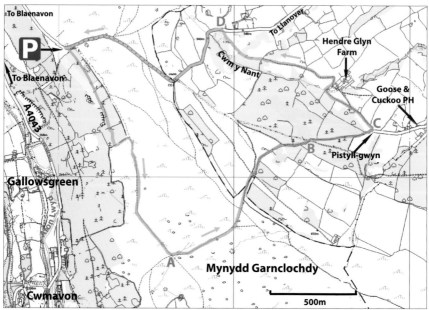

138

Overhead, the mewing of a Buzzard, which seems so evocative of wild, upland areas may be heard, or the deep *gronk* of a Raven; the Red Kite, once scarce but now becoming more widespread, may also be spotted. Listen out for Red Grouse, once preserved on the moors around Blaenavon but now very scarce. Efforts are being made to restore the habitat on nearby Blorenge to encourage a recovery in numbers.

Follow the track down from the ridge, passing between two stone walls and through a gateway, before crossing a wide track and descending alongside a wall to Cwm y Nant forestry. Enter the forestry through a gate and descend to reach a five-way junction (point B). This is some 600m below the ridge. Opposite the junction there is an area of cleared trees where Nightjars may be found.

Continue straight across the junction in the same direction (effectively the second track on the right) and descend on a sunken path. Beware of stones beneath a carpet of leaves. In this area, woodpeckers, Siskin, Treecreeper and Chiffchaff may be noted. After 400m, the track emerges onto the road-head above Llanover (point C). If refreshments are required, the well-known Goose and Cuckoo pub is just 300m down the road. It is open daily, except Mondays, and lunches and real ales are available.

139

Otherwise bear left at the road-head, passing a 'no entry' sign, and descend the track to Hendre Glyn Farm. Do not enter the farmyard but take the stile to the left of the farm gate. Climb the bank alongside some conifers (take care), then bear right and follow the contour around until a track is reached. Now turn left across the fields parallel to the wood. After passing through the second gate continue on the same bearing towards the trees, passing through a gap made through the rocky ridge. Typical farmland species may be spotted here, including finches, Swallows, House Martins and corvids.

700m above the farm, the track emerges onto the Llanover road (point D). Near a cottage to the right, an interesting example of a stone-built beehive pigsty, once common in Gwent, may be seen. Turn left along the Llanover road for 1km to return to the starting point. Look out for Wheatears on the stone walls and rocky outcrops on the way. Just over the crest of the hill, note the 'Mountain Well' to the right. This stone trough was used to refresh cattle returning from Abergavenny market in olden times.

How to get there

About 1 mile SE of Blaenavon

Take the A4043 northwards from Pontypool, passing through Abersychan and Cwmavon, to Blaenavon (6 miles). On entering Blaenavon, take the third exit at a small roundabout signposted Upper Coedcae and Sports Grounds, and drive up the steeply ascending Ton Mawr Street, which becomes Ton Mawr Road. Take the third road on the right, after 300m, which is Llanover Road. This is just before the church on the opposite side of the road.

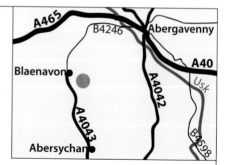

Drive along Llanover Road, leaving the urban area after 0.6 miles at a cattle grid. In a further 0.6 miles, a lone tree with a bench marks the starting point at Capel Newydd (SO270076). There are parking bays on either side of the road.

A T A height of 350m above sea level, this walk on the Gwent part of the mountain straddles the boundary between moor, meadows and the woods of the Clydach Gorge. A good variety of birds may therefore be found though the moors can be pretty lifeless in winter. As well as the birds, walkers may enjoy the spectacular scenery of the Sugar Loaf and Black Mountains and two centuries of industrial archaeology (including the Lonely Shepherd and Giant's Thumb features), marking one of the birthplaces of the Industrial Revolution. Two loop walks off the Hafod Road offer variety according to season. Each loop is about two miles long and may be completed comfortably within two hours. The basic route along Hafod Road is wheelchair friendly.

Three walks

- Two Streams Walk: 1.8 miles (2.9km); moderate
- Moorland Walk: 1.8 miles (2.9km); moderate
- Hafod Road Walk: 3 miles (4.8km); easy

Key points

- Best in spring/ summer
- Public footpaths over private fields and woods
- Excellent viewing from the road
- Take mountain precautions (see p32)
- Only Hafod Road is wheelchair friendly
- Can be bleak and birdless in winter

Target birds

All year: Red Kite 30%, Peregrine 30%, Stonechat 80%
Summer: Cuckoo 60%, Redstart 80%, Whinchat 80%, Wheatear 80%, Tree Pipit 80%
Autumn/winter: Hen Harrier 10%

Other likely species

All year	Grey Wagtail	Wood Warbler
Goshawk	Pied Wagtail	Whitethroat
Common raptors	Reed Bunting	Garden Warbler
Barn Owl	Yellowhammer	Pied Flycatcher
Little Owl		Spotted Flycatcher
Green Woodpecker	*Spring/summer*	Ring Ouzel (on passage)
Great Spotted Woodpecker	Hobby	
Skylark	Curlew	*Winter*
Common woodland birds	Snipe	Merlin
	Hirundines	Jack Snipe
Common finches	Marsh Tit	Winter thrushes
	Summer warblers	Woodcock

Recommended route and birding tips

Two Streams Walk	SO202124 (NP23 4GU)	1.8 miles 🚶/M	Car park P1

P ARK AT P1. From the parking area, the Two Streams Walk takes the track up to the Old Brynmawr Reservoir, sadly now drained, situated just inside the Gwent/Powys border. Check gorse and scrub for Whinchats and Stonechats, particularly around point A. The trees at the top of the farm just beyond point A often hold early arriving Fieldfares and Redwings, with Ring Ouzel possible.

Leave the track to walk up to the reservoir (point B) and check for Wheatears and Reed Buntings. A few Snipe breed in the boggy areas here. Throughout, keep an eye to the sky for passing raptors and Ravens, and check the pylons for Buzzard and Peregrine. From the reservoir, follow the tramroad east, crossing the Nant yr Hafod brook, through the fenced strip marking the route of the natural gas pipeline (point C), and then the track south. Skylarks and Meadow Pipits are common on the open moor.

Rejoin the Hafod road and return to

the start. Common woodland and garden birds may be seen from the road around the farm. Nesting species include Swallow, House Martin, Redstart, Nuthatch, Willow Warbler, Green and Great Spotted Woodpecker. Sparrowhawk is regular, with Hobby occasional in late summer. Check the scrub slope below the road for Bullfinch, Blackcap and Garden Warbler, and the sewage works beyond for wagtails.

Moorland Walk SO221133 (NP7 0LB) 1.8 miles 🚶/M Car park P2

PARK AT P2. Starting further east than the earlier walk, the Moorland Walk heads up the track by Ty-yn-y-Coed to Pant Draenog, originally the quarry manager's cottage. Tree Pipits and Whinchats breed in the area and Little Owls are occasional. In autumn, check early flocks of winter thrushes for passage Ring Ouzels. From Pant Draenog (point D), head up the steep slope to join the tramroad and then walk southwest towards Brynmawr.

Leave the tramroad by the obvious track south back to Hafod Road (not marked on the map) and note the spectacular swallow hole of Pwll Coedog (point E). As well as chats, this area holds breeding Linnet and Goldfinch in the gorse whilst a few wintering Stonechats and Wrens may also be found. Return to the start along Hafod Road, keeping a watch over the spectacular Clydach Gorge for raptors, with Red Kite, Kestrel and Peregrine regular and Hen Harrier and Goshawk occasional.

Hafod Road Walk 3 miles 🚶/E

CAR PARKS P1 and P2 are connected by the Hafod Road, which, in itself, makes an attractive return walk of 3 miles (4.8km). It is dead level, suitable for walkers of all abilities and for wheelchair users. Beware cyclists with whom the road is very popular throughout the year.

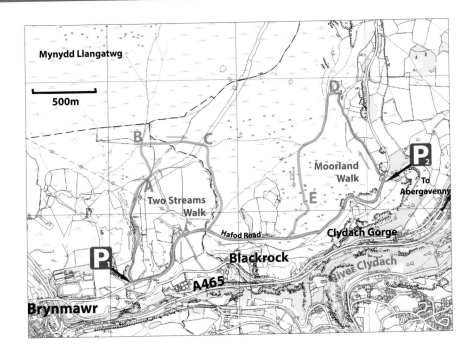

How to get there

About 1 mile NE of Brynmawr

Proceed from the roundabout on the A465 at the head of the Clydach Gorge into Brynmawr on the A4047 (King Street), signposted to Beaufort. After the Bridgend Inn, take the first turning on the right, King Edward Road. At the top of this road turn right into Intermediate Road. Proceed over the bridge and past the entrance to Brynmawr School, then turn left immediately after the 20 MPH speed limit ends into Hafod Road.

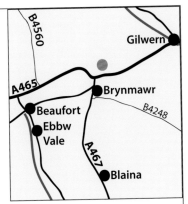

For the Two Streams Walk, continue ¼ mile to car park P1 at SO202125 (NP23 4GU).

For the Moorland Walk, continue just over 3 miles to car park P2 at SO221133 (NP7 0LB).

Key points

- 2.1 miles (3.4km)
- Strenuous walk over rough tracks
- Significant climbs on mountainside
- Open heathland with small wooded areas
- Good variety of upland species
- Telescope useful

THIS IS a walk best undertaken in fine weather. The route climbs 200m in 1200m distance (600 feet in 3/4 of a mile), which is about a third of the total walk. The terrain is field margins and rough tracks.

Target birds

All year: Buzzard 90%, Peregrine 40%, Raven 80%
Spring/summer: Cuckoo 50%, Stonechat 80%, Whinchat 20%, Tree Pipit 60%

Other likely species

All year	Thrushes	Wheatear
Pheasant	Common finches	Tree Pipit
Buzzard		
Kestrel	*Spring/summer*	*Winter*
Regular gulls	Cuckoo	Winter thrushes.
Green Woodpecker	Skylark	Meadow Pipit
Great Spotted	Hirundines	Finches
Woodpecker	Summer warblers	
Common corvids	Spotted Flycatcher	*Occasional*
Treecreeper	Redstart	Goshawk
Wren	Stonechat	Grasshopper Warbler
		Whinchat

Recommended route and birding tips

THIS WALK should be undertaken at a gentle pace, particularly in the initial stages as the route climbs from the start. It is not essential to carry a telescope, but it can be useful, particularly for close views of Stonechat, Whinchat and Wheatear, and also to pick out the raptors that use the updrafts on the mountain flank.

Take the signposted footpath from the start and, following the field border fence, head up towards a stile in the left hand field corner. The hedgerows on the right of the field can hold Whitethroat, Lesser Whitethroat, Chiffchaff and Willow Warbler as well as tits, finches and thrushes. The bramble thickets to the left, towards the stile, have held Whitethroat for a number of years. House Martins and Swallows can also be seen in this area.

Cross the stile and head towards Llanderfel Farm, past the stable yard entrance and over another stile. Hedgerows border both sides of the track, with the brook on the left side. The usual woodland birds can again be seen and heard in this area.

At Llanderfel Farm (point A) turn right in front of the

144

converted barn in front of you and go along the track. Proceed over the stile (steps on a 5-barred gate) and along the sunken path – this area can be wet even after prolonged dry spells so care may be needed. The hedgerow on the right can hold Chiffchaff, Blackcap and Willow Warbler. Wood Warbler has been heard here once. Ravens and both Green and Great Spotted Woodpeckers often overfly the open hill farmland to the left. Buzzards nest locally and can often be seen displaying over the mountain flanks.

Proceed over a wooden stile and continue with the hedgerow to your right until you reach a stone wall. Turn left heading once more uphill. The stone wall should be ideal for Redstart although they have not been seen here recently. Kestrels have nested in the larger trees and Cuckoos can be heard and often seen anywhere along this section. Make your way upwards and towards the right on a diagonal track heading towards the large electricity pylon on the skyline. There is a lone holly bush on the track as a guide. Keep a lookout for Stonechat and Whinchat on the shrubs that are scattered in the area. Grasshopper Warbler has also been heard here in the past.

As you approach the pylon look for a track to the left (about 100m before the pylon) close to a gorse bush (point B). Take this track. You

have now completed most of the climb and are on a fairly level part of the walk. To the right is the moorland of Mynydd Maen whilst to the left there are excellent views of Cwmbran and the surrounding area. On a clear day the Severn Estuary and Somerset coast can be clearly seen.

This area is alive with Skylarks and Meadow Pipits. Buzzard, Kestrel and Peregrine can all be seen over the moorland area. Continue along the track, keeping just above the break in the slope until meeting up with a wider rough track (point C) and bear left downhill. Ahead are the remains of a brick building, a regular site for both Wheatear and Pied Wagtail.

Make your way down to the stone wall surrounding farmland and turn left along the track. Redstarts have been here for a number of years. Look around the stone walls and redundant farm machinery around the field edge. Reed Bunting is an irregular sighting here.

Proceed down the track, over the stile

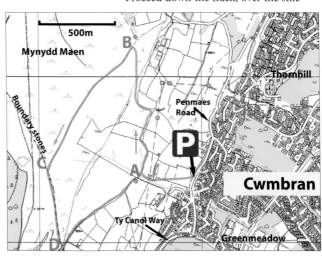

145

(point D) and along the sunken path (part of the Cistercian Way from Llantarnam Abbey to St David's) back towards Llanderfel Farm (point A). (Take care along the sunken path as there is a deep drainage ditch on the left, well hidden by vegetation). At Llanderfel Farm go over the stile and turn right to retrace your steps back to the start point.

How to get there

Immediately W of Cwmbran

The start point is along Penmaes Road, Cwmbran. Parking is on the roadside.

From Cwmbran town centre, head towards Greenmeadow/Fairwater. Take the road to Ty Canol opposite Fairwater High School. Penmaes Road is the second right along Ty Canol Way. Park on the roadside (after about 0.4 miles) where there is a way-mark for the footpath.

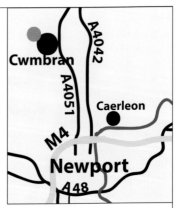

Public transport

By train: regular services run to Cwmbran station from where a short walk will take you to the Town Centre Bus Station.

By bus: regular services from Cardiff, Newport, Blaenavon and Abergavenny stop at Cwmbran Bus Station. From there, the local service to Ty Canol will take you to within 500m of the walk start point. Alight at the Penmaes Road stop. Cross the road and walk Penmaes Road for approx. 500m where there is a way-mark for the footpath.

THE NEDERN Brook Wetlands is an SSSI situated just to the northeast of the town of Caldicot, where periodic flooding of the Nedern Valley creates extensive and persistent pools. In winter, the pools can attract good numbers of wildfowl and waders, notably Bewick's Swans and Redshanks, while in summer, Lapwings breed. The walk begins at Caldicot Castle, is relatively easy, and provides good views across most of the pools (see vantage points A, B and C on the map).

Target birds (when site is flooded)

All year: Little Egret 75%, Kingfisher 15%

Winter: Bewick's Swan 10%, Wigeon 80%, Gadwall 20%, Pintail 20%, Shoveler 80%, Little Grebe 90%, Lapwing 50%, Snipe 60%, Redshank 30%

Passage: Garganey 5%, Common Sandpiper 10%

Other likely species

All year
Mute Swan
Shelduck
Common waterfowl
Grey Heron
Common raptors
Regular gulls
Stock Dove
Little Owl
Tawny Owl
Green Woodpecker
Great Spotted
  Woodpecker
Raven
Tits
Marsh Tit
Common finches

Summer
Cuckoo
Swift
Hirundines
Lesser Whitethroat
Whitethroat
Summer warblers
Spotted Flycatcher

Spring/autumn passage
Green Sandpiper
Grasshopper Warbler
Sedge Warbler
Yellow Wagtail

Winter
Teal
Pochard
Tufted Duck
Jack Snipe
Skylark
Stonechat
Winter thrushes
Reed Bunting

Key points

- 1.8 miles (3km)
- Easy walk, though can be very wet
- Fields with views over flooded areas
- Good only when flooded
- Telescope essential
- Public transport
- Toilets in Castle car park
- Castle café opens 11am-5pm Apr-Oct

Background information

THE NEDERN Brook Wetlands is an area of 'wild' habitat – wild in the sense that it is uncontrollable, at least without great effort and expense. The factor responsible for creating this situation is heavy rainfall, which brings about extensive flooding. The flooding of the valley brings in a wide variety of wildfowl and some wader species, but in the absence of flooding there is comparatively little birding interest.

Typically, flooding takes place following heavy autumn/winter rainfall (November-April) but this is not always the case and in the very wet summers of 2007 and 2008 the Nedern floods reached typical winter levels during July and August (2007) and August onwards (2008). These exceptional summers saw attempted breeding by both Little Grebe (2007) and Black Swan (2008). The Little Grebe attempt failed because the water level fell before breeding could be completed. The Black Swans failed because of the opposite – the flood-levels continued to rise, thus flooding the nest and its five eggs. The winter period, if the floods are present, is certainly the most rewarding, but the time to see birds on the Nedern is after heavy, persistent rain, at whatever season that may be.

Recommended route and birding tips

FROM THE Caldicot Castle car park, walk back up the castle drive to the road (you are once again opposite St Mary's Church). Now turn right and follow the pavement on the right hand side of the road. Continue along the main road past the roundabout and take the first turn on the right into Heol Teifi. Now take the tarmacked path immediately on the left, walking on past the play area to your right and along the backs of houses on your left. After a short distance the path bends to the left where you take the footpath through the small gate on the right. Walk diagonally across the field to the gate at the far corner, immediately beyond which is the first good viewpoint (point A on the map).

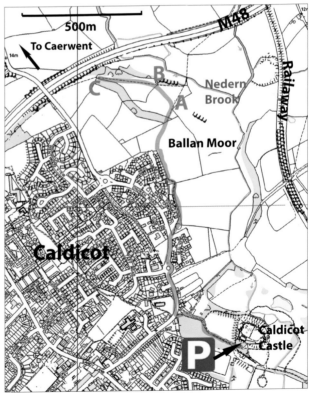

Scan the water for wildfowl, which in winter commonly include Little Grebe, Wigeon and Shoveler, and less frequently Bewick's Swan. Pay particular attention to the edges and shallows where waders such as Redshank and Snipe are likely to be found. In autumn and winter, check suitable perches for a vigilant Kingfisher, and the bushes and hedge tops for Stonechats.

If the floods have persisted into spring, the occasional Garganey is worth looking out for, while a Black Tern or two may accompany the hirundines and Swifts that hawk flies over the water. Careful searching (preferably with a telescope) of the pool edges and any areas of short marginal vegetation may turn up Yellow Wagtail and possibly a Green Sandpiper.

Follow the path on down to reach viewpoints B and C, looking for the same range of species as at viewpoint A. Complete your walk by retracing your outward route.

The walk may be extended on paths around the castle.

How to get there

Immediately NE of Caldicot

The best approach to this site is via Caerwent. Take the A48 from either the Newport or Chepstow direction and turn into the village of Caerwent at the appropriate road sign. Drive into the village and turn south at the crossroads, signposted to Caldicot (this is a right turn if approaching from Newport, or a left turn if approaching from Chepstow). The road now runs parallel to the Roman walls of Caerwent (east wall) for a short distance before carrying on towards Caldicot. Stay on this road, passing over the M48 after about 1 mile and then reaching the suburbs of Caldicot. After the second roundabout turn left (opposite St Mary's Church) down the drive to Caldicot Castle. Park in the Castle car park.

Public transport

A regular bus service (Newport-Chepstow) passes through Caldicot, stopping about five minutes' walk from the castle.

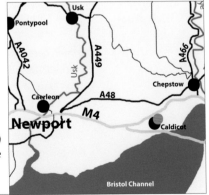

149

Key points

- 1.6 miles (2.6km)
- Easy; can be muddy
- Good birding year-round
- National Nature Reserve
- High tide preferable for waders
- Telescope recommended
- Five hides and viewing platforms

THE CREATION and management of the Newport Wetlands Reserve has provided Gwent with arguably its best birding site. Opened in 2000, the reserve was created as part of the compensation for the destruction of the Taff/Ely Estuary SSSI by the 'development' of Cardiff Bay and incorporates a range of habitats with extensive areas of lagoons, wet grassland, reedbeds and saltmarsh; also smaller areas of scrub and mature hedgerows. The reserve achieved National Nature Reserve status in 2008, which, in addition to the many other designated sites with which it partly overlaps (Nash and Goldcliff SSSI, Whitson SSSI and the Severn Estuary SSSI, SPA, RAMSAR and SAC), underlines its importance at local, national and international levels.

Goldcliff Lagoons

THE LAGOONS and associated habitats at Goldcliff form the eastern end of the reserve. This area is dominated by three large water bodies providing both freshwater and saline habitats for a wide range of feeding and roosting waterbirds. The pools provide year-round birding (with a slight lull in the summer) and, due to the presence of three observation hides, can be 'birdwatched' even on the wettest of days.

Target birds

All year: Shelduck 100%, Gadwall 100%, Teal 90%, Shoveler 100%, Little Egret 100%, Avocet 75%, Ringed Plover 50%, Stock Dove 75%

Summer: Lesser Whitethroat 90%, Whitethroat 90%, Sedge Warbler 100%, Reed Warbler 100%

Winter: Wigeon 100%, Pintail 100%, Merlin 10%, Short-eared Owl 10%

Passage periods: Garganey 10%, Hobby 10%, Little Ringed Plover 50%, Golden Plover 10%, Sanderling 10%, Little Stint 10%, Curlew Sandpiper 10%, Ruff 25%, Black-tailed Godwit 100%, Bar-tailed Godwit 20%, Whimbrel 50%, Spotted Redshank 75%, Greenshank 75%, Wood Sandpiper 10%; also a wide range of county rarities in the form of scarce wildfowl, waders or herons

Other likely species

All year	Curlew	Common Sandpiper	Dunlin
Pochard	Redshank	Green Sandpiper	Kingfisher
Tufted Duck	Raven	Turnstone	Fieldfare
Cormorant		Redstart	Redwing
Grey Heron	*Spring & autumn*	Whinchat	
Little Grebe	*passage*	Wheatear	*Occasional*
Peregrine	Grey Plover	Yellow Wagtail	Mediterranean Gull
Oystercatcher	Knot		A wide range of
Lapwing	Dunlin	*Winter*	scarce waterbirds
	Snipe	Knot	

Recommended route and birding tips

D UE TO the viewing distances and the potential presence of a variety of small waders, a telescope, whilst not essential, will enable you to get more out of your visit; however, if you only possess binoculars the majority of species will still be identifiable and, if push comes to shove, there should usually be somebody around with a telescope who will be willing to help identify a distant speck or two.

The lagoons and surrounding areas of wet grassland provide birding interest throughout the year. In winter large flocks of Wigeon, Teal, Shoveler, Black-tailed Godwit and Lapwing dominate; in the spring and summer the lagoons provide habitat for five or six species of wader; and peak excitement is usually provided by migrating waders in spring, late summer and autumn.

Ideally, a visit to the lagoons should be timed to coincide with a high tide, the higher the better. During these periods waders, pushed

off the estuary, gather to roost or feed on the pools, often in large numbers. Aim to arrive an hour or two before the tide as this will allow you time to comfortably cover the area before the water recedes and the birds move off to feed along the estuary. The route entails walking two and a half

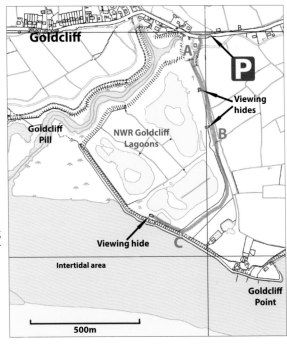

sides of the perimeter of the pools, taking in the hides/observation platforms and seawall, before retracing your steps.

Having parked your car, walk back a few metres towards Goldcliff and turn left onto a track. Before making a headlong dash for the lagoons check the trees and scrub just over the hump-backed bridge (point A); and, likewise, on the way to the first hide, keep an eye and ear on the hedge to your left and take advantage of the gateway to scan the field beyond. All these areas can hold migrants during the spring and autumn with the odd Redstart, Whinchat and warbler in the bushes and Yellow Wagtails in the field beyond.

The first hide provides the best viewing over the northern end of the first lagoon, including the island. Whilst water levels and management activity will dictate the exact distribution of birds, the northern corner (to the right of the hide), the island and the opposite edge of the lagoon (including the area around the small sluice) are often favoured spots. The dominant wader species vary through the year but include Dunlin, Lapwing, Avocet, Ringed Plover, Curlew, Redshank, Black-tailed Godwit and Knot. On most visits something less regular will be present, perhaps a few Greenshanks or Spotted Redshanks feeding in the shallows, or a Little Stint or Curlew Sandpiper amongst the Dunlin; and then, every now and again, a true vagrant will drop in, with visitors from America being more-or-less annual.

Next stop is the first of the observation platforms; this offers a different angle on, and the closest viewing of, the southern end of the island (a popular spot for roosting waders). If time is limited, this platform, and the second hide, can be by-passed with

only a small chance of missing something; however, if you have the time, multiple checks from varying viewpoints are your best chance of finding that skulking scarcity or diminutive rarity asleep amidst a throng of Dunlins.

The second hide provides another angle on the south end of the island and closer viewing of the southern end of the lagoon but, as long as the weather is dry, your time is better spent on the observation platforms which have the additional benefit of allowing you to notice anything interesting flying overhead or flitting along the hedgerow behind you.

The second observation platform (point B) provides a slightly higher viewing point, allowing the two small marshy pools behind the main lagoon to be scanned, but more significantly, also covers the second lagoon. When water levels are low, exposed mud is present in the northeast end of the second lagoon providing further habitat for roosting and feeding waders. This lagoon also often plays host to any diving ducks present on site.

Once content with having checked and re-checked everything on the first couple of lagoons, head towards the seawall. Ideally, aim to be at this point just after the peak of the tide (earlier if the wind is strong and between west and south and likely to produce a seabird or two). Whatever the conditions, a scan over the water may well produce something new for the day – the odd tern, Common Scoter or even porpoise. This is also the only vantage point from which to scan Goldcliff Pill (the grassy saltmarsh off to the right if you are looking out to 'sea'); if the pill hasn't been covered by the tide it is likely to hold the bulk of the roosting Curlew and Whimbrel.

If the tide is still high it is probably worth popping to the third hide but if the water is falling it is best to hang around. As the tide falls the waders will leave the lagoons and, before dispersing more widely, many will initially feed on the exposed mud just beyond the seawall affording you a final opportunity to have a scan. Other areas worth scanning from the seawall are the farm buildings to the southeast, for the odd Wheatear or chat or flock of pipits. The lawns and driveway running up to the house may also hold wagtails and pipits but please be aware the houses at the top are private residences, the occupants of which probably don't want to continually be at the 'wrong' end of a scope. A quick scan with your binoculars will likely turn up anything of note and reduce the likelihood that the reserve staff will get complaints.

Unlike the other hides and observation platforms which face approximately west-southwest, the third hide faces roughly northeast (onto the southwest end of the second and the southeast end of the third lagoon). This makes it ideal on bright, sunny days when the light reduces everything in front of the other hides to silhouettes. The third lagoon does sometimes hold a significant number of waders, particularly during the breeding season, but this lagoon, like the adjacent second, are more likely to produce interest in the form of wildfowl.

Having finished a scan from the third hide it is just a matter of retracing your steps. Any lingering doubts that you may have missed something can be satiated by nipping onto an observation platform or into a hide on the way back.

How to get there

3-4 miles SE of Newport

If travelling on the M4 from the east, exit at J24 and take the first exit at the roundabout onto the Southern Distributor Road/Ringland Way (A48) and follow this for approximately 2.5 miles until, at the fourth roundabout, take the first exit onto Queensway Meadows. At the next roundabout take the third exit onto Meadows Road. Stay on this road (it becomes Nash Road then Goldcliff Road) for 3.3 miles, at which point, a track to the pools leads off to the right (see walk map). Park on the north side of Goldcliff Road, well clear of the bend (ideally east of the national speed limit sign) (ST372830 - NP18 2AX).

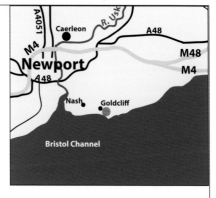

If travelling on the M4 from the west, exit at J28 and take the third exit at the roundabout onto the Southern Distributor Road (A48). Follow this for approximately 4 miles until, at the sixth roundabout, take the second exit onto Queensway Meadows. Then follow directions as above.

Two walks

- Shorter walk: 2.4 miles (3.8km)
- Longer walk: 3.4 miles (5.4km)

Key points

- National Nature Reserve
- Good birding all year round
- Easy walking
- Telescope recommended
- Variety of walks on network of paths
- One hide and several viewing blinds
- Stout footwear essential in winter
- Facilities at Visitor Centre
- Wheelchair accessible on short walk
- Disabled facilities in Visitor Centre
- Public transport

THE REEDBEDS and surrounding habitats at Uskmouth form the western end of the Newport Wetlands Reserve. This area is based on a series of former ash lagoons originally associated with the nearby power station. The lagoons now largely consist of reedbed and areas of open water on the periphery of which are areas of scrub and grassland. The estuary borders the southern edge of the site and the saltmarsh and mudflats can be viewed from the path around the reserve's perimeter. The mix of habitats provides year-round birding.

Whilst a range of waterbirds are present on the lagoons and nearby estuary the primary species of interest are those associated with the reedbeds and wet scrub: Water Rail, Cetti's Warbler and Bearded Tit. The site is yet to regularly attract Bittern but ongoing management will hopefully lead to the increased occurrence of this species.

Target birds

All year: Shelduck 100%, Gadwall 100%, Cetti's Warbler 100% (heard) 50% (seen), Bearded Tit 90% (heard), 75% (seen)
Spring/summer: Water Rail 50% (heard), Cuckoo 90%, Lesser Whitethroat 100%, Whitethroat 100%, Sedge Warbler 100%, Reed Warbler 100%
Winter: Merlin 10%, Water Rail 100% (heard), Short-eared Owl 25%, Kingfisher, 20%
Passage periods: Hobby 20%, Grey Plover 20%, Knot 25%, Black-tailed Godwit 75%, Whimbrel 75%, Grasshopper Warbler 25%

Other likely species

All year	Stock Dove	Short-eared Owl
Pochard	Little Owl	Kingfisher
Tufted Duck	Green Woodpecker	Fieldfare
Cormorant	Raven	Redwing
Little Egret		
Grey Heron	*Spring & autumn*	*Occasional*
Little Grebe	Redstart	Scarce wildfowl
Great Crested Grebe	Whinchat	Bittern
Oystercatcher	Wheatear	Marsh Harrier
Curlew	Yellow Wagtail	Hen Harrier
Redshank		Various scarce migrants
	Winter	
	Merlin	

Recommended route and birding tips

THE LAGOONS and surrounding areas of scrub, grassland and hedgerows, plus the adjacent saltmarsh and mudflats provide year-round birding at Uskmouth. This is *the* Gwent site for Bearded Tit, Cetti's Warbler and Water Rail, all of which are present throughout the year, with numbers of the latter supplemented by immigrant birds in winter. In spring and summer a good mix of warblers includes large numbers of Reed and Sedge plus the odd Grasshopper and, in August, Aquatic Warbler passes surreptitiously through, although usually only detected when caught by ringers. In winter this is the best end of the reserve for Short-eared Owl and diving ducks.

Since the building of the RSPB shop, café, education centre and adjoining playground, the Uskmouth part of the reserve has become very popular with people as a recreational facility. On weekends or during school holidays, particularly those coinciding with warm or sunny weather, you would be best advised to complete most of your chosen route early in the morning.

A telescope will help with scanning the

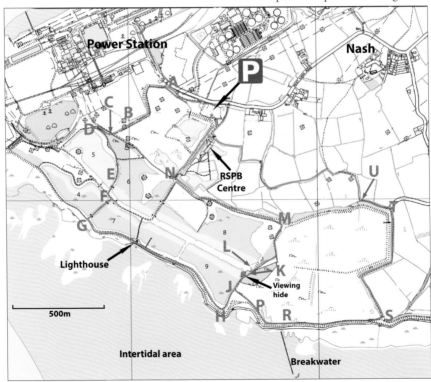

estuary and picking out the odd bird at the back of a lagoon, but for most of the time, and in most of the habitats, binoculars will suffice.

An extensive network of paths means any number of routes can be taken between the lagoons; the two presented here offer a long and a short option – both take in a range of habitats and should result in a reasonable haul of species.

Leave the car park from the northwest corner taking the path that runs parallel to the road. After about 200m you pass through a small copse before turning left at point A to follow the path along the western boundary of the reserve. This area is largely made up of scrub; in spring and summer Whitethroat, Blackcap and Chiffchaff are the dominant warblers but Cetti's are also present in the adjacent ditches and, further up the path where the habitat becomes more open (point B), the odd Grasshopper Warbler may be heard. This species does not regularly breed on

the reserve but every year a few males stop off and sing for a few days. In winter the more open areas are also a good place to look for Stonechat.

As you approach a shelterbelt of alder and other trees, you will arrive at a T-junction in the path (point C). Turn right and then, after about 100m, almost double back on yourself by taking a sharpish left (point D). Whilst undertaking this manoeuvre keep an ear and eye on the shelterbelt – in winter, Siskin and Lesser Redpoll may be present; in spring and autumn check for warblers or maybe a Redstart.

The path now bears round to the right with reedbed on the right hand side, and then passes between Lagoons 5 and 6 (point E). From this point listen for the 'pinging' of Bearded Tits and the squeal of Water Rails – both are possible at any point when alongside the reedbeds. In spring, as you pass between the lagoons, Sedge and Reed Warblers and Reed Buntings will be singing either side of the path. The open water and reed edge can be scanned from the viewing blinds on either side – a range of wildfowl is usually present.

A quick left then right at the next junction (point F) will take you between Lagoons 4 and 7 towards the estuary. Again, blinds provide views of the open water either side of the path but also scan the tops of the reeds for Bearded Tits on the move or, in spring and summer, Cuckoos moving between vantage points.

On reaching the perimeter path alongside the estuary (point G), turn left, and make your way past the pontoon, the lighthouse and on down until the path turns to the left (point H). To your right the extent of the mudflats and saltmarsh will depend on the tide but, throughout most of the year, a good range of wildfowl and waders will be present though often distant (better views of most species can be had at Goldcliff Lagoons). Keep an eye on the landward edge of the saltmarsh and seawall too as at different times of the year pipits, Wheatears, finches and other birds forage among the debris along this stretch.

As you round the left-hand bend in the path you have a decision to make: either turn right after 30m at point J and head off on the longer route (of which more later), or head straight on and up the slope to the hide from which you can view Lagoon 9. In all likelihood, you will see a similar range of waterbirds as already noted on Lagoons 4-7, but if the weather is a bit hit-and-miss this is the best place to sit out a shower on an otherwise fairly exposed walk.

Shorter walk

If taking the shorter route, continue from the hide on the path through the shelter belt/small copse (point K). In winter Siskin and Lesser Redpoll will sometimes be found feeding in the canopy whilst winter thrushes, Chaffinches and even the odd Water Rail might be feeding on the ground. In the breeding season Chiffchaff, Willow Warbler and Blackcap add to the activity of the regular resident Dunnocks, Robins and tits.

As you exit the trees the path continues off to the right, but before carrying on, take the short path opposite to view Lagoon 8 from the raised vantage point (point L). Back on the path, it now passes a scrubby area of willow and alder on the right from which the scratchy song of Whitethroat usually emanates during the spring. Then turn left (point M) and head back towards the RSPB centre and car park. As you go, the reedbed to your left offers more opportunities of Bearded Tit, whilst the scrub on the slope to your right is good for Lesser Whitethroat; and the line of mature willow beyond often holds a Little Owl or two (best viewed by looking northwest about 40m beyond the left turn at point M).

Finally, turn right at the steepish slope (point N) and follow the lane back to the RSPB centre and, just beyond, the car park.

Longer walk

If you have opted for the longer walk, turn right at point J and stay on the path just inland of the seawall. On your left an area of scrub and rough grassland (point P) grades into reedbed. This is a good spot to listen for Grasshopper Warbler in the spring or to look for Stonechat in the winter. Once again the reedbeds may offer up Bearded Tit or the wailing of Water Rails. On the right, the estuary and grassy foreshore is visible from various breaks in the bramble and scrub (point R) which usually hosts displaying Whitethroats in spring. If you have your telescope, scan the old breakwater and other prominent debris for Wheatear and Whinchat in the spring, or Merlin and Stonechat in the winter.

The path then slopes down to a junction

157

(point S). Take the left-hand option, enclosed on both sides with hedgerow and scrub. This zigzags north with largely open scrub on the left and denser scrub and mature hedgerow to the right. This stretch in spring or autumn should produce a good range of warblers, and is often good for Redwing and Fieldfare in the winter. Breaks in the hedge, particularly further along the path, allow scanning of the fields to the east.

At the end of the path, head through the kissing gate (point T) and turn sharp left, keeping the metal security-type fence on your left until it finishes (point U); turn sharp right here. This green lane winds all the way back to the centre and car park and is lined with ditches, hedgerows and a few stands of mature willow. The fields either side often hold thrushes in winter and the ditches and hedgerows will produce a range of species from roving tit flocks to warblers.

How to get there

About 3 miles SE of Newport

If travelling on the M4 from the east, leave the motorway at J24 and take the first exit at the roundabout onto the Southern Distributor Road/Ringland Way (A48). Follow this for approximately 2.5 miles until, at the fourth roundabout, take the first exit onto Queensway Meadows and at the next roundabout take the third exit onto Meadows Road. Stay on this road (it becomes Nash Road) for 1.5 miles, then take the right turn at the staggered crossroads onto West Nash Road towards Nash Village. Follow the road for 1 mile, at which point, the entrance to the reserve car park is on the right at grid reference ST334834. If the car park is locked (early mornings and evenings, i.e. during optimal birding times) a small number of cars can be parked along the road to the water works on the right immediately after the entrance to the car park.

If travelling on the M4 from the west, leave the motorway at J28 and take the third exit at the roundabout onto the Southern Distributor Road (A48). Follow this for approximately four miles until, at the sixth roundabout, take the second exit onto Queensway Meadows. From there follow the route as above.

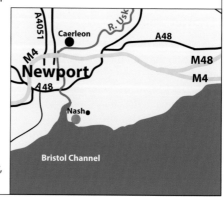

Public transport

From the Kingsway Bus Station in Newport, the Number 63 bus leaves at 7.30am, 9am, 11am, 1.30pm, 3pm, 4.50pm and 6pm and stops at the bus stop in the reserve car park. Alternatively, contact Newport Bus 01633 670563.

LOCATED ON the west side of Tredegar, close to the county border with Glamorgan, Parc Bryn Bach is a popular country park created on the site of former mine workings. A good track around the perimeter of the kilometre-long lake passes through plantations, scrubby woodland and moorland. A circuit can be completed easily in thirty minutes to an hour, though the numerous cyclists and runners proceed considerably faster. Autumn and winter are the best times to see a good variety of waterfowl whilst the right conditions in spring and summer may attract large flocks of hirundines and Swifts.

Key points

- 1.5 miles (2.4km)
- Easy
- Additional public footpaths available
- Telescope recommended
- Very busy in summer and at weekends
- Watch car park closing times
- Café and toilets in visitor centre
- Wheelchair-friendly

Target birds

All year: Mute Swan 90%, Great Crested Grebe 90%, Tufted Duck 90%

Autumn/winter: Goldeneye 30%, Pochard 80%, Goosander 80%

Other likely species

All year	Great Spotted Woodpecker	*Spring/summer*
Canada Goose	Skylark	Hobby
Greylag Goose	Kingfisher	Common Sandpiper
Common waterfowl	Grey Wagtail	Cuckoo
Grey Heron	Pied Wagtail	Hirundines
Cormorant	Tits	Summer warblers
Red Kite	Siskin	Whitethroat
Common raptors	Bullfinch	Garden Warbler
Curlew	Linnet	
Lapwing	Lesser Redpoll	*Winter*
Regular gulls	Reed Bunting	Gadwall
Barn Owl		Teal
Green Woodpecker		Snipe
		Winter thrushes

Recommended route and birding tips

FOLLOW THE perimeter path in either direction around the lake. In winter, flocks of gulls visit to bathe prior to going to roost and these may include scarce species. Water birds often frequent the margins of the three islands, where the resident Mute Swans and Canada Geese nest. Both species have become established only in the last few years. Tufted Ducks first bred in 2013. Goldeneyes tend to frequent the eastern end of the lake. In severe winters the lake is one of the last local water bodies to retain some open water and large numbers of birds may be found crammed into a small area.

The plantations around the park hold the usual species associated with scrubby woodland whilst the moor to the south retains some of the local area's declining population of Lapwings. A network of public footpaths and bridleways through the area provides scope for extending the basic walk round the lake for up to two hours.

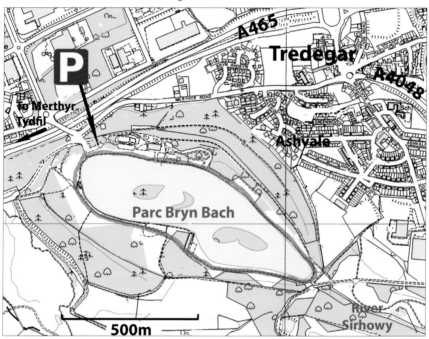

How to get there

Immediately W of Tredegar

Follow signs from the junction of the A465 (Tredegar exit) and A4048. There is ample free parking on site at SO124103 during the day but beware closing times, especially in winter.

Public transport

Regular bus service between Cardiff and Hereford. Alight at Ashvale Crown bus stop from where Bryn Bach is a 10-15-minute walk.

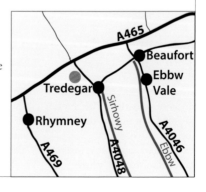

PETERSTONE PILL is probably the best of three good birdwatching sites on the Wentlooge Level coast. The Level is a large low-lying coastal area between Cardiff and Newport, protected from the sea by an earth seawall. It was traditionally pastureland drained by ditches (known locally as reens), but some areas are now pipe-drained and arable, and there are also some land-fill sites, a large industrial complex, a golf course and golf driving range. The seawall gives excellent views over the tidal mudflats and saltmarshes that characterise this stretch of the Severn coast, and also over the adjacent farmland. The top of the seawall has long been used for walking by the public, though it has not had formal public footpath status until recently, when large sections have been incorporated into the Wales Coast Path.

Key points

- **2 miles (3.2km)**
- **Easy**
- **Year-round interest**
- **State of tide important**
- **Very exposed in bad weather**
- **Very limited parking**
- **Facilities at Six Bells pub adjacent to parking**
- **Public transport**
- **Telescope essential**

Target birds

All year: Shelduck 100%, Curlew 70%, Redshank 100% , Cetti's Warbler 20% (80% in spring)

Late April-May: Whimbrel 100%, Lesser Whitethroat 70%

Spring/summer: Reed Warbler 100%

Late August-September: passage waders 90%

Winter: Wigeon 100%, Teal 100%, Pintail 100%, Shoveler 100% (Oct-Dec), Knot 50%, Dunlin 100%, Curlew 100%

Other likely species

All year
Little Egret
Grey Heron
Oystercatcher
Lapwing
Stock Dove
Meadow Pipit
Common finches
Reed Bunting

Spring passage
Great Crested Grebe
Ringed Plover
Little Ringed Plover
Greenshank

Ruff
Yellow Wagtail
Wheatear

Summer
Skylark
Sedge Warbler
Whitethroat

Autumn passage
Golden Plover
Little Stint
Knot
Curlew Sandpiper
Black-tailed Godwit

Snipe
Common Sandpiper
Greenshank
Turnstone

Winter
Grey Plover
Snipe
Spotted Redshank
Turnstone
Buzzard
Peregrine
Merlin
Kingfisher

In addition to those species listed here, a wide range of birds occurs at Peterstone on a more occasional basis (i.e. not necessarily every year) and the total number of recorded species is about 250. Among the more likely occasional species are Bewick's Swan, Garganey, Common Scoter, seabirds (including Manx Shearwater, Gannet, Fulmar and Kittiwake), Avocet, Wood and Green Sandpipers, Little Gull, terns, Short-eared Owl, Black Redstart and Snow Bunting.

Recommended route and birding tips

BROADWAY REEN, which runs across the Wentlooge Level from Marshfield, drains into a large basin known as Peterstone Gout, which in turn drains (via sluices in the seawall) into the estuary where it meanders over the mudflats as Peterstone Pill. The mud surrounding the Pill is a favoured feeding area for wildfowl and waders, and as it is the last area to be covered by the rising tide, there is often a large concentration of birds just prior to full mud cover. However, it requires some local experience to time your arrival to hit this period, as on spring tides full mud cover can be achieved up to 1.5h

prior to high tide, whereas on the lowest neap tides full mud cover is never achieved.

The winter Shoveler flock, which can exceed 300 birds in early winter, is a particular attraction of the site, and there are also good numbers of other duck species throughout the winter season. Apart from the mudflats, the Gout is also of interest, as some wildfowl and waders (particularly Redshank) use it as a high tide roost. In spring and autumn it is a good place to check for passage waders such as Little Stint.

Aim to arrive 2-3h prior to high tide,

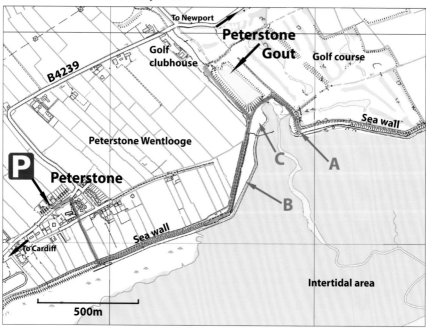

unless it is a small neap tide (say, lower than 10.5m at Cardiff), in which case 1.5-2.00h is usually early enough. From your parking place opposite Peterstone Church, cross the road and take the footpath to the left of the church, continuing along this straight path without deviation, while looking out for a variety of common garden and farmland birds, particularly in the pasture to your right. On reaching the seawall, turn left and walk along the top of the wall. There will be many shorebirds on the mud to your right, but don't spend too much time observing them at this stage, as you should get better views later on. Instead, scan the fields and hedges to your left for Redwings and Fieldfares in winter, while in spring listen for the uninspiring but very distinctive song of the Lesser Whitethroat in the mature hedges, and the harsh, repetive chatter of Reed Warblers in the reedbeds.

Continue along the seawall for about 800m until you reach Peterstone Gout, a rectangular basin on your left that drains into the estuary via concrete sluices. Scan the Gout for waders and ducks (there will often be roosting Redshanks) and check the sluice mechanism for the possibility of a perched Kingfisher. Next, you need to find a vantage point from which you can observe birds feeding around Peterstone Pill on the rising tide. The position of the sun is a major consideration in this. In the morning it is best to cross the sluices and follow the seawall to the east of the pill, and settle at viewing point A, tucking

in below the seaward face of the concrete rampart. In the case of an afternoon visit, retrace your steps a short distance from the sluices, descend to the narrow saltmarsh and settle at viewing point B, sitting on the edge of the turf (preferably on a plastic sheet) with legs behind sea defence rocks which provide cover. Some birders like to watch from point C with their backs to a mud cliff; this has the advantage of being sheltered from northerly winds but the view is not as wide as from other positions.

Wherever you have settled, you are likely to observe a very dynamic scene as the tide rises. Waders will be retreating before the advance of the tide, some becoming marooned on islands of mud and waiting till they are floated off, before reluctantly flying to higher locations, from where they are displaced again as the tide continues to rise. Others will fly off to distant roosts, while new birds, displaced from other nearby sites will drop in for a few minutes to extend their feeding time that little bit longer. Ducks that have been feeding at the edge of the tide, will generally start to drift out to sea before the mud is fully covered, but if you remain still and inconspicuous, many will often swim up the Pill, giving excellent views.

With so much going on close at hand, it is easy to neglect more distant birds out on the estuary, which can include Common Scoter, Great Crested Grebe or passing seabirds.

Point A is also a useful place to monitor the low-level passage of migrant passerines along the coast in late autumn; mid-September through to late October is the best period. The passage starts soon after dawn and peters out in late morning, and is, of course, completely independent of the tides. You need to be stationed on top of the seawall to get the get the widest possible field of view. Visible movements involve a variety of species including Skylark, hirundines, pipits, wagtails and most of the common finches, with numbers getting up to hundreds, or occasionally thousands per hour on very good days.

In spring/summer a walk along the footpath to the west of the Gout will usually produce Whitethroat, Reed Warbler, Blackcap and the song of Cetti's Warbler. Complete your walk by retracing your outward journey back to Peterstone Church.

How to get there

About 5 miles SW of Newport

Peterstone Pill is accessible from the B4239 (the Cardiff to Newport coast road) but parking facilities are not good. We recommend that you start your walk in Peterstone village, parking opposite Peterstone Church (ST268802) in the access road to the houses there (taking care not to provide any obstruction). Your walk begins on the footpath to the left of the church.

Many birders who wish to access the Gout and Pill without the walk from Peterstone Church, park their cars on a small open area near the NW corner of the Gout (ST275808). This area, which has no official status as a car park, is reached from the B4239 by driving through Peterstone Golf Club car park. WE DO NOT RECOMMEND THIS OPTION, partly because the parking area is not officially sanctioned and may, therefore, be closed to cars at some future time, but more importantly because there is a risk of getting locked in if the club closes its gates unexpectedly early – this has indeed happened ocasionally, with the result that people have needed to retrieve their cars the next day. There is a public right of way through the golf course car park, so you can safely use this route on foot.

Public transport

The B4239 is served by bus services 31A and 31C from Newport Bus Station (6-8 buses daily, but no Sunday service).

A N EASY return walk, much of it alongside the River Usk, through sheep- and cattle-grazed pasture with patches of mixed woodland. Common farmland and riverine birds are readily found throughout the year and several summer visitors breed here. Winter brings the possibility of Bewick's Swan (annual in Gwent but found at very few sites) and a fairly regular flock of Goldeneye on the river. A Scaup spent several days here in 2010. Passage birds are, not surprisingly, hit-and-miss but Green Sandpiper is a possibility while Teal and Pied Flycatcher have been seen in recent years. Expect 35-40 species; at least 79 species have been recorded here.

The main walk covers a two-mile stretch of this lovely section of the Usk Valley Walk and takes roughly two hours (there and back) at birding speed, but it is worth spending ten minutes or so in Llantrisant churchyard before setting off across the fields. On reaching Llanllowell another 45 minutes can be taken to include a one-mile loop extension – part of this is along metalled roads.

Key points

- Main walk 3.8 miles (6.1km)
- Optional loop 1.1 miles (1.8km)
- Easy
- Part of the Usk Valley Walk
- Mostly way-marked route; numerous stiles
- Telescope useful
- Good for Bewick's Swans
- Fields are often wet
- Choose another walk if cows with calves are in the fields

Target birds

All year: Kingfisher 10%, Little Owl 10%

Spring: Curlew 20%, Green Sandpiper 5%, Marsh Tit 60%, Yellow Wagtail 5%

Spring/summer: Sand Martin 100%, Spotted Flycatcher 50%

Winter: Bewick's Swan 30% (Dec-Feb), Goldeneye 30%, Goosander 75%

Other likely species

All year	Great Spotted Woodpecker	Sand Martin	Little Grebe
Mute Swan	Marsh Tit	Skylark	Lapwing
Goosander	Nuthatch	Summer warblers	Winter thrushes
Pheasant	Treecreeper	Garden Warbler	Grey Wagtail
Cormorant	Starling	Whitethroat	*Passage*
Grey Heron	Mistle Thrush	Spotted Flycatcher	Green Sandpiper
Common raptors	Bullfinch	Yellow Wagtail	Pied Flycatcher
Moorhen		Reed Bunting	
Stock Dove	*Summer*		*Occasional*
Little Owl	Curlew	*Winter*	Wigeon
Kingfisher	Common Sandpiper	Bewick's Swan	Teal
		Goldeneye	Tree Sparrow

165

Recommended route and birding tips

Main walk	3.8 miles

AFTER PARKING, head back north towards the village. Bear right onto the loop road into Llantrisant village and check the churchyard for finches, Goldcrest and Starling; Spotted Flycatcher is quite likely in summer. Continue to the main road, turn left and within 100 metres you will see a fingerpost pointing to a stile (point A) across the road.

Climb the stile into the field. The trees immediately in front of you and those bordering the small stream are often busy with tits, thrushes, and Nuthatches. Cross the bridge over the stream and scan the

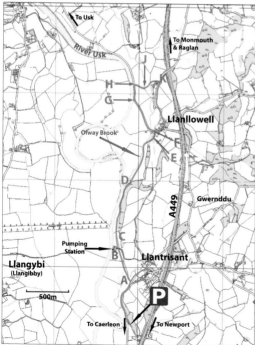

flat expanse of fields for Grey Heron and wagtails; in winter, gull flocks (and the occasional Lapwing) settle on the flashes. Walk along the edge of the field with the hedge on your right – with luck you will see Bullfinch.

Go through the gate into the next field, head toward the right of the brick pumping station (point B) and stand beside the river for a few minutes. Mute Swans and Mallard are regular here, Cormorants fly overhead, the odd Moorhen may be seen skulking under the overhanging vegetation and Kingfisher is a possibility. Common Sandpipers breed further upstream and Green Sandpiper may be spotted on passage. Continue northwards alongside the river, checking the willow scrub in summer for Chiffchaff, Willow Warbler, Spotted Flycatcher and Reed Bunting; Pied Flycatcher is very occasional on passage. Across the field to your right is a steep, wooded bank (point C). The trees hold good numbers of corvids and wintering thrushes as well as Buzzard and Great Spotted Woodpecker.

On reaching the grassy path between the river and woodland, scan the arable fields on the far bank for Bewick's Swans, which, between December and February, are often found feeding with the Mutes. Just before the next stile (point D) the Olway Brook joins the Usk – approach slowly as, when the river is low, Goosanders often rest on the stony islands here. Follow the Olway, checking the alders for Treecreeper and Nuthatch, and walk up into a patch of woodland. This has proved a regular site for Marsh Tit in recent years as well as being frequented by thrushes, warblers (especially Blackcap) and Goldcrest. A final stile (point E) leads to a broad farm track – turn left and go through the gate into the village of Llanllowell. Point F marks the end of the main walk; here you can choose either to retrace your steps to the car or to extend your walk around the optional loop.

Llanllowell loop   1.1 miles

TURN LEFT at point F to start the 'loop' part of the route and walk along the road for 300m. In spring listen for the bubbling call of Curlew and check the hedgerows for Whitethroat. A manure heap just over the hedge on the left has, on occasion, held all three wagtail species – Pied, Grey and Yellow. Approach the wall that backs the lay-by (point G) slowly – Goosanders frequent this stretch of the river and Goldeneyes are possible in winter.

Keep an eye open for otters here, although they are commoner closer to Usk. The trees lining the river attract warblers, Spotted Flycatchers and Treecreepers in spring and summer while Sand Martins may be seen wheeling over the fields – there is a colony further upriver. Little Owl is occasionally found further along the road.

After 200m turn right over the stile (point H) onto the signed footpath and head for the bottom right corner of the field. Cross the stone bridge (point J) over the Olway, bear left up the bank towards the end of the trees and turn right up a fairly steep hill. Pass the old stone farmhouse (point K) and Dutch barn on your right and emerge onto the Usk Flood Route – turn right and walk down the lane back into Llanllowell, checking lone trees for Kestrel. Before turning right again and walking 100m to the track at point F, take a quick look in the churchyard opposite – Blackcap, Chiffchaff and Goldcrest haunt it in summer. Now retrace your steps along the Usk Valley Walk to Llantrisant and your car.

How to get there

3.5 miles SE of Usk

From Usk: at the wonky crossroads on Bridge Street (A472) turn right into Maryport Street and continue along this road to the village of Llanllowell. Keep straight through this village and after just under a mile (grass triangle in road) bear right to Llantrisant. Drive c.350m beyond the village and take the first turning to the left, signed ADH Motors. Park on the wide grass verge at ST389963.

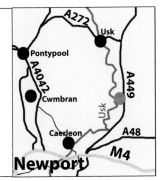

Two walks

- Yellow route
  1 mile (1.5km)
- Blue route
  1.25 miles
  (2km)

Key points

- Walks of
  1.25km, 2km
  or longer
  possible
- Paths are
  steep, slippery
  and uneven in
  places
- Stout
  footwear is
  recommended
- Routes are
  well marked
- Keep to paths
  to avoid
  disturbance to
  breeding birds

THE HIGHEST beech wood in Britain, up to 490m above sea level and one of the most westerly in Europe, Silent Valley has been designated a Gwent Wildlife Trust local nature reserve since 1998; it boasts a wealth of natural and archaeological features. Three way-marked trails provide routes through the main part of the reserve; the longest may be completed in around an hour. A greater variety of habitats may be explored by extending the walk to the highest part of the reserve at its northern extremity. Although well marked, the paths are steep in places and can be slippery. There are a number of information boards around the site and a leaflet published by the Gwent Wildlife Trust (www.gwentwildlife.org) is available. There is no charge for admission to the reserve.

The Silent Valley acquired its name after miners from Abertillery lined the hillside to view the funerals of 52 miners killed in a mining disaster at Cwm Marine Colliery in 1927.

Target birds

All year: Red Kite 30%, Peregrine 30%, Stonechat 80%
Summer: Redstart 80%, Pied Flycatcher 80%, Spotted Flycatcher 20%, Tree Pipit 80%
Autumn/winter: Brambling 50%

Other likely species

All year	Grey Wagtail	Cuckoo
Goshawk	Pied Wagtail	Hirundines
Merlin	Common finches	Ring Ouzel (passage)
Common raptors	Siskin	Marsh Tit
Barn Owl	Lesser Redpoll	Summer warblers
Tawny Owl	Hawfinch	Wood Warbler
Green Woodpecker	Reed Bunting	Whitethroat
Great Spotted Woodpecker	Yellowhammer	Lesser Whitethroat
Lesser Spotted Woodpecker	*Spring/summer*	Garden Warbler
Skylark	Hobby	*Winter*
Dipper	Curlew	Redwing
Common woodland birds	Woodcock	Fieldfare
	Snipe	

Recommended route and birding tips

CHECK THE area around the car park for tits, finches and thrushes. Now follow the wooden boardwalk (taking care if slippery), which commences at the entrance to the car park, and head north for some 250m to the reserve. The latter section is on a gravel path between fences.

At the kissing gate into the reserve, an information board indicates three possible routes: yellow, red and blue. Only the yellow and blue routes are described in this guide. In the woods, the yellow route is well marked with yellow arrows and occasional letters (B, D etc) on short wooden posts; the blue route is well marked with blue arrows and occasional numbers (2, 3 etc) on short wooden marker posts. Not all the original lettered or numbered posts are still present, but several of the remaining ones are mentioned in the text as an aid to route identification. The paths are well defined and by following the route descriptions, with the arrows and posts as aids, there should be no problem in locating the two routes.

Yellow route

IMMEDIATELY THROUGH the reserve gate bear left at post A in the direction indicated by the yellow arrow. Continue past posts B and D along the western side of the reserve. In autumn and winter, Brambling is a good possibility here, feeding with Chaffinches under the beech trees.

Do not drop down towards the Nant Merddog but ascend the slope on the left as indicated by the yellow arrow. Bear

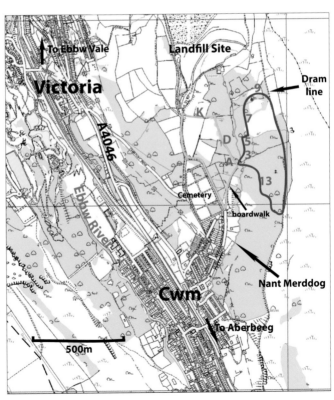

169

left again at the boundary of an exclusion zone (an experimental area to monitor natural processes with minimal human intervention).

Continue ascending alongside a field to the left, pass through a gate and past post K, and finally through a gate onto a tarmac road. This is at the entrance to the Silent Valley Waste Services landfill site.

From here you could retrace your steps back along the yellow route, with the overall distance from and back to the car park being about 1.5km. Alternatively, to complete a circular route, walk down the road, turning left at a junction after 250m. Then follow the road between the reserve and Cwm Cemetery back to the car park. Goldcrests may be found in the conifers.

Blue route

PASS THROUGH the kissing gate into the reserve and go straight ahead in the direction of the blue arrow. Drop down and cross the small wooden bridge over the Nant Merddog, which feeds into the River Ebbw. This route heads into the heart of the reserve and provides the best opportunity for seeing woodland birds.

After passing post 2, climb a flight of steps to post 3 and soon a small clearing is reached. Look out for post 5 where you

bear right uphill onto a narrower path. If you have gone straight on into the trees, staying on the wider path, and into a dell with some large felled tree trunks and evidence of bonfires, you must retrace your steps.

Continue following the blue arrows to posts 6, 7 and 8. The path leads around the base of an old spoil tip before reaching an exclusion zone; this is intended to allow woodland regeneration free of grazing animals. At post 9, there is the opportunity to bear left on a path to explore the northern section of the reserve; this provides the best opportunity for finding upland birds, including Stonechat. However, the description for this particular route is not included here. Continue uphill in the direction of the blue arrow.

Turn left at a junction of paths and then swing up around to the right to join the old dram line. In the late 19th century, ponies were used to haul drams of coal along it; the industrial heritage of Silent Valley is described on an information board here. Views over the reserve and the Ebbw Fawr valley offer chances of seeing raptors (with Red Kite becoming increasingly common) and passing gulls. The ridge to the east

is home to a good number of Ravens, which frequently perform aerobatics in the updraughts.

Now turn southwards and head back down the valley along the dram line. The woods and scrub along the track hold Willow Warbler and Tree Pipit in season; keep an eye out for Redstarts and Pied Flycatchers in the woods. Continue for just over 500m and by a seat and sign, and just before a stile, bear right and descend a flight of steps. Follow the path downwards passing post 13, eventually re-crossing the Nant Merddog and arriving back at the starting point.

How to get there

About 3 miles S of Ebbw Vale

Take the A4046 northwards from Aberbeeg towards Ebbw Vale. Stay on the A4046 Cwm bypass around the village and enter Cwm from the northern side. Take the first turning on the left immediately past the Bailey Arms pub (look out for the brown sign indicating 'Nature Reserve Gwarchodfa Natur' at the junction). This is Cendl Terrace and leads directly to the reserve car park in 0.25 miles.

Alternatively, from the centre of Cwm, proceed northwards along Marine Street, turn right at Cwm Convenience Stores, left over the bypass and railway, and look out for the brown sign indicating the right turn up to the reserve.

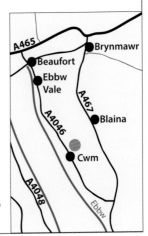

Key points

- Very short walk
- Easy, but may need to climb over farm gate
- Can be very muddy in parts
- Best site in county for Water Pipit
- Good for spring and autumn passage
- Telescope essential

THIS IS a short level walk to view the saltmarsh, the estuary and adjacent reens, and fields with trees and hedgerows. Visiting in the morning an hour before a 'big' high tide, is recommended. April/May and August/September are best for passage waders.

Target birds

All year: Shelduck 90%, Little Egret 80%, Dunlin 90%, Curlew 90%, Redshank 90%

Spring/summer: Lesser Whitethroat 25%, Reed Warbler 90%, Reed Bunting 80%

Winter: Brent Goose 5%, Teal 90%, Pintail 90%, Shoveler 50%, Merlin 10%, Grey Plover 70%, Knot 30%, Bar-tailed Godwit 15%, Black-tailed Godwit 20%, Green Sandpiper 10%, Water Pipit (Nov-Apr) 20%

Passage periods: Whimbrel (mid-April/May) 90%, Greenshank 20%

Other likely species

All year		Passage
Mute Swan	Goldfinch	Garganey
Canada Goose	Linnet	Common Sandpiper
Cormorant	Reed Bunting	Wheatear
Grey Heron		Yellow Wagtail
Common raptors	*Spring/summer*	White Wagtail
Peregrine	Hirundines	
Oystercatcher	Summer warblers	*Occasional*
Lapwing	Whitethroat	Common Scoter
Regular gulls	Sedge Warbler	Seabirds
Stock Dove		Rarer gulls
Collared Dove	*Winter*	Scarcer passage
Little Owl	Wigeon	waders
Skylark	Snipe	Jack Snipe
Meadow Pipit	Turnstone	Golden Plover
	Short-eared Owl	
	Rock Pipit	

Recommended route and birding tips

IT IS best to arrive about an hour before high tide. From the car park, cross the stone bridge and turn immediately left, passing through (if open), or over/under, the steel barrier. Depending on the reed growth, there could be Reed Warblers and Moorhens here. Scan down the banks of the channel for Grey Heron, or Common Sandpiper in spring and July. About 150m down the track you come to a metal farm gate, which you can pass through (if open) or climb over (if locked). Kingfisher is sometimes seen by the reen overflow. The seawall is ahead of you. This area can be very muddy, especially in winter. Walk up the ramp that is a short distance to your left (point A). Proceed slowly and, in the first instance, peep carefully over the top of the seawall, so as not to startle birds on the saltmarsh beyond. Spend some time on the seawall here as the tide comes in. Groups of waders such as Curlew, Dunlin, Knot, Oystercatcher, Grey Plover, Redshank and Lapwing fly past over the sea.

On the sea, check out all the ducks and look for unusual species. Also check the saltmarsh either side. Look for rarer gull species among the Black-headed Gulls. Scan the rocks and bushes to the left and right for Wheatear, Stonechat, Linnet as well as Meadow, Rock and Water Pipits (November to April). Scan the pools for Shelduck, Little Egret, Redshank and other waders. Greenshank, Ruff and Wood Sandpiper have been seen here. In April/ May, Whimbrel forage on the grassy areas.

You can walk some 300m or more towards Newport (point B), to get closer to wader flocks on the outer limit of the saltmarsh. Also check for raptors perched on driftwood out on the saltmarsh and any unusual goose with the Shelducks or Canada Geese, if present. Check the reeds along the reen, and the hawthorns for Reed Warbler, Moorhen and Lesser Whitethroat in summer, and Yellow Wagtail on the grassy areas on passage.

Retrace your steps to point A and continue along the seawall, passing through the kissing gate. Scan again the rocks on the face of the seawall for pipits and the pool for any waders. White Wagtails occur on

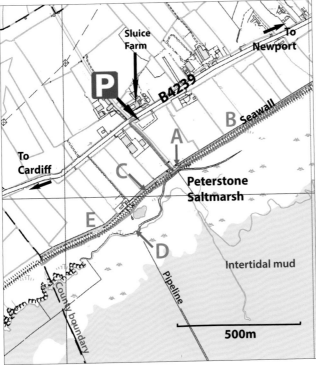

in, Snipe may be displaced from the marsh. Check the bushes on your right for Linnets and Reed Buntings, which also may be seen in the hedges next to the bungalow, flying back and fore to feed in the saltmarsh. Scan to the west down Rumney Great Wharf for the waders roosting at high tide. Also scan the groynes in the sea for roosting waders, and in winter check for any Short-eared Owls hunting. As the tide falls, the pill to the left becomes exposed, as do the inner mudflats, with the possibility of more birds dropping in. You can also move up onto the seawall at point E to get a better view down the Wharf. Retrace your steps and return to your transport.

passage in spring. After 100m walk down the ramp (point C) onto the saltmarsh, and make your way to the rocks at its seaward edge (point D).

This is a good observation point with a wide field of vision. As the tide comes

How to get there

About 2 miles E of Cardiff

From the A48 between Cardiff and Newport, turn off at Castleton for Marshfield. Drive through Marshfield to the junction with the B4239 (2 miles). Be wary of fast traffic and turn right. Drive for 2 miles. Park on a pull-off area on the left, just before a stone bridge over a drainage channel. There are farm buildings to the right and also a short way ahead on the left.

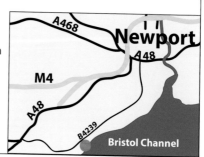

LIKE PETERSTONE Pill, this is a site on the edge of the Wentlooge Level, having the characteristic low-lying farmland drained by reens on one side of the seawall, contrasting with saltmarsh and tidal mudflats on the other. In spring and summer, the main bird interest comprises an attractive selection of breeding species that includes four waders and a number of passerines. From autumn through to spring there is a reliable wader roost that can hold several thousand birds of the commoner species, while during passage periods a sprinkling of more unusual species can be expected. This walk, though categorised as easy, can be very muddy after a season of prolonged rain.

Key points

- 3.2 miles (5km)
- Long walk to reach best locations
- Visit at high tide
- Year-round interest
- Telescope recommended
- Pay & Display car park
- Toilets and food in adjacent pub

Target birds

All year: Ringed Plover 70%, Lapwing 80%, Oystercatcher 100%, Curlew 90%, Redshank 90%

Late April-early May: Sanderling 80%, Whimbrel 90%, Yellow Wagtail 40%

Autumn/winter/spring: Knot 60%, Dunlin 90%, Turnstone 60%, Black-tailed Godwit 40%, Stonechat 50%

Other likely species

All year	*Spring/summer*	
Mute Swan	Raven	Snipe
Shelduck	Sedge Warbler	Bar-tailed Godwit
Cormorant	Reed Warbler	Green Sandpiper
Little Egret	Reed Bunting	Linnet/Goldfinch flocks
Grey Heron		
Common raptors	*Autumn/winter/ spring*	*Passage*
Regular gulls	Merlin	Golden Plover
Skylark	Peregrine	Curlew Sandpiper
Meadow Pipit	Avocet	Whinchat
Reed Bunting	Grey Plover	Wheatear

Recommended route and birding tips

ARRIVE AT the Lighthouse Inn car park during the high tide period and, having 'paid & displayed', leave the car park via the gate and climb the steps to the top of the seawall. From here you can make your first scan of the estuary, looking for wildfowl on the sea. During the summer months a complete lack of birds would not be surprising, but in winter

175

you are likely to find a straggling line of Shelducks a few hundred metres offshore, stretching parallel to the coast for as far as you can see, and your count could top 500. The large area of well-grassed saltmarsh to your left can be covered by about 10cm of water on the very highest tides, but these are unusual, as evidenced by the fact that Redshanks usually breed successfully on the marsh. Normally then, you can safely follow a path eastward along the seaward edge of the saltmarsh turf without danger of getting your feet wet.

From late autumn through to spring, the boulders that protect the saltmarsh from wave action, often have small roosts of Ringed Plover, Dunlin and Turnstone. The small rocky promontories toward the eastern end of the marsh are favourite places for Turnstones. During passage periods look out for Wheatears, which occur reliably on the saltmarsh, whereas White Wagtails, Yellow Wagtails and Whinchats are more occasional. Skylarks are present year round and breed. Large flocks of Linnets, Goldfinches and Meadow Pipits

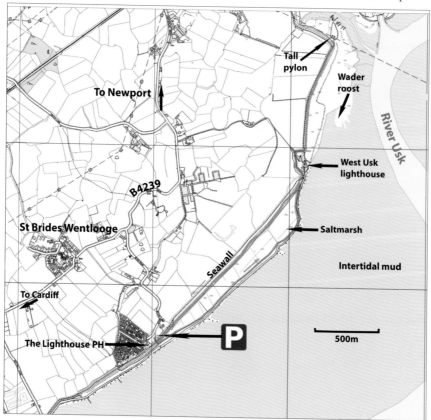

occur in winter, and a few of the latter stay to breed. In spring and early summer you are likely to stir up at least one pair of anxious Redshanks that have eggs or chicks nearby – if this is the case, please move on quickly so as to cause minimal disturbance.

Reaching the end of the saltmarsh, mount the seawall and follow it around the left side of the West Usk Lighthouse. The beach that now becomes visible is a very reliable winter wader roost that on good days can hold Knot and Dunlin by the thousands, Ringed Plover, Black-tailed Godwit and Curlew by the hundreds, smaller numbers of Oystercatchers and Grey Plovers, and the occasional Bar-tailed Godwit. It is best to remain on the seawall when observing the roost as closer approach is likely to cause disturbance. In early May you would be unlucky not to see a few Sanderlings, which are easy to find because they spend their time twinkling along the tideline rather than roosting. In the breeding season, Oystercatchers and Ringed Plovers have nests in the shingle area at the top of the beach, and a careful telescope scan from the vantage of the seawall will often reveal the sitting birds.

From here you can either return to the car park or continue northward along the seawall for about 800m to the large pylon at the mouth of the River Ebbw, which is often used as a nest site by Ravens. Adjacent fields form the winter home for Gwent's largest Mute Swan flock with as many as 100 birds in some years. From the pylon, a winter Redshank roost holding up to about 300 birds can usually be located. Its position varies, but the banks of the Ebbw upstream from the pylon or the old pier that extends from Newport Docks on the far side of the rivermouth are frequent locations.

To return to the car park, retrace your steps to the West Usk Lighthouse and then continue along the top of the seawall, concentrating your observations on the fields to your right. Redshank and Lapwing both breed, as do Reed and Sedge Warblers, and Reed Bunting. In most winters a few Stonechats can be found perching on high points such as dead reed stems, while in spring, Whimbrel flocks feed in the pastures. On reaching the Lighthouse pub, descend to the car park.

How to get there

About 3 miles S of Newport

Coming from Cardiff or Newport, turn south off the A48 at Castleton and follow this road through the village of Marshfield, reaching a T-junction with the B4239 after two miles. Turn left and follow the B4239 for 1.5 miles to St Brides; after a further 400m turn right into Beach Road, signposted Lighthouse Inn. Follow this road to its end and park in the Lighthouse Inn car park which is Pay & Display.

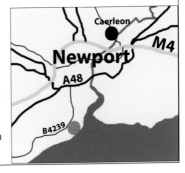

Key points

- 4 miles (6.4km)
- Moderate
- Stout footwear required
- Good range of upland & woodland species
- Spring/ summer

THE PARK walk is a gradual climb up what is commonly known to the locals as St David's Vale. The best time to see birds here is from April to June. It is a long walk of approximately three hours, suited to the reasonably fit, with a fairly dry terrain at this time of year, but stout footwear is required. The walk encompasses oakwoods, beechwoods, scrubland and moorland.

Target birds

All year: Red Grouse 25%, Red Kite 40%, Raven 70%
Spring/summer: Cuckoo 80%, Wood Warbler 50%, Garden Warbler 30%, Whitethroat 40%, Dipper 15%, Spotted Flycatcher 20%, Redstart 20%, Whinchat 70%, Stonechat 60%, Wheatear 45%, Pied Flycatcher 50%, Tree Pipit 50%, Meadow Pipit 60%

Other likely species

All year		*Spring/summer*
Common raptors	Skylark	Hobby
Hobby	Common woodland birds	Swift
Peregrine	Marsh Tit	Swallow
Green Woodpecker	Pied Wagtail	House Martin
Lesser Spotted Woodpecker	Grey Wagtail	Summer warblers
Common corvids	Common finches	Grasshopper Warbler
		Lesser Whitethroat

Recommended route and birding tips

FROM THE car park, there is a view down the valley where Red Kite, Buzzard and Sparrowhawk may be seen. The field below is a good place to see Green Woodpecker, Pied Wagtail, Jackdaw and Swallow.

Make your way up the lane signposted Porth-y-Parc to the old farmhouse. Go past the recently renovated barn – a chance to see Swallow and House Martin here – to the first stile, marked with the National Trust logo (point A).

Keeping to the lower path on your right, passing through good habitat for Garden Warbler, Chiffchaff and Song Thrush, you will quickly reach the second stile (point B). Over the stile are sheep fields and wooded areas of oak and beech. Keen eyes will pick out Greater and Lesser Spotted Woodpeckers, Redstart and Pied Flycatcher.

Carry on to the next stile

(point C), then cross the small stream to another wooded area of sessile oak. At point D, keep to the track bearing right, avoiding the marked path that branches left. You are likely to see Wood Warbler, Pied Flycatcher and Redstart here. Go through a gate (point E) and keep to the path straight ahead, ignoring both paths on your right and left. This lovely natural woodland has Treecreeper, Great Spotted Woodpecker, Tree Pipit, Blue and Great Tits. Listen out for Cuckoo and you may even see a Tawny Owl.

Continue walking through the woodland, going through a series of further gates along the way, until the trees gradually begin to thin and the path opens out into scrubland and sheep fields on either side. Pause to take in the beautiful panoramic view. This is an excellent spot for warblers, Yellowhammer, Whitethroat, Goldfinch, Buzzard and Raven. Lizards, grass snakes and adders are also present in this area.

Moving on, the path takes you over a small stream into a woodland of dwarf oak trees. Look out for orange tip and speckled wood butterflies, as well as emperor moth. When you reach the end of the woodland, climb over the stile (point F) and step into upland heath. Look out for Red Grouse, Yellowhammer, Whinchat, Stonechat, Whitethroat, Meadow Pipit, Willow Warbler and Skylark. If you are lucky, you might catch sight of a Hen Harrier.

Follow the left hand path,

which runs alongside a bank-cum-stone wall. This walk is the boundary of The Park. You will see the Sugar Loaf mountain above you in the distance. Listen out for the distinctive sound of Grasshopper Warbler while looking for Linnet, Cuckoo, Meadow Pipit and Wheatear. Kestrel, Hobby and Peregrine have also been seen here.

After about 800m, you start to go downhill. Walk a further 1.5km, ignoring the footpath marked to the left at point G, until you reach the end of the fence (point H). Take the path going about 45 degrees to the left, and head back down into woodland where Jay, Wood Warbler and

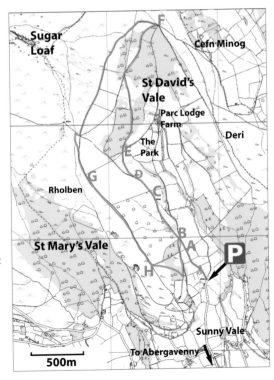

179

Looking across to St Davids Vale and the Sugar Loaf

Dave Brassey

Bullfinch are all likely. The path continues through the woodland until it joins an adjacent path. Follow this path left and upwards until you come to the clearing between stiles (A) and (B). Head back to the gate and stile with the National Trust Logo, and passing through the farm, return to the car park.

Although covering quite a large area, this is a very worthwhile walk, with a good variety of birds, plants and habitat and a possibility of seeing some of the less common species. You shouldn't be disappointed.

How to get there

Immediately N of Abergavenny

Take the A40 (Brecon Road) out of Abergavenny. At a set of pedestrian crossing lights, just before a roundabout, turn right into Chapel Road. Proceed for about 0.5 miles to the end of the road, bearing to the right as it joins Pentre Road. At the junction of Pentre Lane and Chain Road go straight ahead up the dead-end road and continue northwards for about 0.7 miles until you reach a pull-in on the right, large enough to take around ten cars. Park here.

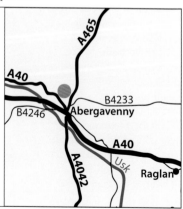

SITUATED ON the east side of the Sirhowy Valley above Tredegar, St James Forestry contains coniferous plantations of varying ages, clear-felled areas, moorland and a lake. The old conifers support breeding Crossbills, with good numbers of Lesser Redpolls in the dense young stands and Tree Pipits around the margins. Snipe and Wheatear can be present on the moor and Goosanders use the lake in winter. The walk includes a steady but not steep climb to the ridge and may comfortably be completed in around ninety minutes to two hours.

Key points

- 2.5 miles (4km)
- Moderate
- All-year interest
- Stout footwear
- Forestry operations may change habitats and paths
- An Ordnance Survey map is recommended

Target birds

All year: Red Kite 20%, Peregrine 20%, Stonechat 60%, Lesser Redpoll 70%, Crossbill 70%

Spring/summer: Wheatear 70%, Tree Pipit 70%

Autumn/winter: Goosander 50%

Other likely species

All year	Skylark	Curlew
Canada Goose	Goldcrest	Cuckoo
Common waterfowl	Nuthatch	Swift
Grey Heron	Treecreeper	Redstart
Cormorant	Tree Pipit	Summer warblers
Goshawk	Pied Wagtail	Whitethroat
Common raptors	Siskin	Garden Warbler
Regular gulls	Bullfinch	
Tawny Owl	Linnet	*Winter*
Green Woodpecker	Reed Bunting	Snipe
Great Spotted Woodpecker		Jack Snipe
	Spring/summer	Winter thrushes
	Hobby	

Recommended route and birding tips

EXPLORE THE area around the lake for tits, warblers and finches, including Crossbills in the tall trees. From the car park follow the track to the left of the reservoir and up through the forest in a southeasterly direction. Check the clear-felled areas above the track for Stonechat, Tree Pipit and Willow Warbler. Cross the cattle-grid, passing the forestry sign indicating you are on Manmoel Common, and continue onto the moor.

The track bends to the left and eventually reaches Manmoel Road (point A), which is also the Sirhowy Valley Walk at this point. Turn left (north) here and follow this rough road just over 1km to the mast. Wheatears are possible around the rock piles and dry-stone walls. Raptors and Ravens are likely overhead.

181

After the mast continue downhill to a point just past a green building on the right (point B), and turn left across the moorland via an indistinct path to a clearly visible green stile (point C) at the edge of the forestry. Cross the stile and follow the path, which can be boggy in places, to the left of the pool. Much of this area has been cleared and the reservoir marked on the map has been drained, leaving a boggy area that can hold Snipe or Jack Snipe in winter.

When a broad track is reached, turn right for about 200m until another forestry track is reached (point D) (a mast should be about 100m to your right at this point). Turn left and follow the track for about 150m to a forest road, where you should

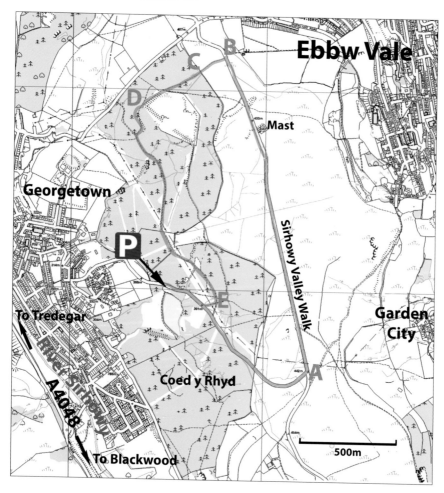

also turn left, continuing for about 1km. The dense plantations on the track back to the lake provide the most likely sites for Lesser Redpoll and Bullfinch.

As the forest track begins to peter out take a path on the right (point E) just prior to a point where the track is covered in a depth of stones. Descend for 100m, and cross a fence to turn right onto a track that returns you to the starting point.

How to get there

Immediately SE of Tredegar

Leave the A4048 at the Bedwellty House roundabout (B4256 south of Tredegar) – (this roundabout provides access for the leisure centre, which is signposted) and take the easterly turn signposted Georgetown. Continue along this road (Vale Terrace) for about 200m before turning left into Poplar Road. Drive for about 0.3 miles to negotiate a sharp right-hand bend, before taking the second road on your left. Proceed uphill past the new St James Park estate to the parking area on the edge of the forestry. The car park

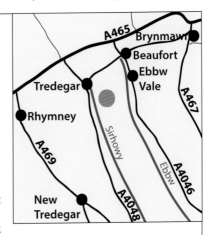

is at SO155080, overlooking the reservoir. If you have a satnav, the postcode NP22 4NH will take you to the St James Park estate. From here drive left through the estate and bend around right and uphill to the reservoir.

Key points

- About 1 mile (1.6km) to cover all areas of the park
- Easy
- Good range of woodland birds
- Interesting trees
- Pay & Display parking
- Wheelchair friendly in most areas
- Refreshments Apr-Oct
- Toilets (unreliable in winter)

SITUATED OFF the A48 just to the west of Newport, this site offers an interesting mix of parkland habitats that can be covered easily in the space of an hour. There is a good range of the commoner bird species, and any visitor with a botanical interest cannot fail to be impressed by the collection of exotic trees that includes dozens of ancient giant redwoods.

Most areas are accessible to wheelchairs, the exception being the lakeside path close to the northwest end of the lake, where exposed tree roots make wheelchair passage impossible.

Target birds

All year: Mute Swan 90%
Spring/summer: Cetti's Warbler (heard) 50%, Reed Warbler 80%
Winter: Kingfisher 20%, Jackdaw roost 100%, Redwing 40%, Fieldfare 20%

Other likely species

All year		
Canada Goose	Grey Heron	Common woodland birds
Pochard	Little Grebe	Thrushes
Tufted Duck	Regular gulls	Common finches
Common waterfowl	Hirundines	Siskin

Recommended route and birding tips

TREDEGAR HOUSE, together with the gardens, café and gift shop, is open from early April to mid-October, but the adjacent park is open all year. The car park is Pay & Display.

From the car park take the path through numerous outbuildings to Tredegar House and pass to the right of the house into the park, then bear right until you reach the lake. It is worthwhile to walk right around the lake in either direction. The path around the lake is wooded at the northern end and down the eastern side. The major trees are mostly exotic conifers, but none the less impressive for that. Some areas are birdless owing to a dense understorey of rhododendrons, but in other areas, native broad-leaved trees have invaded and provided a habitat rich in the commoner woodland species; these include Great Spotted and Green Woodpeckers,

Blackcap, Chiffchaff, Goldcrest, Nuthatch, Treecreeper and a range of finches including Siskin.

In winter, Kingfishers frequently feed from tree branches that overhang the lake. The lake itself is usually rather species-poor, but has breeding Mute Swans, Mallard and Coots; Cormorants, Swallows and House Martins use it for feeding, and other duck species occur in winter on an occasional basis.

After exploring the lake, cross the grasslands, or follow the surfaced path at the southern end, westwards to the children's playground, behind which is a large pond with an extensive reedbed. In summer the reeds hold both Reed and Cetti's Warblers, while Coots and Moorhens breed around the pond margins.

Little Grebe breeds in some years.

The open grasslands are good for winter thrushes, and a big Jackdaw roost is present around the house and in the woodlands during winter.

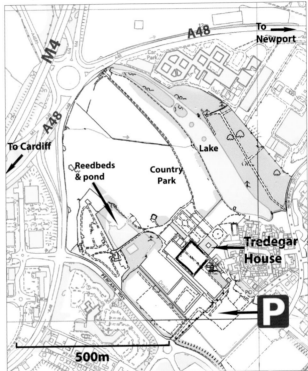

How to get there

Adjacent to A48 W of Newport

Starting at j28 on the M4, take the A48 westwards (signed to Castleton and St Mellons) and turn left at the first traffic lights, signed Superstore and Imperial Park. The first exit from the next roundabout will take you into the Tredegar House car park. There is a £2.00 charge for all-day parking.

185

Key points

- Moderate/strenuous
- Best in spring
- Take great care around rock faces of quarries
- Do not venture above the quarries in bad weather or low cloud
- Keep out of the active workings at all times
- Stout footwear required
- Facilities in pub in village
- Ordnance Survey map recommended

ALTHOUGH THE old Trefil quarries have traditionally been a reliable site for Ring Ouzel, this species is now no more than a scarce passage migrant. However, you may hit lucky on a visit in spring. A variety of other typical upland birds, including raptors, may nevertheless be found in the surrounding area. The walk is moderately strenuous with a fairly steep climb to the quarries and the moor above them. It may comfortably be completed in around ninety minutes to two hours.

Target birds

All year: Red Grouse 30%, Red Kite 20%, Peregrine 20%, Little Owl 10%, Stonechat 30%
Spring/summer: Common Sandpiper 30%, Wheatear 90%
Autumn/winter: Hen Harrier 10%, Merlin 10%
Passage: Ring Ouzel 10%

Other likely species

All year	Regular gulls	Swift
Mallard	Skylark	Tree Pipit
Moorhen	Blackbird	Goldfinch
Buzzard	Pied Wagtail	Linnet
Kestrel		Reed Bunting
Curlew	*Spring/summer*	
	Cuckoo	

Recommended route and birding tips

FROM YOUR car, walk north along the quarry road. Check the pond to the west for Common Sandpiper and wagtails. 150m beyond the access barrier, and past a large brick shed and small stand of conifers, take a stony track up the slope to the right (SO118132). Follow the perimeter fence of the active quarries. Wheatears abound in this area in spring and may include birds of the Greenland race passing through. The gorse-covered slope below the track holds Linnets and Goldfinches. The valley provides a flyway into Brecknockshire: movement of gulls, hirundines and other birds may be observed. Watch across the valley for raptors hunting.

At the top of the track, cross the quarry access road. Bear left for 40m and then head right into the old quarries to the north of the active workings. Although these are ideal Ring Ouzel habitat, Blackbirds are much more commonly found nowadays. Kestrels and Little Owls may be seen around the crags, with Peregrine or Raven overhead. A faint path may be followed through the old workings; take care scrambling out at the northern end onto the open moor. The moor above the quarries is open access land but the terrain is rough and there are no well-defined tracks. Skylarks are numerous and a few Red Grouse remain in the denser heather. Bear right and work your way back above the eastern side of the old quarries, keeping well back from the edge (as mentioned above, do *not* attempt in poor weather conditions). On reaching the boundary of the active quarry, bear right and descend to the access road; retrace your steps back to the barrier.

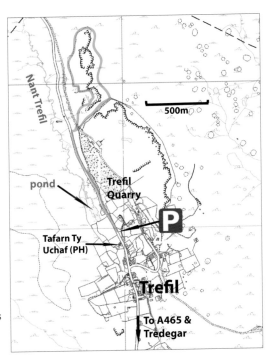

How to get there

About 2 miles N of Tredegar

Heading west on the A465 Heads of the Valleys road from Abergavenny, turn off right (3rd exit) at the main Tredegar roundabout near Dukestown. The advance direction sign indicates the A4048 to Tredegar to the left, Trefil to the right. Continue north for 2 miles to Trefil village.

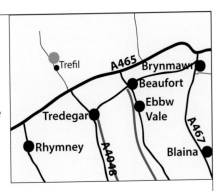

Park on the roadside in Trefil village. There is space for a couple of cars just before you reach the barrier, beyond which is a private road and bridleway (access permitted on foot, horseback and bicycle). A notice by the barrier states 'The barrier will be closed and locked between 17.00 - 08.00h and at weekends'. A pedestrian gate may be used when the barrier is closed.

Key points

- 3.7 miles (6km)
- Easy
- All-year interest
- Can be very muddy in parts

THIS WALK takes you through the farmland and woodland around Treowen, a privately owned historic house. The land was in the Tir Gofal scheme and is managed sympathetically for plants and birds. There are four ponds and a small lake, diverse woodland, many new hedges, streamsides, pastures and arable land. Of particular note is winter stubble, which has helped a small population of Linnets and Yellowhammers to survive. Wetland birds move between Treowen and two nearby sites to the west – Dingestow Court and The Warrage, which is covered elsewhere in this book.

Target birds

All year: Goshawk 5% (higher probability in Feb/March), Snipe 5%, Stock Dove 90%, Marsh Tit 80%, Linnet 80%, Yellowhammer 80%

Summer: Woodcock 15%, Firecrest 5%, Redstart 75%, Spotted Flycatcher 50%, Hawfinch 5%

Other likely species

All year	Marsh Tit	Summer warblers
Mute Swan	Raven	Whitethroat
Canada Goose	Common corvids	Garden Warbler
Common waterfowl	Common finches	
Tufted Duck		*Winter*
Common raptors	*Spring/summer*	Starling
Common woodland birds	Goldcrest	Siskin
	Hirundines	Lesser Redpoll

Recommended route and birding tips

FROM THE car park in Dingestow village, walk past the caravan site to the bridge over the River Trothy. Here look out for Dippers. Turn left at point A onto a path into the woodland (not the vehicular track) and follow the path to a gate (point B) out into a pasture. Cross this field to another gate into a cereal field and walk up the hill to join a wide track (the driveway to Treowen House) at point C. Turn left, keeping on this track past the farm buildings and house. Turn left again, just past a large cow shed (point D) and follow the waymark signs, leaving the woodland at point E and passing through two fields on your way down to the Afon Trothy (point F).

Turn right at the footbridge (do not cross it) and head for the far side of the field. After crossing the concrete bridge (point G) bear right and aim for the highest point of the hill; the next gate (point H) (halfway along the hedgerow ahead) can be seen from just over the top of the hill. Follow the waymark signs through the fields until you come to the Hendre road (point J). Turn right, and right again at a crossroads with a bridleway (point K); this will bring you back to the cow shed and Treowen

House, from where you can retrace your outward steps back to your car.

The birds of Treowen are typical farmland birds, but the water bodies attract a range of other species and the mixed woodland affords habitat for many woodland species. Yellowhammers and Linnets are frequent through the year, especially evident in the autumn on stubble fields. There is a thriving colony of House Sparrows around the buildings at

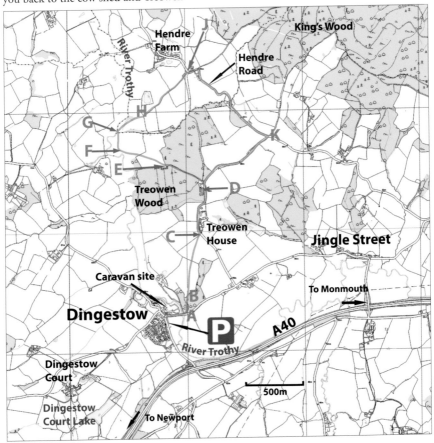

Treowen and several pairs of Swallows. In the summer, one or two pairs of Spotted Flycatchers may be heard or seen along the main track near the farm buildings, whilst Stock Doves and sometimes a pair of Redstarts nest in the many old parkland trees. The wetland birds are largely common and widespread species such as Mallard, Tufted Duck, Coot and Moorhen; Canada Geese are not tolerated. Occasional visitors such as Pochard and Wigeon appear in the winter. Snipe may be flushed in the winter especially where rush-lined tiny streams enter the ponds.

How to get there

About 4 miles ENE of Raglan

From Monmouth take the Wonastow road past the industrial estates, continuing through Wonastow and Jingle Street to Dingestow. Alternatively go to Dingestow from the Raglan to Mitchel Troy road. – driving north along the A449, turn off to Raglan and after 650m turn right across the carriageway, and right again onto the road signposted to Mitchel Troy. After 2.9 miles turn left to Dingestow. There is car parking in Dingestow opposite the village hall at SO458102.

THIS IS an excellent walk for a birder with between 40 minutes and an hour (or more) to spend while in Monmouth itself. It is readily accessible from the centre of the town but holds the prospect of a good variety of birds in all seasons and, if luck holds, it may be possible to find something out of the ordinary. The walk, of just under a mile, is alongside two rivers – the Monnow and the Wye and their confluence. It is entirely on flat terrain, at first along a gravelled road and then in a field, though on well-maintained footpaths. It is a great place for hirundines and Swifts in the spring and autumn; there is a well-established Cormorant day-roost and the breeding birds are interesting. Mute Swans breed, Kingfisher is often seen and Goosander is usually present in winter.

Key points

- 0.9 miles (1.5km)
- **Easy walking, easy access**
- **Good birding all year round**
- **Pay & Display car park**
- **Can be linked with shopping trip**
- **All facilities (toilets, food, drinks) are on hand**
- **Wheelchair accessible only along the track**

Likely species

All year
Mute Swan
Mallard
Grey Heron
Cormorant
Buzzard
Sparrowhawk
Regular gulls
Kingfisher

Common woodland/ garden birds
Reed Bunting

Spring/summer
Swift
Hirundines
Warblers including Sedge and Garden
Common Sandpiper (passage)

Autumn/winter
Goosander
Winter thrushes

Occasional
Red Kite
Kestrel
Dipper

Recommended route and birding tips

THIS WALK merits an early start, as this is a popular area, especially in fine weather. 8am or earlier is appropriate in spring, summer and early autumn; before 9am in late autumn and winter. Note that it is at its best when water levels in the two rivers are relatively low. The full walk, taken at a slow birding pace, will take between an hour and an hour-and-a-half, though most of it may be covered more quickly if time is pressing.

Once parked (and paid & displayed) walk towards the old fortified bridge – do not climb the embankment between the car park and the river as it is steep and often slippery. Join the track that parallels the Monnow on your side of the river. You will see a weir (point A) 30m downstream from the bridge. There is a permanent gathering of Mallard here. Mute Swans are regular and Grey Wagtails are often present near the weir, with Pied Wagtails in the car park or on surrounding buildings.

In summer there is a small Sand Martin colony, nesting in the drain holes in the wall adjacent to the bridge, on the east side of the river; and Swifts nest in the roof of the bridge itself. In winter, gulls are usually in the vicinity, with Black-headed the most likely, though Common, Lesser Black-backed and Herring are often seen, sometimes in double-figure numbers. Mediterranean Gull has occurred here, proving that even small gull flocks are worth studying!

Follow the track downstream towards the Two Rivers Meadow (about 600m). Keep a sharp eye open for Kingfishers, which often perch on stems overhanging the water; they can be very inconspicuous but on this stretch (point B) are not particularly shy. In winter, Goosanders may appear at any point from here onwards, though usually in small numbers, while more Mallard and Mute Swans are near certain. Grey Wagtail may occur anywhere.

Passing under two road bridges one arrives at allotments. Follow the footpath to the right (south) of the allotments, along the river bank, scanning the allotments for common passerines as you go. Within 50m one enters the Meadow. One may wander anywhere within it (though obviously not in the allotments) but it is best to continue along the footpath, with large willows on the right, beside the River Monnow. These trees may hold finches and tit flocks in winter, while in summer a variety of warblers can be found. Many species overfly this area so the sky should not be neglected.

The footpath leads to the confluence of the Rivers Wye and Monnow (point C). This area and the immediate upstream section of the Wye are well worth some scrutiny. There will be at least one and usually two or more families of Mute Swans, with numbers sometimes reaching 20 or more. Goosanders are often here in winter, either hunting in the river or preening on the shingle on the east bank. Mallard may be numerous.

In spring, all three hirundines appear over

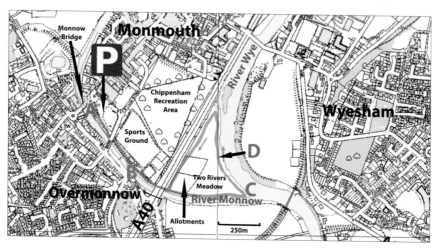

the Wye, often early and in considerable numbers, while Swifts arrive a little later, but again are often present in good numbers. It is worth remembering that Gwent has only two records of Alpine Swift and both came from this spot.

In summer, Sedge Warbler and Reed Bunting both breed here in the dense riverside vegetation and Garden Warbler, Blackcap and Whitethroat are also present and usually obvious.

There is an obvious daytime roost of Cormorants in poplar trees on the large island in the Wye, easily viewed from point D. Numbers may be into double figures outside the breeding season, but some birds may be present even in late spring and through the summer. Grey Herons frequently roost in the same trees and Kingfisher is not uncommon on this stretch of the Wye.

Buzzards are usually to be seen soaring over the area, or a little to the south of it, and a hunting Sparrowhawk may flash through. Commoner passerines are always around and there is a rookery, part of a scattered group

of 50 or so nests within the town, across the dual carriageway, in Chippenham Park. The antics of the colony while nest-building in March can be an amusing diversion.

There are benches at several places overlooking the Wye and it is worth taking advantage of these; wait and see what flies by. One may return to the car park by continuing a circumnavigation of Two Rivers Meadow, though this means walking for about 300m quite close to the busy A449 dual carriageway. Though the field is well below the level of the road, traffic noise can be an issue, but in spite of this, small passerines seem to like the dense blackthorn bushes that grow on the embankment. Alternatively, walk back through the centre of the field and skirt the allotments (passing either side of them) before retracing your steps on the track by the Monnow, to the car park.

Expect to see somewhere between 25 and 35 species on this walk, though with more time spent here in late spring or early summer something nearer 40 species may well be possible – but only for the early riser.

How to get there

Adjacent to Monmouth town centre

Head for Monmouth town centre and find the main street (Monnow Street). Monnow Bridge is at the lower end of this street and the car park is 100m to the east of the bridge across the road from Waitrose. It is easily found.

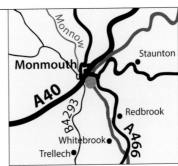

Alternatively, heading north to Monmouth on the A40, turn off onto the B4293 immediately after the tunnel. Take the second exit at the first (mini) roundabout, and then turn right at the traffic lights, signposted Town Centre. Take the first left at the mini roundabout just over the bridge and enter the Pay & Display car park on your left.

OS map OL14 SO432086 (NP15 2EU) 0.3 miles 🚶E

Key points

- Very short walk
- Easy, but can be muddy
- Best in winter
- Good site for Wigeon
- Telescope useful

THIS IS a short walk on a footpath across private land, leading to an artificial lake that holds good numbers of wildfowl in winter.

Target birds
Winter: Wigeon 80%

Other likely species

All year
Canada Goose
Mallard
Gadwall
Grey Heron

Great Crested Grebe
Moorhen
Coot

Spring/summer
Hirundines

Reed Bunting

Winter
Wigeon
Goosander

Recommended route and birding tips

Having parked, look for the three oak trees in the lay-by. A path leads down just east of the third oak tree and over a stile into a field. Walk diagonally left across the pasture (about 250m) to two oak trees in a tall hedge and look at the lake through the gap.

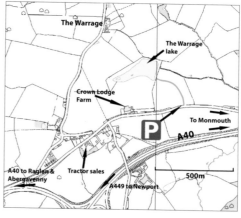

The lake is most interesting in winter when there can be up to 300 Wigeon plus a few Goosander and various other ducks and gulls. It also holds breeding Canada Geese, Great Crested Grebes and Coots, which are present year-round, while Reed Buntings are seen in spring. Please be careful not to disturb Wigeon in the winter months as they graze on the grass on the top of the dam.

How to get there

About 1 mile NE of Raglan

Driving north along the A449, turn off to Raglan and after 650m, turn right across the carriageway, and right again onto the road signposted to Mitchel Troy. Continue for just under a mile to a lay-by on the left at SO432086 (NP15 2EU).

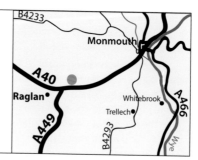

THIS IS a large area of moorland and bog situated in the northwest of the county. The site holds only a small range of species but this includes a number of raptors that are not widely encountered in the county. Either of two routes can be walked but, using a telescope, most of the target species can be seen from the car park. The walks overlap to some extent with the Coity Mountain walk (Walk 12).

Target birds

All year: Red Kite 70%, Raven 90%
Spring/summer: Grasshopper Warbler 70%, Whinchat 60%, Stonechat 80%
Winter: Hen Harrier 30%, Merlin 40%, Short-eared Owl 60%, Stonechat 20%

Other likely species

All year	Common finches	Thrushes
Common raptors	*Spring/summer*	Wheatear
Peregrine	Curlew	Meadow Pipit
Red Grouse	Snipe	*Winter*
Little Owl	Skylark	Jack Snipe
Tawny Owl	Hirundines	Barn Owl
Common corvids	Summer warblers	Winter thrushes
Pied Wagtail	Whitethroat	

Key points

- Each walk is about 1.5 miles (2.4km) return
- Easy
- Best in winter for birds of prey
- Warm clothing essential in winter
- Raptor watching can be done from the car
- Keep to hard tracks
- Telescope recommended
- Public transport

Recommended route and birding tips

START YOUR visit at the roadside lay-by where you have a choice of two walks – one (the Railway Walk) heads southeast and the other (the Road Walk) heads south. Both routes cover similar habitats, open moorland and bog being most prevalent, and both involve retracing your steps along the same track to return to your car. The Railway Walk is an easy, firm path that follows the former railway line. It descends into a cutting so the bog itself is only easily visible for the first 100m or so but the track passes through some thicker cover that holds chats and Grasshopper Warblers in spring

and summer. The Road route (now barred to vehicles) goes along a surfaced road and gives good, generally unimpeded views over the moorland and bog. On both routes, it is a case of walking as far as you wish (up to about a mile) and then returning. If, however, your main aim is to see the raptors that frequent the site in winter, the best plan is to set up your telescope in the car park and wait and watch from there. The site may be used by paragliders on windy days.

The site is at its best in winter when the species for which it is well known are present. Short-eared Owls are regular visitors during

195

December, January and February, and during these months you have an excellent chance of seeing them in picturesque surroundings, with the Brecon Beacons National Park in the background. Dusk is by far the best time for the owls as they emerge to hunt over the open moorland. Up to six have been present in the past, sometimes staying well into the spring if food is still plentiful. Hen Harriers are also present during the winter but are less likely to be spotted than the owls, as they hunt over vast areas, covering several square miles in a single day.

Merlin is also often present, along with increasing numbers of Red Kites, which are almost guaranteed during a winter visit. Barn Owl, Tawny Owl and Little Owl have all been spotted here though these are much more difficult to see as they are often hidden during the day in old farm buildings to the southeast of the site. You also have a reasonable chance of seeing Red Grouse, as the site is adjacent to Gwent's stronghold for this species.

Spring and summer can be pleasant on and around the

bog, as upland species such as Wheatear, Whinchat and Meadow Pipit are present. Skylarks can be heard singing overhead. Grasshopper Warblers breed in areas of heather and rushes along the old railway track. Snipe also breeds on the bog and Jack Snipe occurs, but only during winter.

Another charismatic species to look for at Waun Afon Bog is the Raven. These impressive birds can regularly be seen flying over the site, calling to their mates.

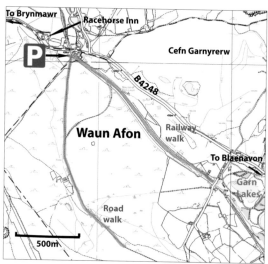

How to get there

2.5 miles NW of Blaenavon

Park in the large lay-by opposite the Racehorse inn, on the B4248 about 2.5 miles northwest of Blaenavon. The bog can be viewed from the lay-by.

Public transport

Regular buses between Blaenavon and Brynmawr.

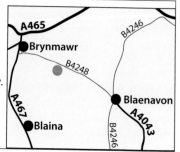

W ENTWOOD IS the largest ancient woodland in
Wales, dating back many centuries. There are
ancient burial sites from the Bronze Age on the south side
of Gray Hill. In more recent times, forestry, especially the
planting of quick-growing conifers such as larch, has led to
the creation of different habitats but also to the destruction
of much of the old oak and broad-leaved woodland. The
forest is currently managed by Natural Resources Wales
for the commercial exploitation of the area, and by The
Woodland Trust, which is trying to preserve and re-establish
areas of the ancient forest.

Target birds
All year: Willow Tit 20%, Marsh Tit 60%, Crossbill 70%, Lesser
Redpoll 50%
Spring/summer: Goshawk 70%, Woodcock 90%, Cuckoo 90%,
Nightjar 90%, Wood Warbler 80%, Tree Pipit 95%
Winter: Goldeneye 20%, Great Grey Shrike 10%

Other likely species

All year		Winter
Canada Goose	Grey Wagtail	Mandarin Duck
Common wildfowl	Pied Wagtail	Wigeon
Cormorant	Common finches	Teal
Grey Heron	Siskin	Gadwall
Great Crested Grebe	Yellowhammer	Winter thrushes
Little Grebe	Reed Bunting	Brambling
Common raptors	*Spring/summer*	
Regular gulls	Hobby	*Occasional*
Common woodland birds	Hirundines	Red Kite
Dipper	Summer warblers	Peregrine
Thrushes	Whitethroat	Hawfinch
Stonechat	Whinchat	
	Spotted Flycatcher	
	Pied Flycatcher	

Recommended route and birding tips

M OST OF the forest is
open for public access
and is used by many as a
recreational area for activities
such as mountain biking,

horseriding and walking –
especially dog walking. Less
desirable uses include cross-
country motorcycling.

The forest has many

Two walks
- Cadira Beeches: 2.5 miles (4km); easy
- Gray Hill: 1 mile (1.6km); moderate

Key points
- Forest used for recreational activities
- Numerous paths so easy to get lost – take a map
- Can be very muddy in parts
- Torch recommended when looking for night birds
- Telescope recommended for reservoir
- Wheelchair accessible at least part of the way between Cadira Beeches and Five Paths

197

footpaths and bridle paths and it is easy to get lost, even for those who know the forest. It is advisable, therefore, to carry an OS map. Some of the tracks can be very muddy, especially bridle paths. If venturing out at night for Nightjars, remember to take a torch and have a safe route back to your car.

| Cadira Beeches | ST422948 (NP15 1NA) | 2.5 miles 🚶/E | Car park P1 |

This easy walk starts at Cadira Beeches car park (P1). An early start is recommended, when the birds are often most active, and before the walkers and dog walkers arrive. It is worth spending some time within 100m of the car park, as the area is open but with some tall, established trees, and many species are most easily seen here. Look for Crossbill, Siskin, Lesser Redpoll and Goldcrest. Firecrests have also been seen here in several years. In the winter period there may be flocks of Chaffinches and other finches, including Brambling, feeding on beech mast. Nuthatch, Treecreeper, Mistle Thrush and other common birds are present all year. In the summer months Chiffchaff and Willow Warbler are very common, but Wood Warbler may need some searching for. Spotted and Pied Flycatchers are also present.

Turn your back on the road and take the wide forest track, which leads in a roughly easterly direction towards the Five Paths (point C). Along this route look and listen for the same species as above and also for Whitethroat, Garden Warbler and Tree Pipit in the scrubbier areas. After about 600m, where the path descends steeply (point A), there are the options of continuing straight ahead to Five Paths, or turning left down a similar track to reach the Five Paths by a rectangular route (A-B-C), turning right at point B immediately after the clear-fell area.

Nightjars and Tree Pipits occur in the clear-fell area. At the Five Paths there is a large open area surrounded by trees –

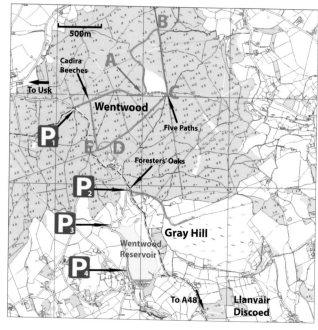

this is another place in which Firecrest has occurred. In the open areas keep checking for raptors such as Goshawk, which is not uncommon in the forest, whereas Buzzard is very common. In summer there are many flowering plants, such as broad-leaved helleborine and other orchids, here.

Ignoring the other paths take the main track (just south of the track from Cadira Beeches) in a southwesterly direction. On your left is an area of clear-fell which has been a reliable place for Nightjars and roding Woodcocks. In mid-summer you may have to wait until after 10.00pm before they appear, so take sensible precautions. There is also the option of

arriving at 4.00am! The track then drops somewhat and the forest becomes damper and more scrubby. There is a stream here and this area has been good for Willow Tit. The track then begins to climb and there is a left fork, which leads to the Nine Wells and the Foresters House and eventually the main road. Ignore this and keep on the upper track.

You should soon see a parking area (point D) on the left (where they sell Christmas trees). Immediately on your right (just as you enter the conifer trees) and about 50m from the main road, there is a bridle path (point E), which goes up to the original Cadira Beeches-Five Paths path. Just before you reach this there is a pond fed by a stream that can be good for seeing finches and other birds as they come down to drink. The path is usually very muddy at this point. A Water Rail overwintered here once. Carry on to the main path where you turn sharp left and head back to Cadira Beeches.

Gray Hill & Wentwood Reservoir ST428939 (NP26 3AZ) 1 mile 👣/M P2

From Cadira Beeches car park, turn left onto the road and head downhill, passing the foresters' houses on the left. The Foresters' Oaks car park (P2) is on the right, shortly after the turning to Llanvaches. This is a good base for exploring Gray Hill. Having parked, return to the road, cross over and head up the main tarmac path ahead. After passing a large house on your right, keep straight on, with the open fields on the your right. As the path narrows, turn through the wooden gate and up the steep (often muddy) slope to the summit. Here you can have glorious views over the Severn Estuary to the south and the forest to the north. This is a more open area in which Meadow Pipit, Wheatear, Whinchat and Stonechat are possible in season. It is also a good raptor-watching site and gives a good view of Wentwood Reservoir. Retrace your steps to the road.

Wentwood Reservoir itself is best viewed from the road above or below the reservoir, but there are only very limited stopping points if going by car. There is just about space for roadside parking of one car at (P3; ST426934), or for a few at (P4; ST428930), but to view the reservoir from the upper road it is best to park at the Foresters' Oaks car park and walk down the road. The reservoir usually holds Great Crested and Little Grebes as well as Coot, Moorhen and Mallard. In recent winters there has been a large flock of diving ducks – mainly Tufted Duck and Pochard but also with an occasional Goldeneye. Gadwall and Wigeon are recorded in small numbers and Mandarin Duck is occasional.

How to get there

About 5 miles SE of Usk

Leave Usk in a southwesterly direction on Maryport Street, towards Llanllowel. Continue on this road, passing under the A449, and ignoring any side roads (to Llantrisant for instance). The road soon climbs up into Wentwood and after about 6 miles reaches Cadira Beeches on the left side (ST422948). The Foresters Oaks car park is

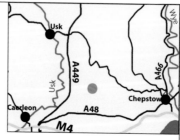

further on down the hill on the right side just above Wentwood reservoir (ST428939).

From J24 of the M4 take the A48 eastwards. Continue for 6.5 miles, through Langstone and Penhow, until you reach the sign to Caerwent on the right. Take the turning immediately on the left to Llanvair Discoed, and turn right at the T-junction in the village, signed Wentwood and Usk. Follow this road, passing Wentwood Reservoir after 1.25 miles, and go past the entrance to P2 (signed Foresters Oaks Picnic Site) on your left. Continue a further 0.75 miles to Cadira Beeches car park (P1) on your right.

T HIS IS a scenically spectacular area with limestone cliffs of the Wyndcliff and Blackcliff, rich woodland and the tidal River Wye. There are a number of stunning viewpoints, notably at the Eagle's Nest, Lovers' Leap and the Giant's Cave, from which you can scan the skies for raptors, the river for Goosanders, Teal, Mallard and Shelduck, and the tree tops for an elusive Hawfinch. There is a heronry on Piercefield cliffs so Grey Herons are regularly seen flying up and down river and perhaps a Little Egret or two. Three pairs of Peregrines breed on cliffs between Chepstow and Tintern, as do Ravens. This is also an excellent area for some unusual and rare plant species.

Target birds

All year: Goshawk 5%, Peregrine 50%, Lesser Spotted
    Woodpecker 5%, Marsh Tit 75%, Hawfinch 5-10%
Spring/summer: Wood Warbler 80%
Late winter/spring: Goshawk 10%

Other likely species

All year	Raven	Summer warblers
Cormorant	Common woodland	
Grey Heron	birds	*Winter*
Little Egret		Goosander
Buzzard	*Spring/summer*	Teal
	Shelduck	

Recommended route and birding tips

Wyndcliff circuit 2.5 mls

S TART OFF by visiting the nearby viewpoint (point A), which is about 30m down a path from the north end of the car park (P1). Return to the car park and follow the path to the south for the Wye Valley walk. This path meanders through superb woodland. There are gentle descents and climbs with steps in some sections, but beware the steep slope to your left down to the river. The woodland has oaks and beeches and some fine stands of large-leaved lime and hornbeam, the latter providing seed sought out by Hawfinches in the winter. A good range of woodland birds occurs here.

There are tantalising glimpses of the river below, more visible in winter without the leaves, but once you pass through the Giant's Cave there is a superb viewpoint where you can scan

Two walks

- Wyndcliff circuit: 2.5 miles (4km)
- Piercefield extension: 3 miles (5.8km)
- Chepstow Castle spur: 0.6 miles (1km)

Key points

- Some steep sections and a ladder
- Can be muddy in parts
- Moderate fitness required
- Walking boots recommended
- The Giant's Cave can be used for shelter
- Stunning views (best in winter when trees are not in leaf)
- Telescope useful
- Good botanical interest

the river for birds such as Shelduck in summer or Goosander in winter. Make sure you also look at higher levels for soaring raptors. At this point you can, if you wish, extend the walk to Chepstow Castle and return via Piercefield Park (see below). To complete the Wyndcliff circuit, turn sharp right at point B, just beyond the Giant's Cave, onto a path that goes up through to the top of the wood. Follow this path for about 0.5 km to the main road near St Arvans, detouring a few metres off the path to see the spectacular views from Lovers' Leap viewpoint, which will be evident from the path. At the main road pass through an impressive pair of tall gate-posts (point C), turn left (take care) and then take the right fork onto the small road that goes up to the Upper Wyndcliff car park (P3). Follow the road to the car park and take the broad bridleway to the left of the car park and walk uphill (do not go onto the footpath across the fields) – keep following the broad track and 100m after a bench, turn right to the viewpoint from the Eagle's Nest (point D). Enjoy the

spectacular view over the Llancaut meander of the River Wye and beyond to the Severn Estuary, and in the spring look out for soaring raptors (the longer you watch, the more likely you will see Goshawk). Now retrace your steps and take a signposted left turn off the track to lead you to the start of the 365 steps (point E). Beware, as there is one steep, ladder section. Follow the steps down to the A466 through predominantly yew woodland (berries good for wintering

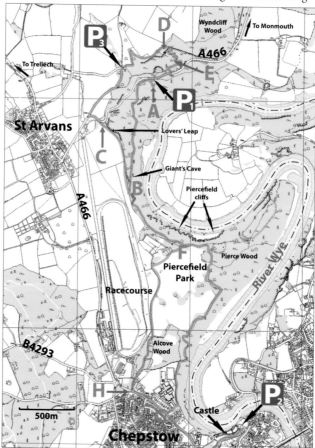

202

thrushes) and cross the road with care back to the car park.

Piercefield extension 3 miles

AT POINT B, there is the option to extend your walk to Chepstow. Follow the Wye Valley Walk south (ignoring the right turn at point F) all the way to Chepstow Leisure Centre car park, and exit onto the B4293 road (point G). You then have two options.

Chepstow Castle spur: turn left on the B4293 and carry on to Chepstow Castle (turn left just after Dell primary school and walk down the Dell to the castle) or

Piercefield Park: turn right to complete a circular walk though points H and F to point B. The return path starts just before Crossway Green roundabout and is marked by a footpath signpost directing you through an open gateway in a stone wall (point H). From here, follow the path through woodland to Piercefield Park (there are posts marking the path). The track runs alongside the racecourse before veering right in front of Piercefield House ruins, and into the woodland where you can rejoin the Wye Valley walk at point F. Turn left and retrace your steps to point B. From this point on follow the directions given in the Wyndcliff walk above to return to your car.

An alternative strategy for the walk is to leave a car at both Wyndcliff (P1) and Chepstow Castle (P2) car parks, and take a linear walk from one to the other.

A useful booklet *Picturesque Piercefield*, is available from the Wye Valley AONB office or tourist boards, provides information on walks as well as much historical information about Piercefield House and sites on the way.

How to get there

2 miles N of Chepstow

Park in the lower car park P1 (at ST526972) in woodland below the Wyndcliff; this is on the left (marked with a viewpoint sign) as you are driving south on the A466 from Tintern and on the right if coming from St Arvans. Drive slowly and keep a sharp look out, as there is no advance warning of the car park entrance and it is easily missed. There are several walks from here, which take in broad-leaved woodland on the limestone cliffs and slopes as well as spectacular views down to the River Wye. If parking at Chepstow Castle, turn left off the B4293 (Welsh Street) at the T-junction wih High Street, then left again into Bank Street. Continue along this one-way, narrow road as it becomes Bridge Street and turn left just after the Three Tuns Inn into the Pay & Display car park (P2) at ST535941 (NP16 5HD).

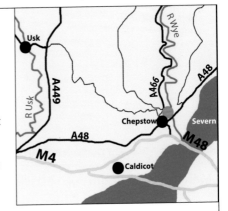

Key points

- Allow a full day for the extended walk
- All-year birding interest
- Walking boots or wellingtons after rain
- Public transport
- Facilities and shelter at the Boat Inn, Redbrook
- Wheelchair friendly on the rail track section of the Redbrook-Whitebrook walk

THESE WALKS, always close to the River Wye, take you through extensive woodlands, and provide an attractive range of river and forest birds. They are easy, but long, walks on mostly well-maintained footpaths, though some sections can be very wet and muddy at certain times of the year and several areas are a little rough. The main walk comprises a circular route from Monmouth to Redbrook and back. The walk from Redbrook to Whitebrook and back can be tackled as an extension to the main route or as a separate walk, much of it along a former railway track that is wheelchair accessible.

Target birds

All year: Goshawk 5% (higher in Feb/March), Lesser Spotted Woodpecker 5%, Hawfinch 5%

Spring/summer: Hobby 10%, Sedge Warbler 75%, Reed Bunting 75%

Winter: Goosander in winter 95%

Other likely species

All year	Raven	Wood Warbler
Mute Swan	Marsh Tit	Garden Warbler
Mandarin	Common woodland birds	
Cormorant		*Winter*
Grey Heron	Grey Wagtail	Goosander
Common raptors		Regular gulls
Green Woodpecker	*Spring/summer*	Dipper
Great Spotted Woodpecker	Hobby	Winter thrushes
Kingfisher	Common Sandpiper (passage)	Common finches
Common corvids	Hirundines	Lesser Redpoll
	Summer warblers	

Recommended route and birding tips

Monmouth to Redbrook   SO509127 (NP25 3XP) 6.7 miles

FROM THE car park near Monmouth School (P1), turn left and retrace your way to the Queen's Head pub. There, turn right and use the underpass to cross the busy A40 dual carriageway. Cross Wye Bridge.

From the car park at the southern end of the town (P2), or if your arrival has been by bus, make your way up Monnow Street (the main street) and take the first turn to your right after 400m or so, into Glendower Street. Walk along this road to the Police

204

Station, at which you should bear left and follow the road (200m) to Monmouth School (on your right). Continue ahead to the Queen's Head pub, turn right, and use the underpass beneath the A40 and cross Wye Bridge.

At the end of the bridge, turn right into Monmouth School playing field car park (SO512127) – note that parking here is not permitted! – and walk behind the pavilion, between the playing field fence and the line of large conifers, onto a footpath that follows the riverbank. Sand Martins nest in a few holes and pipes in the walls alongside the bridge and Grey Wagtails sometimes

nest here too.

The first section is always good for Mute Swans and Mallard and, in the winter, for a Goosander or two, often near the mouth of the River Monnow on the opposite bank. There is a small day-roost of Cormorants in large overhanging willow trees. In the spring and summer, Sedge Warblers and Reed Buntings may be heard or seen in riverside willows and tall riparian vegetation. The playing field is a good site for Black-headed Gulls in winter and there is always a chance of spotting a Mediterranean Gull among them. Pied Wagtails that roost in Monmouth often gather on the fields before

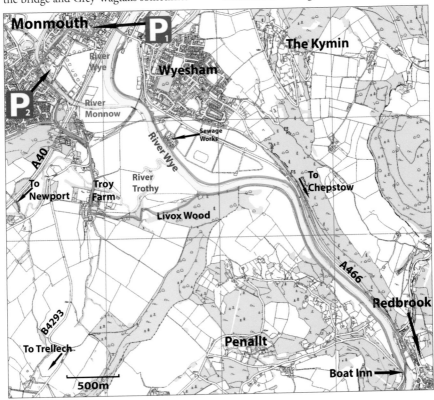

dusk or in the morning.

Continue on under the iron bridge and shortly after, under the remains of the old stone viaduct. Jackdaws nest in crevices in the stonework and a colony of Sand Martins nest high in the crevices. Just after you cross a tiny stream look out for Monmouth sewage works behind a fence on your left. In severe weather the filter beds attract large numbers of Meadow Pipits, wagtails and Chaffinches, as they always remain free of snow and are full of small worms and other invertebrates.

To the right are the Trothy meadows that, when flooded, attract some wildfowl and soon you will see Livox Wood across the river and some rapids. Goosanders and

Grey Wagtails typically occur here and Reed Buntings breed in riverside vegetation. The footpath soon leaves the fields, home to Monmouth Show, and meanders through woodland before emerging again in another field. Follow the river edge to Redbrook, looking out for Kingfishers and Moorhens. The path takes you along the road for 100-200m and then turns off from the road, bringing you to the old rail bridge over the river, which you can cross for refreshments at The Boat Inn. Grey Wagtails frequent this spot and Kingfishers can often be seen from the pub. The valley here is favoured by feeding House Martins and occasionally a Hobby can be seen.

From here you can return to Monmouth via Troy Farm on the west bank or, if you wish, you can extend your walk to Whitebrook (see below).

If returning to Monmouth, follow the footpath along the west bank of the river; this eventually goes through Livox Wood and brings you out into fields. At this point follow the fence-line away from the river, head through the gateway and follow the track up the slope and then down towards Troy Farm. On approaching the farm follow the main track ahead then turn sharp right, go through the farmyard, walk past Troy House and over the River Trothy. Turn right on joining the road and follow this, without diverting, down to the

mini-roundabout by a filling station. Turn left here, walk about 300m and then turn right at the next roundabout to walk over the old fortified Monnow Bridge (the only remaining mediaeval fortified river bridge in Britain) into Monnow Street. Take the first right onto Blestium Street to return to the car park (P2) or the first left to return to the bus station. If parked at P1, continue along Monnow Street and follow the directions given at the beginning of this section above.

Redbrook to Whitebrook extension SO537098 (NP25 4LR) 4.2 mls E

FROM THE river crossing at Redbrook, you can continue to Whitebrook by following the Wye Valley Walk under the rail bridge near the Boat Inn on the west side of the river for about 3.5km. The path comes away from the river up onto a disused railway line which you can follow back to the Boat Inn and then return to Monmouth either on the west bank via Troy Farm (as detailed above), or by retracing your outward route along the east bank.

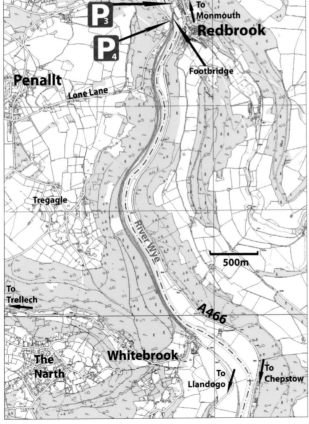

If you choose to include this extension, you will find, in spring and summer, that the woodland edge on the west bank is alive with birds – numerous Blackcaps and smaller numbers of Garden Warblers and Marsh Tits; even a Lesser Spotted Woodpecker, Hawfinch or Pied Flycatcher is possible. A Dipper is often seen on the rocks below Redbrook or at the mouth of the culvert that carries the Red Brook below the main Monmouth to Chepstow road. Lesser Redpoll and Siskin are common in riverside alders in winter. In February as you walk along the river look out for Goshawks displaying over woodland early in the morning. Buzzards and Ravens are frequently seen.

How to get there

Walk starts in Monmouth town centre

When approaching Monmouth on the A40 from the northeast, take the third exit off the roundabout just north of the town and head for the town centre. Pass the large secondary school on your left and at the traffic lights (NOT the lights on the dual carriageway – if you find them you have gone too far!) turn left. Follow the road to a roundabout (in St James's Square) with a war memorial and a large tree in its centre and take the second exit. After 200m, at the Queen's Head public house, go straight on (note that this is a 'Stop' junction). You will pass Monmouth School on your left, and as the road veers right, you will find a large Pay & Display car park (P1) at SO509127. Park there.

If approaching on the A40 from the southwest, turn left onto the B4293 immediately after passing through the road tunnels. Pass the filling station on your left, go straight

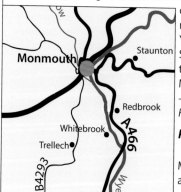

over the mini-roundabout and after 100m, turn right at the traffic lights and drive over the bridge. You will see a large Pay & Display car park (P2) at SO505124 on your left; park there. Exit the car park, turn left along Blestium Street and then right into Monnow Street and make your way to Wye Bridge – see detailed directions as to how to do this in *Recommended route and birding tips* above.

Public transport

From Monmouth Bus Station, turn left into Monnow Street and make your way to Wye Bridge as in *Recommended route and birding tips*.

Redbrook to Whitebrook as independent walk SO537098 (NP25 4LR) P3

This section could be treated as a separate walk, and has the advantage of using the former railway track, which is wheelchair friendly. If you wish to make it a circular walk, you can follow the railway path one way and the river path (not wheelchair friendly) on your return. Although there are two separate paths, they are so close together that they are not always distinguishable on the map.

After parking in Redbrook at P3 (SO537098), cross the bridge (navigable by wheelchair) to the Boat Inn, walk a short distance up the road to Penallt and turn left onto the wheelchair-friendly disused railway line. If you've parked at P4 (SO535097) just walk back up the road and turn left onto the track. This railway track leads south to Whitebrook but before reaching the village you will see the river path (not suitable for wheelchairs) veering off to the left – this will take you back to Redbrook along the Usk Valley Walk, unless you wish to retrace your route along the railway line. The birds likely to be seen on this walk are given in the Redbrook to Whitebrook extension above.

How to get there

Walk starting from Redbrook

Drive to Redbrook village (on the east bank) and park in the village car park (P3), which is well signed (SO537098; NP25 4LR). Alternatively, if prepared to risk losing your way in the maze of narrow lanes when approaching from the west, drive down Lone Lane in Penallt until you reach the river, where there are a few parking places (P4) near the Boat Inn (SO535097; NP25 4AL). From here, walk a short way back up Lone Lane and proceed as above.

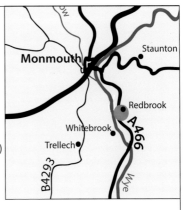

Key points

- Reservoir Walk 1 mile (1.6km)
- Reservoir plus Fourteen Locks 2 miles (3.2km)
- Easy/moderate
- Steep hill down to reservoir
- Wellington boots recommended for longer walk
- Telescope recommended for reservoirs
- Public transport
- Café and toilets at Fourteen Locks Canal Centre (check opening hours)

YNYSYFRO RESERVOIRS lie close to the M4 on the northwest side of Newport and within sight of the residential area of High Cross. Its immediate surroundings, however, comprise grazing fields, part of a golf course and a mixed conifer and larch plantation, giving it an appearance that is at least semi-rural. Its main ornithological attraction is as a wintering site for small to moderate numbers of water birds; usually only a few of these remain during the breeding season. Periods of rough weather can occasionally bring in more unexpected species.

All of the upper pool, and most of the lower, can be viewed from public footpaths, and are thus accessible at any time. Access to the banks of the lower pool requires a permit, obtainable from Welsh Water. For the more energetic bird-watcher, a visit to the site may be incorporated into a circular walk, of up to three hours' duration, which covers a greater variety of habitats, and also includes the Fourteen Locks heritage site.

Likely species

All year
Mute Swan
Canada Goose
Common waterfowl
Little Grebe
Great Crested Grebe
Tufted Duck
Sparrowhawk
Buzzard
Green Woodpecker
Great Spotted Woodpecker

Skylark
Common woodland birds

Spring/summer
Hirundines
Summer warblers
Whitethroat

Winter
Regular gulls
Mediterranean Gull
Great Black-backed Gull

Redwing
Pochard
Meadow Pipit
Common finches

Occasional
Goosander
Goldeneye
Teal
Gadwall
Wigeon
Shoveler
Rarer grebes

Recommended route and birding tips

Reservoir only	1 mile

FROM THE Fourteen Locks Canal Centre car park walk out of the main entrance and turn right. After 30m turn right again, down the (private) road towards the reservoir; the public footpath runs along this road. The road descends a fairly steep hill (point A) and reaches the causeway (point B) between the two pools of the reservoir. From here the whole of the upper pool is well within the range of most binoculars. Little Grebe, Tufted Duck, Pochard and Coot are regular winter species here, often joined by Mute Swan and Canada Goose, and occasionally by other ducks also. The winter gull flock usually consists of 100 or more Black-headed Gulls, with a small number of Common, Herring and Lesser Black-backs among them; when on the upper pool, the flock is worth checking for scarcer gulls, such as Mediterranean, among them. The gulls return to the coast to roost every day, and have usually gone by mid-afternoon. From time to time the water level is lowered, exposing areas of mud, mainly on the far side, and at such times small numbers of Teal, Gadwall and Shoveler may appear; by contrast, waders visit very rarely, even when the exposed mud looks inviting.

The plantation to the east (best seen from point C) and the small copse to the west frequently host Jays and woodpeckers, while Buzzard and Sparrowhawk also appear overhead. The plantation is also a good spot to listen for early Chiffchaffs and Willow Warblers. During the

breeding season, the small patch of reeds in the far corner has hosted breeding pairs of Coot, Mute Swan, Moorhen and Little Grebe (occasionally). Skylark and (in winter) Meadow Pipit may also be seen or heard over the fields at the bottom of the hill.

Beware anglers casting from the slope adjacent to the railings – their flying tackle passes close to head height, and they may not always be aware of people on the causeway.

Only part of the lower pool is readily visible from the causeway; access to the bank requires a permit from Welsh Water. Great Crested Grebes are regular in winter on the lower pool, while other grebes

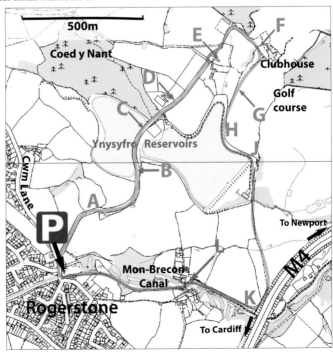

and Goosanders make the occasional appearance. Cormorants (to the anglers' annoyance) also favour the lower pool, perching conspicuously along the dam wall, while (again in winter) a pair of Great Black-backed Gulls sometimes perches on the dam railings. In spring and summer, Swifts and hirundines appear in small to moderate numbers, while warblers breed in the surrounding hedgerows.

To return to the car park, the only route is back along the road up the hill; this may prove very steep for wheelchair users. If you wish to extend your walk around a circular route that takes in more of the Fourteen Locks Heritage site, continue as described below.

Extension to Fourteen Locks Centre   2 miles

Follow the road from the causeway past the plantation and the stables (point D) towards three houses (point E). The hedge on the left, and the field behind, is a favoured spot for finches and Redwings in winter, while on the right there is a partial view of the northern arm of the lower pool. The path then passes the houses on their left and joins the access road towards the golf club car park. The conifer plantation here is also favoured by winter finches, especially Goldfinch and Siskin.

In front of the golf clubhouse (point F), the path turns sharp right and follows another hedge (point G) down to the eastern edge of the lower pool and the vantage point (H), from which most of the lower pool, out of range of the causeway, can be fairly well seen. On this stretch, note that the path runs alongside the first hole of the golf course, and that players tee off from near the clubhouse at regular intervals. Again it is wise, in the interests of both safety and good relations, to observe the standard golf course etiquette of standing still while strokes are being played. A good rule of thumb is that, when golfers are walking, it is safe for birders to walk too. Skylarks seem to have little difficulty

coexisting with golf, and this stretch of the circuit may also yield their song or call.

The path then leaves the golf course, turning sharp right at point J into a small thicket, down which it runs to a stile into the field at the bottom. Buzzards often appear from the wood on the left, while Pied Wagtails, Meadow Pipits and (in winter) Redwings use the fields and surrounding trees. The path crosses the fields via two more stiles, the first being close to the solitary oak and the second in the far corner of the fields, close to the M4. A small stream runs across the second field, passing under the path through a culvert. A short stretch of fenced-in path now leads to the canal towpath (K), close to the M4 underpass. The route then follows the towpath up the staircase of locks, where Kingfishers are sometimes to be seen, and over a bridge at Pensarn Cottage. The cottage owners keep their bird tables well stocked; Nuthatch and Coal Tit often feed among the visiting hordes of House Sparrows, while in hard winter weather Brambling has appeared there.

Above Pensarn there is a choice of paths (point L), along the towpath or through the woods, to return to the visitor centre.

Nuthatch and Great Spotted Woodpecker are regular here, while Treecreeper and Green Woodpecker appear occasionally, and in winter there are small parties of Siskins, with the occasional Lesser Redpoll among them, in the alders on the north side. Grey Wagtails are also most likely to appear around one of the pools on this upper part of the Fourteen Locks site.

Parts of this circuit, especially on the golf course and across the fields between points J and K, can become very muddy, even in moderately dry weather. After prolonged wet weather, it can become impassable, which is a good reason to do the walk in reverse, thus having a shorter return walk if an impasse is reached. The reverse walk also allows you to keep a better eye on the golfers and thus minimise any disruption that your passing might cause.

How to get there

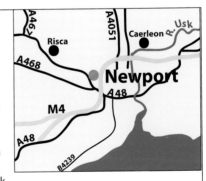

On NW fringe of Newport

From Junction 27 on the M4, follow the B4591 towards High Cross. In about half a mile, past a filling station on the left and a car sales site on the right, take the turn to the right signposted to the Fourteen Locks Canal Centre. After 200m, cross a narrow hump-backed bridge – beware! cars often approach the bridge at speed from the other direction! – and turn right into the visitor centre car park just beyond it. Note that the car park is closed daily at 4.45pm, and that a lot of traffic uses Cwm Lane as a through route, so parking there is best avoided. For after-hours parking, there is space in Brunel Avenue, opposite the car park entrance.

Public transport

From Newport Market Square, there are frequent bus services to Risca and Blackwood or Tredegar, which travel along the B4591 (currently services 56, R1 and R2 pass Fourteen Locks but check before travelling). The nearest stop to Fourteen Locks is the second stop after crossing the M4, and is nearly opposite the car sales site described above, and only a short distance from the signposted road off the B4591.

Key points

- 2.3 miles (3.7km)
- Moderate (one steep descent)
- Year-round birding interest
- Cattle and horses likely to be encountered
- Numerous stiles
- Outstanding views
- Parts can be muddy

YSGYRYD FACH (Little Skirrid) is one of Abergavenny's lesser-known hills, not as visually prominent as the Blorenge, Sugar Loaf or Ysgyryd Fawr. It is located just to the east of Abergavenny and is mostly tree covered, and, being at a lower elevation than the other hills, lacks moorland on the summit. A Monmouthshire County Council way-marked circular trail will take you through farmland and woodland, including mature trees, restocks and clear-felled areas.

The woodland is privately owned, and although there are a number of forest tracks on and around the hill, none of these are public rights of way. During the winter months there are organised Pheasant shoots, usually on alternate Saturdays.

Target birds

All year: Red Kite 20%, Goshawk 20%, Peregrine 20%
Spring/summer: Hobby 10%, Lesser Spotted Woodpecker 10%, Tree Pipit 100%
Winter: Woodcock 80%, Redwing 100%, Fieldfare 100%, Crossbill 50%

Other likely species

All year	Common farmland birds	Lesser Whitethroat
Barn Owl		Redstart
Little Owl	*Spring/summer*	Spotted Flycatcher
Raven	Summer warblers	
Common woodland birds	Wood Warbler	
	Whitethroat	

Recommended route and birding tips

THE WALK starts immediately at the southern end of the lay-by, just past a brook adjacent to a stile on the left with a yellow way-mark arrow. Cross the stile and follow the direction of the arrow up the field path with the hedge and brook on your left. At the top of this first field the path crosses a bridge over the brook before reaching a stile with three way-mark arrows. Keep straight on up the hill with the hedge, brook and tree line now on your right. Continue uphill to cross another stile adjacent to a metal gate. Continue along another field with the tree line on your right to another stile and ditch, and head towards the electricity pylons.

On reaching the pylons (point A), pause for a while to take in the view over the Coldbrook valley. The former estate house in the bottom of the valley has long been demolished but many of the former parkland trees are still evident. The farmland is a mixture of pasture and crop cultivation, and hosts typical farmland bird species. The late summer/autumn can see large numbers of Stock Doves congregating on the pastures (following muck-spreading), with up to 100 sometimes recorded. In the autumn, flocks of several thousand Woodpigeons fly over as they follow the edge of the Black Mountains/coalfield hills southwards. The hill and surrounding farmland are good for birds of prey and owls. In addition to the more common raptors, look out for Red Kite (mainly in the spring), Peregrine (at any time of year – generally sitting on one of the pylons waiting for a passing meal), Hobby and Goshawk. Little Owls can be heard setting up their territories at dusk on autumn evenings, Barn Owls hunt the Coldbrook valley and Tawny Owls are common.

To continue, keep the hedge on your right and the wood (approx 100m away) on the left. The gradient levels and after about 800m you reach a stile in the far corner of the field. Cross the stile and brook to see a white house on the left (Keeper's Cottage). Walk a short distance straight ahead with the house and garden on your left, then cross the stile and immediately turn left (follow the arrow) to climb the short steep bank into a field that usually has cattle in it. The route begins to climb gently again, following the woodland edge, and a stile in the top corner leads into a second field with a stile in the top left corner. Cross the stile onto a wide track. Ahead you will see a Pheasant release pen; turn right and follow the track uphill along the edge of the wood. After about 200m you will arrive at a T-junction of tracks where you turn left and continue to follow the woodland edge.

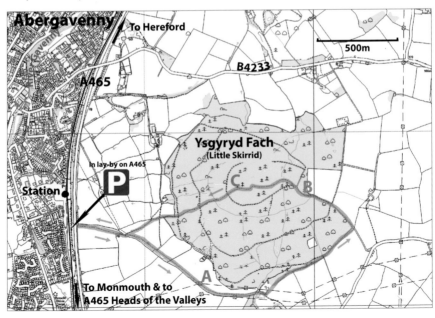

During the winter months there are usually good numbers of Redwings and Fieldfares roosting in the more sheltered parts of the woodland (in the Coldbrook valley or on the northeastern flank), and watching from this eastern edge of the woodland (point B) at dusk can reveal several thousand birds flying in. Also look out for Woodcocks as they flight out, after resting in the woodland during the day, to feed in the farmland during the night. Up to 20-30 are usually flushed during the Pheasant shoots, but they normally stay hidden from the occasional walker. Raven numbers generally build up to 30-40 at their winter roost in the taller evergreen trees.

After about 300m you will now have to leave the stone track and continue straight ahead onto a grassy path to take you to the summit (point C). The summit was cleared of trees early in 2011, revealing extensive views in all directions. It will likely be a further ten years or so before the next generation of tree planting once again closes off the views.

A few Crossbills can usually be heard flying overhead and flocks of up to 50 Siskins are common. A few pairs of Tree Pipits and Linnets have colonised the summit since the trees were cleared, and Nightjar is always a possibility (though not yet recorded).

Continue straight across the summit to pick up a narrow path (usually muddy) with a steep descent for about 800m. You will cross two stone tracks and a third grassy track, before climbing a stile into pasture again. Cross the stile in the bottom right corner of the field and continue down the field with the hedge on your right. You will now recognise your earlier route in the fields below you. At the bottom of the field look for a metal gate on the left, which is near a yellow way-mark arrow that directs you over a stile and across the brook to rejoin the lay-by and start point.

How to get there

Immediately E of Abergavenny

The way-marked route leaves Abergavenny railway station and crosses the main Hereford Road, but to avoid the parking charge and having to cross the busy trunk road (there is no pedestrian crossing facility), it is suggested you park in the long lay-by on the right-hand side (driving north) of the A465, Abergavenny-Hereford trunk road. From the complex roundabout at the junction of the A40 and A465, take the A465 to Hereford and park in the lay-by on the right after about 0.3 miles (SO306135). Depending on traffic conditions, it may be safer to continue north along the A465 for another half-mile, where you can leave the main road, turn around and rejoin, driving south for easier parking in the lay-by.

Best walks for disabled access

Contributors of walks were asked to provide information on disabled access. The following list comprises all walks that were considered to be wholly or partially accessible to wheelchair users. In most cases the recommended tracks will be hard and even, but please bear in mind that some may be uneven and more difficult. Some walks are along metalled country roads that may be narrow in places and lack pavements.

Afon Lwyd at Cwmbran
All main paths are hard-surfaced and wheelchair accessible.

Bargoed Woodland Park
The various access points to the park are all wheelchair accessible, as are the main paths, though a few sections are moderately steep.

Black Rock and Sudbrook
The main route along the Wales Coast Path is wheelchair accessible, though optional detours onto the adjacent saltmarsh are not.

Brynmawr Ponds
The main routes around both Dunlop Semtex and Machine Ponds, and the recommended routes between them, are all wheelchair accessible. We have been advised by a disabled user that there are two short sections where the 'pusher' needs to be fairly fit.

Bulmore Lakes
Apart from a short optional detour, this walk is routed along a minor road that carries little traffic outside of rush hours, but has no pavements and is narrow in places. It is usable, with care, by wheelchairs. However, to obtain adequate views of the lakes and river the user would need to be able to stand on occasions.

Castle Meadows, Abergavenny
The main paths are all wheelchair accessible.

Cwmtillery Lakes
The path beside the lower lake is wheelchair friendly but the lake can no longer be circumnavigated by wheelchair.

Garn Lakes
The Local Nature Reserve section is wheelchair accessible but not the mountain walk.

Goetre House Wood
The canal section of the walk. It can be accessed from the road at points G and H (bridges 72 and 74) and followed to point C, or along the road to point F (but not through points D and E).

Graig Goch Woods
The described walk is not wheelchair accessible, but from the car park there is a very pleasant walk along the old railway track through the Sirhowy Valley Country Park. This route has many of the birds listed for the Graig Goch Walk but none of the upland species.

Llandegfedd Reservoir
Wheelchair accessible at the dam and in the immediate vicinity; the user would need to stand to see over the wall. The reservoir is also visible from the anglers' car park at the northern end but the walks leading off from the car park are not suitable for wheelchairs.

Best walks for disabled access

Lower Monnow Valley

Only the metalled road is wheelchair accessible, but this is the largest section of the walk. It is a relatively wide country road with good visibility and light traffic.

Magor Marsh

The hard paths are suitable for wheelchairs but not the boardwalks, which are in need of repair. The hide is wheelchair friendly but is currently inaccessible, as the boardwalks need to be crossed to reach it. The Gwent Wildlife Trust plans to do the required repairs. Disabled visitors are advised to contact GWT beforehand to ascertain the current position.

Minnetts Wood

Wheelchair access is limited to Minnetts Lane, much of which has a moderately steep gradient.

Mynydd Garnclochdy

From the car park, wheelchair users can undertake a half-kilometre section of the walk in the reverse direction along the Llanover road. At the cattle grid, the road leads very steeply downhill. Other sections of the walk are not wheelchair accessible.

Mynydd Llangatwg

The Hafod Road walk is, as the name might suggest, along a road; it is wheelchair usable but has no pavement and is narrow in places. The other two walks are not suitable.

NWR – Uskmouth Reedbeds

The Reserve Centre and the shorter walk are fully wheelchair accessible; the longer walk is not. Disabled facilities are available at the Visitor Centre.

Parc Bryn Bach

Fully wheelchair accessible.

The Blorenge

The Tramroad walk is wheelchair usable for a considerable distance until it starts to descend.

Tredegar Park, Newport

Many of the paths are hard-surfaced and wheelchair friendly. A section of path on the northwest edge of the lake has too many exposed tree roots for wheelchair use, but is easily by-passed.

Two Rivers Meadow, Monmouth

Wheelchair accessible only along the track.

Waun Afon Bog

Using a telescope, many birds can be seen from the car park; this is one of the options recommended for the able-bodied birder as well.

Wentwood

The section of track from Cadira Beeches car park to Five Paths (omitting the diversion to the north) is hard-surfaced but stony and it descends gradually. Accessible by wheelchair but rather bumpy.

Wye Valley South of Monmouth

The Redbrook to Whitebrook walk is wheelchair accessible from the car park through to Whitebrook if following the disused railway track. The river path is not suitable.

The Gwent bird list

The following list is based on the latest Gwent avifauna, *The Birds of Gwent* (Venables *et al.*, 2008. Christopher Helm, London) and the Annual Bird Reports produced by the Gwent Ornithological Society.

All 301 species, including vagrants, recorded up to the end of 2012, are listed in the table below. The first two columns are blank to allow you to record species you see. The third, fourth and fifth columns give, respectively, the English (BOU) vernacular name, scientific name and Welsh name. A brief note of each species' current status is given in the fifth column, while the final column indicates your chance of seeing the species.

The likelihood of seeing any given species is indicated by a simple code, as follows:

1 Should be seen almost anywhere in the countryside

2 Should be seen on a visit but only in appropriate habitat/season

3 Maybe, but scarce and/or irregular

4 Very unlikely in a short visit – this species is rare

5 Not a chance!

		English Name	Scientific Name	Welsh Name	Status in Gwent	Chance
		Mute Swan	*Cygnus olor*	Alarch Dôf	Widespread	1
		Bewick's Swan	*Cygnus columbianus*	Alarch Bewick	Uncommon winter visitor	3
		Whooper Swan	*Cygnus cygnus*	Alarch y Gogledd	Very scarce & irregular winter visitor	4
		Bean Goose	*Anser fabalis*	Gŵydd y Llafur	Very rare winter visitor	5
		Pink-footed Goose	*Anser brachyrhynchus*	Gŵydd Droed-binc	Rare winter visitor	5
		White-fronted Goose	*Anser albifrons*	Gŵydd Dalcen-wen	Very scarce & irregular winter visitor	4
		Greylag Goose	*Anser anser*	Gŵydd Wyllt	Scarce on passage; feral birds widespread	1
		Greater Canada Goose	*Branta canadensis*	Gŵydd Canada	Locally common resident	1
		Barnacle Goose	*Branta leucopsis*	Gŵydd Wyran	Rare winter visitor; feral birds irregular	4
		Brent Goose	*Branta bernicla*	Gŵydd Ddu	Uncommon winter visitor	3
		Egyptian Goose	*Alopochen aegyptiaca*	Gŵydd yr Aifft	Rare visitor	4
		Shelduck	*Tadorna tadorna*	Hwyaden yr Eithin	Locally common resident	2
		Mandarin Duck	*Aix galericulata*	Hwyaden Gribog	Resident in small numbers	3
		Wigeon	*Anas penelope*	Chwiwell	Common winter visitor/passage migrant	2
		American Wigeon	*Anas americana*	Chwiwell America	Very rare vagrant	5
		Gadwall	*Anas strepera*	Hwyaden Lwyd	Common resident in wetlands	2
		Teal	*Anas crecca*	Corhwyaden	Common winter visitor; rare breeder	2
		Green-winged Teal	*Anas carolinensis*	Corhwyaden Asgell-werdd	Very rare vagrant	5
		Mallard	*Anas platyrhynchos*	Hwyaden Wyllt	Common resident	1
		Pintail	*Anas acuta*	Hwyaden Lostfain	Fairly common winter visitor	2

The Gwent bird list

		English Name	Scientific Name	Welsh Name	Status in Gwent	Chance
		Garganey	*Anas querquedula*	Hwyaden Addfain	Scarce passage migrant; very rare breeder	3
		Shoveler	*Anas clypeata*	Hwyaden Lydanbig	Common winter visitor; rare breeder	2
		Red-crested Pochard	*Netta rufina*	Hwyaden Gribgoch	Scarce visitor	4
		Pochard	*Aythya ferina*	Hwyaden Bengoch	Fairly common winter visitor	2
		Ring-necked Duck	*Aythya collaris*	Hwyaden Dorchog	Very rare vagrant	5
		Ferruginous Duck	*Aythya nyroca*	Hwyaden Lygadwen	Very rare vagrant	5
		Tufted Duck	*Aythya fuligula*	Hwyaden Gopog	Common winter visitor; scarce breeder	2
		Scaup	*Aythya marila*	Hwyaden Benddu	Uncommon winter visitor	3
		Lesser Scaup	*Aythya affinis*	Hwyaden Benddu Leiaf	Very rare vagrant	5
		Eider	*Somateria mollissima*	Hwyaden Fwythblu	Scarce and irregular, mostly in spring	4
		Long-tailed Duck	*Clangula hyemalis*	Hwyaden Gynffon-hir	Scarce winter visitor	4
		Common Scoter	*Melanitta nigra*	Môr-hwyaden Ddu	Regular in small nos, mostly summer; non-breeding	3
		Velvet Scoter	*Melanitta fusca*	Môr-hwyaden y Gogledd	Rare on passage/in winter	4
		Goldeneye	*Bucephula clangula*	Hwyaden Lygad-aur	Uncommon winter visitor	3
		Smew	*Mergellus albellus*	Lleian Wen	Very scarce winter visitor	4
		Red-breasted Merganser	*Mergus serrator*	Hwyaden Frongoch	Very scarce winter visitor	4
		Goosander	*Mergus merganser*	Hwyaden Ddanheddog	Uncommon winter visitor; scarce breeder	3
		Ruddy Duck	*Oxyura jamaicensis*	Hwyaden Goch	Rare visitor, post national cull	5
		Quail	*Coturnix coturnix*	Sofliar	Very scarce summer visitor	4
		Red-legged Partridge	*Alectoris rufa*	Petrisen Goesgoch	Uncommon resident; most introduced for shooting	3
		Red Grouse	*Lagopus lagopus*	Grugiar	Uncommon resident on heather uplands	2
		Black Grouse	*Tetrao tetrix*	Grugiar Ddu	Former resident; no records since 1977	5
		Grey Partridge	*Perdix perdix*	Petrisen	Now a very scarce resident	4
		Pheasant	*Phasianus colchicus*	Ffesant	Common resident; many introduced for shooting	1
		Red-throated Diver	*Gavia stellata*	Trochydd Gyddfgoch	Rare winter visitor	4
		Black-throated Diver	*Gavia arctica*	Trochydd Gyddfddu	Very scarce in winter or on passage	4
		Great Northern Diver	*Gavia immer*	Trochydd Mawr	Rare winter visitor	4
		Fulmar	*Fulmarus glacialis*	Aderyn-Drycin y Graig	Scarce; mostly storm-blown, spring to autumn	3
		Cory's Shearwater	*Calonectris borealis*	Aderyn-Drycin Cory	Very rare storm-blown vagrant	5
		Manx Shearwater	*Puffinus puffinus*	Aderyn-Drycin Manaw	Regular in summer, often storm-blown	3
		Storm Petrel	*Hydrobates pelagicus*	Pedryn Drycin	Very scarce wind-blown vagrant, mostly summer	4
		Leach's Petrel	*Oceanodroma leucorhoa*	Pedryn Gynffon-fforchog	Rare wind-blown vagrant, mostly in autumn	5

220

The Gwent bird list

		English Name	Scientific Name	Welsh Name	Status in Gwent	Chance
		Gannet	*Morus bassanus*	Hugan	Uncommon visitor, often wind-blown	3
		Cormorant	*Phalacrocorax carbo*	Mulfran	Fairly common resident & winter visitor	1
		Shag	*Phalacrocorax aristotelis*	Mulfran Werdd	Very scarce visitor, usually in autumn	5
		Bittern	*Botaurus stellaris*	Aderyn y Bwn	Very scarce but regular winter visitor	4
		American Bittern	*Botaurus lentiginosus*	Aderyn-bwn America	Very rare vagrant	5
		Little Bittern	*Ixobrychus minutus*	Aderyn-bwn Leiaf	Very rare vagrant	5
		Night-heron	*Nycticorax nycticorax*	Crëyr y Nos	Very rare vagrant	5
		Squacco Heron	*Ardeola ralloides*	Crëyr Melyn	Very rare vagrant	5
		Cattle Egret	*Bubulcus ibis*	Crëyr y Gwartheg	Very rare vagrant	5
		Little Egret	*Egretta garzetta*	Crëyr Bach	Fairly common on coast; breeds	2
		Great White Egret	*Ardea alba*	Crëyr Mawr Gwyn	Rare vagrant, becoming more regular	4
		Grey Heron	*Ardea cinerea*	Crëyr Glas	Fairly common resident	1
		Purple Heron	*Ardea purpurea*	Crëyr Porffor	Very rare vagrant	5
		White Stork	*Ciconia ciconia*	Ciconia Gwyn	Rare summer visitor	5
		Glossy Ibis	*Plegadis falcinellus*	Crymanbig Ddu	Rare visitor	5
		Spoonbill	*Platalea leucorodia*	Llwybig	Very scarce summer visitor, now annual	3
		Little Grebe	*Tachybaptus ruficollis*	Gwyach Fach	Uncommon resident	1
		Great Crested Grebe	*Podiceps cristatus*	Gwyach Gopog	Uncommon winter visitor; scarce resident	2
		Red-necked Grebe	*Podiceps grisegena*	Gwyach Yddfgoch	Rare in winter or on passage	4
		Slavonian Grebe	*Podiceps auritus*	Gwyach Gorniog	Rare in winter or on passage	4
		Black-necked Grebe	*Podiceps nigricollis*	Gwyach Yddfddu	Very scarce in winter or on passage	4
		Honey-buzzard	*Pernis apivorus*	Bod y Mêl	Rare summer visitor & passage migrant	4
		Black Kite	*Milvus migrans*	Barcud Du	Very rare visitor	5
		Red Kite	*Milvus milvus*	Barcud Coch	Scarce resident	2 / 3
		Marsh Harrier	*Circus aeruginosus*	Bod y Gwerni	Scarce passage migrant & winter visitor	3
		Hen Harrier	*Circus cyaneus*	Bod Tinwen	Scarce in winter & on passage	3
		Montagu's Harrier	*Circus pygargus*	Bod Montagu	Very rare in summer & on passage	5
		Goshawk	*Accipiter gentilis*	Gwalch Marth	Uncommon resident	2 / 3
		Sparrowhawk	*Accipiter nisus*	Gwalch Glas	Fairly common resident	2
		Buzzard	*Buteo buteo*	Bwncath	Common resident	1
		Rough-legged Buzzard	*Buteo lagopus*	Bod Bacsiog	Very rare winter visitor	5
		Golden Eagle	*Aquila chrysaetos*	Eryr Euraid	Very rare vagrant	5
		Osprey	*Pandion haliaetus*	Gwalch y Pysgod	Scarce passage migrant	3
		Kestrel	*Falco tinnunculus*	Cudyll Coch	Fairly common resident but declining	1
		Merlin	*Falco columbarius*	Cudyll Bach	Uncommon winter visitor & very scarce breeder	3
		Hobby	*Falco subbuteo*	Hebog yr Ehedydd	Uncommon summer visitor; breeds	2
		Peregrine	*Falco peregrinus*	Hebog Tramor	Uncommon resident	2
		Water Rail	*Rallus aquaticus*	Rhegen y Dŵr	Uncommon resident & winter visitor	3
		Spotted Crake	*Porzana porzana*	Rhegen Fraith	Scarce passage migrant	4
		Corncrake	*Crex crex*	Rhegen yr Ŷd	Rare passage migrant	5

The Gwent bird list

	English Name	Scientific Name	Welsh Name	Status in Gwent	Chance
	Moorhen	*Gallinula chloropus*	Iâr Dŵr	Common resident	1
	Coot	*Fulica atra*	Cwtiar	Common resident	2
	Crane	*Grus grus*	Garan	Very rare visitor	5
	Stone-curlew	*Burhinus oedicnemus*	Rhedwr y Moelydd	Rare visitor	5
	Black-winged Stilt	*Himantopus himantopus*	Hirgoes	Very rare visitor	5
	Avocet	*Recurvirostra avosetta*	Cambig	Uncommon passage migrant; regular breeder	2
	Oystercatcher	*Haematopus ostralegus*	Pioden y Môr	Fairly common, winter & on passage; scarce breeder	2
	American Golden Plover	*Pluvialis dominica*	Corgwtiad Aur	Very rare visitor	5
	Golden Plover	*Pluvialis apricaria*	Cwtiad Aur	Uncommon winter visitor & passage migrant	3
	Grey Plover	*Pluvialis squatarola*	Cwtiad Llwyd	Fairly common winter visitor	2
	Lapwing	*Vanellus vanellus*	Cornchwiglen	Common winter & on passage; uncommon breeder	2
	Little Ringed Plover	*Charadrius dubius*	Cwtiad Torchog Bach	Scarce summer breeder & on passage	3
	Ringed Plover	*Charadrius hiaticula*	Cwtiad Torchog	Mainly a passage migrant; scarce breeder	2
	Kentish Plover	*Charadrius alexandrinus*	Cwtiad Caint	Very rare visitor	5
	Greater Sand Plover	*Charadrius leschenaultii*	Cwtiad y Tywod Mwyaf	Very rare vagrant	5
	Dotterel	*Charadrius morinellus*	Hutan y Mynydd	Very rare passage migrant	5
	Whimbrel	*Numenius phaeopus*	Coegylfinir	Uncommon passage migrant	2
	Curlew	*Numenius arquata*	Gylfinir	Common in winter & on passage; scarce breeder	2
	Black-tailed Godwit	*Limosa limosa*	Rhostog Gynffonddu	Fairly common winter & on passage; some summer	2
	Bar-tailed Godwit	*Limosa lapponica*	Rhostog Gynffonfrith	Uncommon on passage; scarce in other seasons	2
	Turnstone	*Arenaria interpres*	Cwtiad y Traeth	Fairly common in winter & on passage	2
	Knot	*Calidris canutus*	Pibydd yr Aber	Common winter visitor	2
	Ruff	*Calidris pugnax*	Pibydd Torchog	Uncommon passage migrant	3
	Broad-billed Sandpiper	*Calidris falcinellus*	Pibydd Llydanbig	Very rare vagrant	5
	Curlew Sandpiper	*Calidris ferruginea*	Pibydd Cambig	Uncommon on passage especially in autumn	3
	Temminck's Stint	*Calidris temminckii*	Pibydd Temminck	Rare passage migrant	4
	Sanderling	*Calidris alba*	Pibydd y Tywod	Uncommon passage migrant	3
	Dunlin	*Calidris alpina*	Pibydd y Mawn	Common winter visitor & passage migrant	2
	Purple Sandpiper	*Calidris maritima*	Pibydd Du	Scarce visitor in passage periods	4
	Baird's Sandpiper	*Calidris bairdii*	Pibydd Baird	Very rare vagrant	5

The Gwent bird list

	English Name	Scientific Name	Welsh Name	Status in Gwent	Chance
	Little Stint	*Calidris minuta*	Pibydd Bach	Scarce passage migrant	3
	White-rumped Sandpiper	*Calidris fuscicollis*	Pibydd Tinwen	Very rare vagrant	5
	Buff-breasted Sandpiper	*Calidris subruficollis*	Pibydd Bronllwyd	Very rare vagrant	5
	Pectoral Sandpiper	*Calidris melanotos*	Pibydd Cain	Rare vagrant	3
	Semipalmated Sandpiper	*Calidris pusilla*	Pibydd Llwyd	Very rare visitor	5
	Red-necked Phalarope	*Phalaropus lobatus*	Llydandroed Gyddfgoch	Rare vagrant	4
	Grey Phalarope	*Phalaropus fulicarius*	Llydandroed Llwyd	Rare passage migrant, usually in autumn	4
	Common Sandpiper	*Actitis hypoleucos*	Pibydd y Dorlan	Uncommon passage migrant & breeder	2
	Spotted Sandpiper	*Actitis macularius*	Pibydd Brych	Very rare vagrant	5
	Green Sandpiper	*Tringa ochropus*	Pibydd Gwyrdd	Uncommon passage migrant	2
	Spotted Redshank	*Tringa erythropus*	Pibydd Coesgoch Mannog	Scarce passage migrant; occasionally over-winters	2
	Greenshank	*Tringa nebularia*	Pibydd Coeswerdd	Uncommon passage migrant; few winter records	2
	Lesser Yellowlegs	*Tringa flavipes*	Melyngoes Bach	Very rare vagrant	5
	Wood Sandpiper	*Tringa glareola*	Pibydd y Graean	Scarce passage migrant	3
	Redshank	*Tringa totanus*	Pibydd Coesgoch	Fairly common, winter & on passage; scarce breeder	2
	Jack Snipe	*Lymnocryptes minimus*	Giach Fach	Uncommon winter visitor	3
	Long-billed Dowitcher	*Limnodromus scolopaceus*	Giach Gylfin-hir	Very rare vagrant	5
	Woodcock	*Scolopax rusticola*	Cyffylog	Uncommon winter visitor; uncommon breeder	2
	Snipe	*Gallinago gallinago*	Giach Gyffredin	Fairly common winter visitor & scarce breeder	2
	Black-winged Pratincole	*Glareola nordmanni*	Cwtiadwennol Aden-ddu	Very rare vagrant	5
	Pomarine Skua	*Stercorarius pomarinus*	Sgiwen Frech	Scarce passage migrant	4
	Arctic Skua	*Stercorarius parasiticus*	Sgiwen y Gogledd	Uncommon passage migrant	3
	Long-tailed Skua	*Stercorarius longicaudus*	Sgiwen Lostfain	Very rare passage migrant	5
	Great Skua	*Stercorarius skua*	Sgiwen Fawr	Scarce visitor in all seasons	3
	Puffin	*Fratercula arctica*	Pâl	Very rare visitor	5
	Razorbill	*Alca torda*	Llurs	Very scarce visitor, usually storm-blown	4
	Little Auk	*Alle alle*	Carfil Bach	Very rare visitor	5
	Guillemot	*Uria aalge*	Gwylog	Very scarce visitor, usually storm-blown	4
	Little Tern	*Sternula albifrons*	Morwennol Fechan	Very scarce passage migrant	4
	Gull-billed Tern	*Gelochelidon nilotica*	Morwennol Ylfinbraff	Very rare vagrant	5
	Whiskered Tern	*Chlidonias hybrida*	Corswennol Farfog	Very rare vagrant	5

	English Name	Scientific Name	Welsh Name	Status in Gwent	Chance
	Black Tern	*Chlidonias niger*	Corswennol Ddu	Fairly common passage migrant	3
	White-winged Black Tern	*Chlidonias leucopterus*	Corswennol Adeinwen	Very rare vagrant	5
	Sandwich Tern	*Sterna sandvicensis*	Morwennol Bigddu	Scarce passage migrant	4
	Common Tern	*Sterna hirundo*	Morwennol Gyffredin	Fairly common passage migrant	3
	Roseate Tern	*Sterna dougallii*	Morwennol Wridog	Very rare visitor	5
	Arctic Tern	*Sterna paradisaea*	Morwennol y Gogledd	Fairly common passage migrant	3
	Sabine's Gull	*Xema sabini*	Gwylan Sabine	Very scarce passage migrant	4
	Kittiwake	*Rissa tridactyla*	Gwylan Goesddu	Uncommon visitor, usually storm-blown	3
	Black-headed Gull	*Chroicocephalus ridibundus*	Gwylan Benddu	Common, winter/on passage; uncommon summer	1
	Little Gull	*Hydrocoloeus minutus*	Gwylan Fechan	Scarce passage migrant	3
	Mediterranean Gull	*Larus melanocephalus*	Gwylan Môr y Canoldir	Scarce passage migrant & winter visitor	3
	Common Gull	*Larus canus*	Gwylan y Gweunydd	Common in winter & on passage	2
	Ring-billed Gull	*Larus delawarensis*	Gwylan Fodrwybig	Very rare vagrant	5
	Lesser Black-backed Gull	*Larus fuscus*	Gwylan Gefnddu Leiaf	Common; increasingly breeds	1
	Herring Gull	*Larus argentatus*	Gwylan y Penwaig	Common; breeds	1
	Yellow-legged Gull	*Larus michahellis*	Gwylan Goesmelyn	Very uncommon visitor	4
	Iceland Gull	*Larus glaucoides*	Gwylan yr Arctig	Very scarce winter visitor	4
	Glaucous Gull	*Larus hyperboreus*	Gwylan y Gogledd	Very scarce winter visitor	4
	Great Black-backed Gull	*Larus marinus*	Gwylan Gefnddu Fwyaf	Fairly common resident breeder	2
	Feral Pigeon	*Columba livia*	Colomen Ddôf	Feral birds only	1
	Stock Dove	*Columba oenas*	Colomen Wyllt	Fairly common resident	2
	Woodpigeon	*Columba palumbus*	Ysguthan	Abundant resident	1
	Collared Dove	*Streptopelia decaocto*	Turtur Dorchog	Common resident	1
	Turtle Dove	*Streptopelia turtur*	Turtur	Rare passage migrant - formerly bred	4
	Ring-necked Parakeet	*Psittacula krameri*	Paracit Torchog	Rare visitor	4
	Cuckoo	*Cuclus canorus*	Cog	Fairly common summer visitor	2
	Barn Owl	*Tyto alba*	Tylluan Wen	Uncommon resident	2
	Snowy Owl	*Bubo scandiacus*	Tylluan yr Eira	Very rare visitor	5
	Little Owl	*Athene noctua*	Tylluan Fach	Uncommon resident	2
	Tawny Owl	*Strix aluco*	Tylluan Frech	Common resident	2
	Long-eared Owl	*Asio otus*	Tylluan Gorniog	Scarce breeder winter visitor	3
	Short-eared Owl	*Asio flammeus*	Tylluan Glustiog	Uncommon winter visitor/passage migrant	3
	Nightjar	*Caprimulgus europaeus*	Troellwr	Uncommon summer visitor	2
	Swift	*Apus apus*	Gwennol Ddu	Common summer visitor	2
	Alpine Swift	*Apus melba*	Gwennol Ddu'r Alpau	Very rare visitor	5

	English Name	Scientific Name	Welsh Name	Status in Gwent	Chance
	Little Swift	*Apus affinis*	Gwennol Ddu Fach	Very rare visitor	5
	Kingfisher	*Alcedo atthis*	Glas y Dorlan	Uncommon resident	2
	Bee-eater	*Merops apiaster*	Gwybedog y Gwenyn	Very rare vagrant	5
	Roller	*Coracias garrulus*	Rholydd	Very rare vagrant	5
	Hoopoe	*Upupa epops*	Copog	Very scarce passage migrant	4
	Wryneck	*Jynx torquilla*	Pengam	Rare passage migrant, mainly in autumn	4
	Green Woodpecker	*Picus viridis*	Cnocell Werdd	Fairly common resident	1
	Great Spotted Woodpecker	*Dendrocopos major*	Cnocell Fraith Fwyaf	Common resident	1
	Lesser Spotted Woodpecker	*Dendrocopos minor*	Cnocell Fraith Leiaf	Very scarce resident	3
	Golden Oriole	*Oriolus oriolus*	Euryn	Rare passage migrant	5
	Red-backed Shrike	*Lanius collurio*	Cigydd Cefngoch	Rare passage migrant - formerly bred	5
	Great Grey Shrike	*Lanius excubitor*	Cigydd Mawr	Scarce winter visitor	3
	Woodchat Shrike	*Lanius senator*	Cigydd Pengoch	Very rare passage migrant	5
	Chough	*Pyrrhocorax pyrrhocorax*	Brân Goesgoch	Very rare vagrant	5
	Magpie	*Pica pica*	Pioden	Common resident	1
	Jay	*Garrulus glandarius*	Ysgrech y Coed	Common resident	1
	Nutcracker	*Nucifraga caryocatactes*	Malwr Cnau	Very rare visitor	5
	Jackdaw	*Corvus monedula*	Jac-y-do	Common resident	1
	Rook	*Corvus frugilegus*	Ydfran	Common resident	1
	Carrion Crow	*Corvus corone*	Brân Dyddyn	Common resident	1
	Hooded Crow	*Corvus cornix*	Brân Lwyd	Rare visitor	5
	Raven	*Corvus corax*	Cigfran	Common resident	1
	Goldcrest	*Regulus regulus*	Dryw Eurben	Common resident	1
	Firecrest	*Regulus ignicapilla*	Dryw Penfflamgoch	Scarce passage migrant, occasional breeder	3
	Blue Tit	*Cyanistes caeruleus*	Titw Tomos Las	Common resident	1
	Great Tit	*Parus major*	Titw Mawr	Common resident	1
	Coal Tit	*Periparus ater*	Titw Penddu	Common resident	1
	Willow Tit	*Poecile montana*	Titw'r Helyg	Scarce resident	4
	Marsh Tit	*Poecile palustris*	Titw'r Wern	Fairly common resident	2
	Bearded Tit	*Panurus biarmicus*	Titw Barfog	Uncommon resident in coastal reedbeds	3
	Woodlark	*Lullula arborea*	Ehedydd y Coed	Rare visitor - has bred	4
	Skylark	*Alauda arvensis*	Ehedydd	Common resident	1
	Sand Martin	*Riparia riparia*	Gwennol y Glennydd	Common summer visitor	2
	Swallow	*Hirundo rustica*	Gwennol	Common summer visitor	2
	House Martin	*Delichon urbicum*	Gwennol y Bondo	Common summer visitor	2
	Red-rumped Swallow	*Cecropis daurica*	Gwennol Dingoch	Very rare visitor	5
	Cetti's Warbler	*Cettia cetti*	Telor Cetti	Resident in coastal wetlands	2
	Long-tailed Tit	*Aegithalos caudatus*	Titw Gynffon-hir	Common resident	1
	Yellow-browed Warbler	*Phylloscopus inornatus*	Telor Aelfelyn	Rare visitor	4

	English Name	Scientific Name	Welsh Name	Status in Gwent	Chance
	Wood Warbler	*Phylloscopus sibilatrix*	Telor y Coed	Fairly common summer visitor	2
	Chiffchaff	*Phylloscopus collybita*	Siff-saff	Common summer visitor	2
	Iberian Chiffchaff	*Phylloscopus ibericus*	Siff-saff Iberia	Very rare visitor	5
	Willow Warbler	*Phylloscopus trochilus*	Telor yr Helyg	Common summer visitor	2
	Blackcap	*Sylvia atricapilla*	Telor Penddu	Common summer visitor	1
	Garden Warbler	*Sylvia borin*	Telor yr Ardd	Fairly common summer visitor	2
	Barred Warbler	*Sylvia nisoria*	Telor Rhesog	Rare visitor on passage	5
	Lesser Whitethroat	*Sylvia curruca*	Llwydfron Fach	Uncommon summer visitor	2
	Whitethroat	*Sylvia communis*	Llwydfron	Common summer visitor	2
	Dartford Warbler	*Sylvia undata*	Telor Dartford	Rare	4
	Marmora's Warbler	*Sylvia sarda*	Telor Marmora	Very rare vagrant	5
	Subalpine Warbler	*Sylvia cantillans*	Telor Brongoch	Very rare visitor	5
	Grasshopper Warbler	*Locustella naevia*	Troellwr Bach	Uncommon summer visitor	3
	Melodious Warbler	*Hippolais polyglotta*	Telor Pêr	Very rare visitor	5
	Aquatic Warbler	*Acrocephalus paludicola*	Telor y Dŵr	Rare visitor - usually seen only by ringers	5
	Sedge Warbler	*Acrocephalus schoenobaenus*	Telor yr Hesg	Fairly common summer visitor	2
	Marsh Warbler	*Acrocephalus palustris*	Telor y Gwerni	Very rare visitor	5
	Reed Warbler	*Acrocephalus scirpaceus*	Telor y Cyrs	Fairly common summer visitor	2
	Waxwing	*Bombycilla garrulus*	Cynffon Sidan	Rare winter visitor	4
	Nuthatch	*Sitta europaea*	Delor y Cnau	Common resident	1
	Treecreeper	*Certhia familiaris*	Dringwr Bach	Common resident	1
	Wren	*Troglodytes troglodytes*	Dryw	Abundant resident	1
	Starling	*Sturnus vulgaris*	Drudwen	Common resident	1
	Rose-coloured Starling	*Pastor roseus*	Drudwen Wridog	Very rare vagrant	5
	Dipper	*Cinclus cinclus*	Bronwen-y-Dŵr	Fairly common resident	2
	Ring Ouzel	*Turdus torquatus*	Mwyalchen y Mynydd	Scarce passage migrant	3
	Blackbird	*Turdus merula*	Mwyalchen	Abundant resident	1
	Fieldfare	*Turdus pilaris*	Socan Eira	Common winter visitor	2
	Song Thrush	*Turdus philomelos*	Bronfraith	Common resident	1
	Redwing	*Turdus iliacus*	Coch Dan-aden	Common winter visitor	2
	Mistle Thrush	*Turdus viscivorus*	Brych y Coed	Common resident	1
	Spotted Flycatcher	*Muscicapa striata*	Gwybedog Mannog	Uncommon summer visitor	2
	Robin	*Erithacus rubecula*	Robin Goch	Abundant resident	1
	Nightingale	*Luscinia megarhynchos*	Eos	Rare summer visitor	4
	Bluethroat	*Luscinia svecica*	Bronlas	Very rare migrant	5
	Pied Flycatcher	*Ficedula hypoleuca*	Gwybedog Brith	Fairly common summer visitor	2
	Black Redstart	*Phoenicurus ochruros*	Tingoch Du	Scarce winter visitor & passage migrant	3

The Gwent bird list

	English Name	Scientific Name	Welsh Name	Status in Gwent	Chance
	Redstart	*Phoenicurus phoenicurus*	Tingoch	Fairly common summer visitor	2
	Whinchat	*Saxicola rubetra*	Crec yr Eithin	Fairly common summer visitor	2
	Stonechat	*Saxicola rubicola*	Clochdar y Cerrig	Uncommon resident	2
	Wheatear	*Oenanthe oenanthe*	Tinwen y Garn	Fairly common summer visitor	2
	Desert Wheatear	*Oenanthe deserti*	Tinwen y Diffaethwch	Very rare visitor	5
	Dunnock	*Prunella modularis*	Llwyd y Gwrych	Abundant resident	1
	House Sparrow	*Passer domesticus*	Aderyn y Tô	Abundant resident	1
	Tree Sparrow	*Passer montanus*	Golfan y Mynydd	Very rare resident	4
	Yellow Wagtail	*Motacilla flava*	Siglen Felen	Uncommon summer visitor	3
	Grey Wagtail	*Motacilla cinerea*	Siglen Lwyd	Fairly common resident	1
	Pied Wagtail	*Motacilla alba*	Siglen Fraith	Common resident	1
	Richard's Pipit	*Anthus richardi*	Corhedydd Richard	Very rare vagrant	5
	Tawny Pipit	*Anthus campestris*	Corhedydd Melyn	Very rare vagrant	5
	Tree Pipit	*Anthus trivialis*	Corhedydd y Coed	Fairly common summer visitor	2
	Meadow Pipit	*Anthus pratensis*	Corhedydd y Waun	Common resident, passage migrant, winter visitor	1
	Rock Pipit	*Anthus petrosus*	Corhedydd y Graig	Uncommon winter visitor; rare resident	3
	Water Pipit	*Anthus spinoletta*	Corhedydd y Dŵr	Uncommon winter visitor	3
	Chaffinch	*Fringilla coelebs*	Ji-binc	Abundant resident	1
	Brambling	*Fringilla montifringilla*	Pinc y Mynydd	Fairly common winter visitor	2
	Greenfinch	*Chloris chloris*	Llinos Werdd	Common resident	1
	Goldfinch	*Carduelis carduelis*	Nico	Abundant resident	1
	Siskin	*Carduelis spinus*	Pila Gwyrdd	Uncommon resident; common winter visitor	1
	Linnet	*Carduelis cannabina*	Llinos	Common resident	1
	Twite	*Carduelis flavirostris*	Llinos y Mynydd	Rare visitor	4
	Lesser Redpoll	*Carduelis cabaret*	Llinos Bengoch Leiaf	Fairly common winter visitor; uncommon breeder	2
	Common Redpoll	*Carduelis flammea*	Llinos Bengoch	Very rare visitor	5
	Crossbill	*Loxia curvirostra*	Gylfin Groes	Uncommon resident/winter visitor; variable nos.	2
	Common Rosefinch	*Carpodacus erythrinus*	Llinos Goch	Very rare visitor	5
	Bullfinch	*Pyrrhula pyrrhula*	Coch y Berllan	Common resident	1
	Hawfinch	*Coccothraustes coccothraustes*	Gylfinbraff	Uncommon breeding resident	2
	Snow Bunting	*Plectrophenax nivalis*	Bras yr Eira	Very rare visitor	4
	Lapland Bunting	*Calcarius lapponicus*	Bras y Gogledd	Very rare visitor	4
	Yellowhammer	*Emberiza citrinella*	Melyn yr Eithin	Uncommon resident	2
	Cirl Bunting	*Emberiza cirlus*	Bras Ffrainc	Former breeder, long since gone	5
	Reed Bunting	*Emberiza schoeniclus*	Bras y Cyrs	Common	1
	Corn Bunting	*Emberiza calandra*	Bras yr Ŷd	Former breeder, now rare visitor	4
	Common Yellowthroat	*Geothlypis trichas*	Gyddf-felyn	Very rare visitor vagrant	5

Useful contacts

Gwent wildlife recorders

Birds
Chris Jones, 22 Walnut Drive, Caerleon, Gwent NP18 3SB
Tel: 01633 423439   email: countyrecorder@gwentbirds.org.uk
(Gwent Ornithological Society)

Mammals
Jan Kinchington   email: info@themammalssociety.org
(The Mammal Society)

Bats
Ian Rabjohn   email: ian.jessica123@btinternet.com
(Gwent Bat Group)

Amphibians and Reptiles
Melanie Dodd (GWENTARG) c/o SEWBReC   email: info@sewbrec.org.uk
(Gwent Amphibian and Reptile Group)

Butterflies and Moths
Butterflies and macro-moths
Martin Anthoney   email: martin@chemlep.demon.co.uk
Micro-moths
Sam Bosanquet   email: sam.bosanquet@cyfoethnaturiolcymru.gov.uk
(Monmouthshire Moth and Butterfly Group)

Dragonflies
See British Dragonfly Society below

Grasshoppers and Crickets
Steve Williams   email: steven71296@aol.com
(National Orthoptera Recording Scheme)

Plants
Stephanie Tyler   email: steph_tyler2001@hotmail.com
(Botanical Society of Britain and Ireland)

Mosses and Liverworts
Sam Bosanquet   email: sam.bosanquet@cyfoethnaturiolcymru.gov.uk
(British Bryological Society)

Gwent wildlife organisations

Gwent Ornithological Society

www.gwentbirds.org.uk
Secretary
Trevor Russell, The Pines, Highfield Road, Monmouth NP25 3HR
Tel: 01600 716266   email: secretary@gwentbirds.org.uk

Gwent Wildlife Trust

www.gwentwildlife.org
Seddon House, Dingestow, Monmouth NP25 4DY
Tel: 01600 740600   email: info@gwentwildlife.org

Monmouthshire Meadows Group

www.monmouthshiremeadows.org.uk
Secretary
Maggie Biss   email: monmouthshiremeadows@aol.com

Gwent Badger Group

www.gwentbadgergroup.org.uk   email: secretary@gwentbadgergroup.org.uk

Gwent Bat Group

www.gwentbatgroup.co.uk

Gwent Amphibian and Reptile Group

www.sewbrec.org.uk/garg.page   email: gwentarg@hotmail.co.uk

Monmouthshire Moth and Butterfly Group

www.chemlep.demon.co.uk/
Secretary
Kevin Dupé, 44 Melbourne Road, Newport, NP20 3RF
Tel: 01633 263374   email: smallranunculus@btinternet.com

Useful contacts

Wildlife organisations (rest of UK)

British Trust for Ornithology (BTO)
Wales Office
www.bto.org/national-offices/wales
Thoday Building, Deiniol Road, Bangor, Gwynedd LL57 2UW
Tel: 01248 383285   email: info@bto.org

Gwent BTO Representative
Jerry Lewis, Y Bwthyn Gwyn, Coldbrook, Abergavenny NP7 9TD
Tel: 01873 855091   email: jmsl2587@yahoo.co.uk

Royal Society for the Protection of Birds (RSPB)
www.rspb.org.uk/about/offices/wales/wales.aspx
Wales Headquarters, Sutherland House, Castlebridge, Cowbridge Road East, Cardiff CF11 9AB
Tel: 029 2035 3000   email: cwmru@rspb.org.uk

Natural Resources Wales
http://naturalresourceswales.gov.uk
Tŷ Cambria, 29 Newport Road, Cardiff CF24 0TP
Tel: 0300 0653000

Butterfly Conservation
www.butterfly-conservation.org
Manor Yard, East Lulworth, Wareham BH20 5QP
Tel: 01929 400209

British Dragonfly Society
www.british-dragonflies.org.uk
Lyn Curry, Membership Office, 23 Bowker Way, Whittlesey, Peterborough PE7 1PY
Tel: 01733 204286

The Woodland Trust
www.woodlandtrust.org.uk
Headquarters, Kempton Way, Grantham NG31 6LL
Tel: 01476 581111

Useful contacts

Other useful contacts

South East Wales Biodiversity Records Centre
13 St Andrews Crescent, Cardiff, CF10 3DB
Tel: 029 2064 1110
www.sewbrec.org.uk/   email: info@sewbrec.org.uk

Wye Valley Area of Outstanding Natural Beauty (AONB) Office
Hadnock Road, Monmouth, Monmouthshire NP25 3NG
AONB Officer
Andrew Blake Tel: 01600 713977   email: aonb.officer@wyevalleyaonb.org.uk

Tourist Information Centres

Abergavenny
Swan Meadow, Monmouth Road, Abergavenny NP7 5HL
Tel: 01873 853254   email: abergavennyic@breconbeacons.org

Blaenavon
Blaenavon World Heritage Centre, Church Road, Blaenavon, Torfaen NP4 9AS
Tel: 01495 742333   email: blaenavon.tic@torfaen.gov.uk

Caerphilly
Lower Twyn Square, Caerphilly CF83 1JL
Tel: 02920 880011   email: tourism@caerphilly.gov.uk

Chepstow
Castle Car Park, Bridge Street, Chepstow NP16 5EY
Tel: 01291 623772   email: chepstow.tic@monmouthshire.gov.uk

Monmouth
Shire Hall, Agincourt Square, Monmouth NP5 3DY
Tel: 01600 713899   email: monmouth.tic@monmouthshire.gov.uk

Newport
Museum & Art Gallery, John Frost Square, Newport NP20 1PA
Tel: 01633 842962   email: newport.tic@newport.gov.uk

Useful contacts

Help and advice regarding injured birds and other animals

City Wildlife Care

www.citywildlifecare.org.uk
Albert Avenue, Newport, Gwent NP19 8FT
Tel: 07794 179207

RSPCA

National contact number for all sick and injured birds and other animals
Tel: 08705 813182

Wildlife crime

If you think a crime against wildlife or the environment has been committed in your local area, report it immediately on 101.

Gwent Wildlife Crime Officers

Blaenau Gwent

Abertillery – PC 1494 Rob Heel   email: robert.heel@gwent.pnn.police.uk
Ebbw Vale – PC 207 Ian Withers   email: ian.withers@gwent.pnn.police.uk

Caerphilly

Bedwas – PC 1150 Mark Wilkinson   email: jonathan.wilkinson@gwent.pnn.police.uk
Risca – PC 2005 Alan Tinsley   email: alan.tinsley@gwent.pnn.police.uk

Monmouthshire

Chepstow – PC 2058 Peter Lewis   email: peter.lewis@gwent.pnn.police.uk
Abergavenny – PC 576 Maldwyn John   email: maldwyn.john@gwent.pnn.police.uk

Newport

Marshfield – PC 986 Adrian Walters   email: Adrian.walters@gwent.pnn.police.uk
Llanmartin – PC 682 Anthony Williams email: Anthony.williams@gwent.pnn.police.uk

Torfaen

Cwmbran – PC 668 Mark Ruddick   email: mark.ruddick@gwent.pnn.police.uk

Further reading

Birds of Gwent, The. 1977. Ferns *et al.* Gwent Ornithological Society.
  ISBN 0 9505760 0 X

Birds of Gwent, The. 2008. Venables, W A *et al.* Helm, London.
  ISBN 978-0-7136-7633-4

Birds in Wales 1992-2000. 2002. Green, J; Welsh Ornithological Society.
  ISBN 0 9542145-0-1

Birds in Wales. 1994. Lovegrove, R, Williams, G & Williams I. T & A D Poyser, London.
  ISBN 0-85661-069-0

Flora of Monmouthshire, The. 2007. Evans, T. The Chepstow Society.
  ISBN 0 900278-49-8

Gwent Atlas of Breeding Birds, The. 1987. Tyler *et al.* Gwent Ornithological Society.
  ISBN 0 950 5760 9 3

Gwent Bird Report. Published annually. Gwent Ornithological Society

Gwent Wildlife Trust's Nature Reserves. 2013. (Ed) Rappel, I. Gwent Wildlife Trust

Monmouthshire Lepidoptera. 1994. Horton, G A N. Comma International Biological
  Systems.
  ISBN 0 9513979-5-3

Time to Stare: Wildlife in a Corner of Britain. 2005. Armstrong, R. Grice Chapman
  Publishing.
  ISBN-10: 0954572661, ISBN-13: 978-0954572662

Where to Watch Birds in Wales. 2008. Saunders, D & Green, J; Helm, London.
  ISBN 978-0-7136-7484-2

Wildflower Meadows in Monmouthshire. 2013. (Eds) Biss, Margaret et al.
  Monmouthshire Meadows Group.
  ISBN 978-0-9576424-0-9

Wildlife in Gwent Post Millennium. 2006. Titcombe, C *et al.* C Titcombe, Llandogo.
  ISBN 0 9532756 1 2

Wye Valley (Collins New Naturalist Library No. 105). 2008. Peterken, G. Harper
  Collins, London.
  ISBN 10: 0007160682 / 0-00-716068-2, ISBN 13: 9780007160686

Gwent Ornithological Society website: www.gwentbirds.org.uk

Index of Target birds

THIS INDEX contains all the species listed in the **Target birds** sections of each walk. The reference is to the **walk number**.

Map of walks

SO	23				
	22	32	42		
11	21	31	41	51	
10	20	30	40	50	
	19	29	39	49	59
	18	28	38	48	58
ST	27	10km squares of the National Grid			

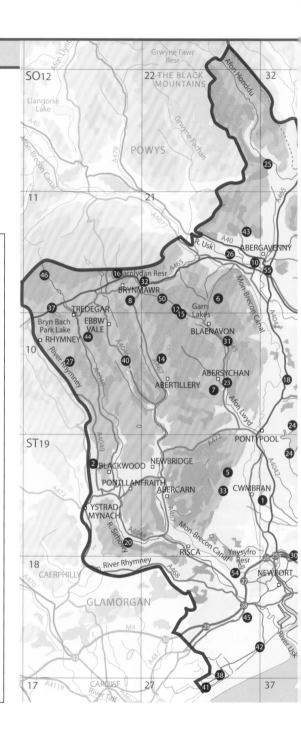

236

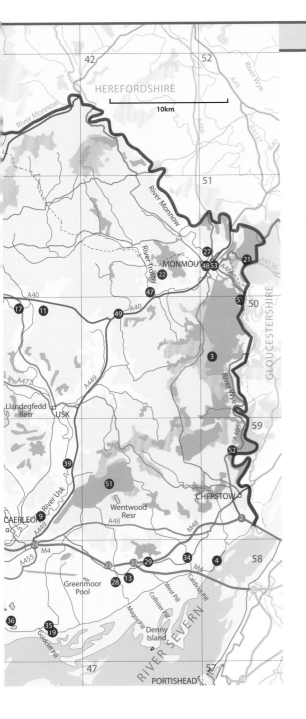

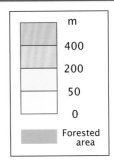

m	
	400
	200
	50
	0
	Forested area

29 Minnetts Wood
30 Moorings, The, River Usk
31 Mynydd Garnclochdy
32 Mynydd Llangatwg
33 Mynydd Maen
34 Nedern Brook Wetlands
35 NWR – Goldcliff Lagoons
36 NWR – Uskmouth Reedbeds
37 Parc Bryn Bach
38 Peterstone Pill & Gout
39 River Usk & Olway Brook
40 Silent Valley
41 Sluice Farm Saltmarsh
42 St Brides Coast
43 St David's Vale
44 St James Forestry
45 Tredegar Park
46 Trefil Quarry
47 Treowen
48 Two Rivers Meadow
49 Warrage, The
50 Waun Afon Bog
51 Wentwood
52 Wye Valley at Wyndcliff
53 Wye Valley S of Monmouth
54 Ynysyfro Reservoirs
55 Ysgyryd Fach

Gwent Ornithological Society

GWENT ORNITHOLOGICAL Society (GOS) was founded some fifty years ago, by a small group of birdwatching beginners, who wanted to improve their birding skills by sharing information and experiences. Although GOS has grown greatly in the ensuing years (with membership currently standing at over 300) the society has never lost its roots – retaining a friendly informal style, and welcoming beginners and experts alike.

GOS offers numerous services and activities, and members are welcome to attend/participate in as many, or as few, as they wish.

Indoor meetings
Fortnightly programme: September to Easter

Indoor meetings take place in the evening at the Goytre Village Hall (about 3 miles NE of Pontypool), beginning with a talk from an invited speaker and concluding with the opportunity to meet other birders and chat informally over a cup of tea/coffee and biscuits. The talks are illustrated by superb photographs and range widely over all aspects of birds and birdwatching.

Field outings
Every 2-3 weeks year-round

The field meetings comprise local walks or visits to good birding sites, both within the county and further afield. Typically, they involve small groups of about 8-15 people, led by a local expert who will help with bird identification and answer other related questions. Occasionally, weekends away are arranged at birding hotspots such as Portland Bill.

Participation in surveys

Many GOS members participate in both national and local bird surveys, and the large-scale involvement of members has allowed the production of two breeding bird atlases for the county, covering the years 1981-85 and 1998-2003. The Society has also produced two county avifaunas: *The Birds of Gwent* (1977) and *The Birds of Gwent* (2008).

Newsletter

A quarterly newsletter, *The Dipper*, provides interesting articles and snippets about birds as well as reporting on Society events and giving updates on birds that have been seen recently in the county.

The Gwent Bird Report

This is published annually and gives details of all the year's sightings in the county, submitted by over 160 birdwatchers. It also has knowledgeable articles on a wide range of avian topics and is a showcase for some stunning photos taken by members.

The Library

The Society has an extensive DVD and book library containing hundreds of titles relating to birds and birdwatching. These are freely available to members for reference or borrowing.

Goytre House Wood

GOS owns an 11-acre woodland nature reserve, adjacent to the Monmouthshire and Brecon Canal, to which members have free access.

GOS website: www.gwentbirds.org.uk

The website gives the very latest bird sightings and society news. The Members' Forum can be used to ask questions, arrange lifts, buy and sell etc. Details of how to join are also found here.

Field outing at Graig Goch Woods   *Al Venables*